Organizations for
Policy Analysis

edited by

Carol H. Weiss

Organizations for Policy Analysis
Helping Government Think

 SAGE PUBLICATIONS
The International Professional Publishers
Newbury Park   London   New Delhi

For information address:

SAGE Publications, Inc.
2455 Teller Road
Newbury Park, California 91320

SAGE Publications Ltd.
6 Bonhill Street
London EC2A 4PU
United Kingdom

SAGE Publications India Pvt. Ltd.
M-32 Market
Greater Kailash I
New Delhi 110 048 India

Printed in the United States of America

Library of Congress Cataloging-in-Publication Data

Organizations for policy analysis : helping government think / edited by
Carol H. Weiss.
    p.   cm.
    Includes bibliographical references and index.
    ISBN 0-8039-4359-8 (c). — ISBN 0-8039-4360-1 (p)
    1. Government consultants—United States.   2. Policy sciences.
3. Research institutes—United States.   4. Group problem solving—
United States.   I. Weiss, Carol H.
JK458.C7074   1992
353.09'3—dc20   91-12233
                                                                        CIP

FIRST PRINTING, 1992

Sage Production Editor: Judith L. Hunter

Contents

Preface

This is a book about policy analysis organizations that provide advice to government. Its purpose is to describe a variety of such organizations and the work they do. It explores how they fit into American political culture and why they have grown and flourished in this environment.

Organizations for policy analysis are inventions of the twentieth century, although they have roots in traditions of advice-giving that go back through the millennia. Like the priests and soothsayers, chamberlains and kitchen cabinets before them, they exist to help government officials in the formulation of public policy. The world is a more complicated place than it was in the past, and government is called upon to perform a range of tasks that go far beyond the functions of earlier times. Officials are buffeted by demands, increasingly constrained in resources, under constant scrutiny from the media and the public. The agencies that they govern are "pluralistic, divided, under-informed, short-sighted, only partly in control of their own processes, and unable to guarantee the outcomes which they promise. There are enormous gaps, and sometimes no linkages at all, between realities, perceptions, decisions, actions, and consequences" (Blackstone & Plowden, 1990, p. 12).

In this situation, officials turn to may advisers to help them through the day. But given the complexity of the issues with which they deal and the tangled interconnections among them, they need specialized forms of knowledge and analysis. Enter the policy analysis organization.

One of the distinguishing features of these organizations is the tools they use. Particularly in the United States, their stock in trade consists of empirical evidence and systematic techniques for processing and analyzing that evidence as the basis for the advice they give. The analysts who staff these organizations are not the entire cast of "policy intellectuals" who provide consultation for government. They are the particular subset who lay claim to specialized knowledge for making plausible and relevant sense of data.

For many problems in the analytic world, it turns out that sophisticated methodology is overkill. Analysts make much of their contribution through reliance on a few basic principles, intelligence, logic, systematic reasoning, and a willingness to think in unorthodox ways (Nelson, 1987). But method has given them their claim to authoritativeness. Largely on the basis of method, they have become players in the policy game.

The chapters in this book give a historical view of the genesis, activities, and orientations of 14 policy analysis organizations. Almost all were written by analysts who themselves are or have been members of the units under discussion. The authors write about the founding, funding, and findings of the organizations and try to place them within the political and economic context of the period.

Characteristics of Organizations for Policy Advice

The organizations about which the authors write are analytic units inside government agencies and free-standing nonprofit organizations outside government. The latter commonly are called "think tanks," a term that came into currency in the 1950s (Smith, 1989).

The characteristics of these organizations that offer to "help government think" are:

1. They are permanent organizations with specialized staff.

2. They do not have responsibility for operations. Even those that are part of government departments are separate from regular line functions of government.

3. Their staffs have special expertise. Most commonly the expertise is methodological, and the methods may be those of the policy sciences, which Lasswell (1971) listed as operations research, linear and dynamic programming, program budgeting, cost-benefit analysis, systems analysis, computer simulation and gaming, social accounting, brainstorming, and sensitivity training. The last few items on his list look old-fashioned today, and skills now in demand include statistical analysis, program evaluation, decision analysis, survey research, econometric modeling, forecasting, risk analysis, qualitative analysis of interviews and documents, argumentation, and analysis of the arguments of others. Historical analysis is increasingly relevant as well.

Knowledge of the policy domain is important in the course of work. Here analysts face competition from line staff in the department who have often spent their careers on agency issues. Analysts tend to acquire knowledge about the substance of policy on the job. In some cases, when staff in the analytic unit have served longer than program staff, they become the repository of substantive expertise for the department.

As Dror (1980, 1987) reminds us, knowledge of government and its practices and knowledge of politics are useful resources for analysts to have. Without such kinds of understanding, they are ill equipped to gauge the latitude they have—how innovative they can be or how practical they must be, how and to whom they should communicate, where resistance is likely to arise, and what if anything can be done to counter it.

4. They are policy oriented, and their primary purpose is to improve the process and content of public policies. A number of them also aim to contribute to general knowledge. They publish magazines; their staff write books, contribute to academic journals, and give papers at disciplinary meetings. But the main rationale of the organization, and its appeal to sponsors and contributors, is the enhancement of public policy-making. Many staffs judge their success by the influence of their work on government policy (Pugliaresi & Berliner, 1989), a difficult and elusive test. Their main influence is apt to be on policy actors' understanding and interpretation of issues (Feldman, 1989).

5. Their main output is analysis and advice. As Prince (1983) writes about British governmental analytic units, its output is paper. Again, the more academically oriented think tanks take pride in the books they publish and the education they provide to the field. The RAND Corporation even runs a degree-granting graduate program. (See chapter 3 on RAND.) But the name of the business is policy advice.

6. Policy analysis units place a heavy emphasis on communicating the results of their work to those engaged in making policy. As the chapters in this book demonstrate, most of the units wish they did a better job of it. They tend to spend a great deal of time and effort disseminating their reports through a variety of channels to reach those in a position to put the results to work. A premium is put on clear writing, brevity, good graphics, multiple messages—memos, bulletins, magazine stories, op-ed pieces, articles in house organs, incorporation into training programs, tapes, and videodiscs, and personal contact and suasion.[1] If they are to influence policy, a necessary (although not sufficient) first step is to see that their message is heard.

With all these commonalities, however, analytic organizations show considerable diversity. Some (both inside and outside government) have a long time horizon and a research-oriented perspective. They stress original data collection, sophisticated statistical analysis and modeling, and analysis of long-term trends. Others respond to immediate requests for information and advice, and they favor quick back-of-the-envelope calculations. Units vary as well in their efforts to maintain neutrality. Some place enormous emphasis on checking and rechecking the factual evidence they report, and they go to great lengths to try to keep their own opinions out of the work. This position is particularly common in analytic units that work for legislatures and in outside units that seek contracts from governments of different persuasions. The unit has to be seen as impartial and objective by representatives of the whole political spectrum, or else it loses credibility and support. Others are, in the word of Willetts (1987, p. 450), "viewy." Their policy preferences are obvious in the way they frame the analytic question and the range of options they consider.

Outside think tanks tend to take a wider view than internal units. Although generalizations are risky, it is probably fair to say that they take a longer term view and a more critical stance toward current policy. Inside units often have better access to data, more sustained interaction with programmatic staff and departmental decision makers, and continuing chances to advance their interpretation of policy options.

Organizations That Are Included

Of the 14 organizations profiled here, five are external to government. They are nonprofit "think tanks."[2] They range from the Brookings Institution, the oldest of the policy analysis organizations described in the book, through the conservative American Enterprise Institute, the research-oriented RAND Corporation, to the liberal and relatively new Center for Budget and Policy Priorities. The last of them, the Center for Policy Research in Education, is a hybrid. It is funded by the Department of Education but located in a university, staffed by scholars from several universities, and charged with responsibility for doing research that is relevant to state and local decision makers.

The next four organizations in the book are units within executive agencies: Executive Office of the President, the Department of Interior, and two units within the Department of Health and Human Services (HHS). The first of the HHS units is the Office of the Assistant Secretary for Planning and Evaluation, which has passed its 20th anniversary and has been regarded as the premier analysis unit in the domestic agencies of the U.S. government. The other is the Office of the Inspector General, a part of the auditing/oversight apparatus of the department, which has evolved into an empirically oriented evaluation unit. Because of its responsiveness to immediate issues and its quick turnaround time, it appears to have become the departmental workhorse for practical program review.

Of the policy analysis organizations inside government, five work for the legislative branch. They are the Congressional Research Service, the General Accounting Office, the Congressional Budget Office, and the Office of Technology Assessment—all of which are agencies of the U.S. Congress—and the Office of the Legislative Analyst of the State of California. In discussions of policy analysis organizations, organizations that work for the legislative branch often are overlooked. Unlike their executive-agency counterparts, they do not serve one client with an "Administration" point of view. Rather, they work for many masters and have to satisfy the wants and needs of legislators of many political hues.

Organizations That Are Not Included

I have limited this volume to policy analysis organizations in the United States. Although many other countries have internal analysis units within government bureaucracies, and a number have outside analysis organizations, I have concentrated solely on the United States in order to cover a range of organizational creatures in this one institutional zoo. An intriguing development of recent years, however, is the appearance of external think tanks in countries around the world. This development suggests that some of the conditions that gave rise to them in the United States (see the next chapter) are becoming visible in other Western-style democracies and would-be democracies.

I have excluded university-based policy research organizations.[3] Hundreds of research centers and institutes exist in universities with at least a titular allegiance to policy relevance. But on the whole they are caught in a tension between the values of the policy world that they presumably are serving and the values of the university that determine their standing and the advancement and career chances of their staffs. In most of the university policy institutes that I know, the values of the university prevail. Relevance to policy fades before the pressure to publish in academic journals. Interdisciplinary work founders because disciplinary departments usually determine promotion and tenure. Prompt and lively communication to policy audiences wins few kudos on campus. Therefore, university policy units tend to remain academic institutions more than advisers to government.

To stake out a place for them in the advising system, some commentators have suggested an ordered continuum of research and analysis, with basic research at one end, leading on to policy research, and then to policy analysis. In this view, university departments conduct basic research, develop theory, and improve research methods. University policy research centers draw on basic research to develop policy-oriented research, which takes a long-term perspective on issues in the policy domain. Policy analysis units tailor policy-oriented research to the operational constraints of the policy world. This neat division among the three entities has a pleasing plausibility, but there is a paint-by-the-numbers artificiality to it. Many university centers do good and important work, but the work does not necessarily fit immediate analytic demands; it usually serves a more general "enlightenment" purpose. Policy analysis groups not infrequently find little to draw on when faced with concrete problems.

The book also omits consulting firms and other for-profit research organizations. They are a diverse lot, some of outstanding quality, but one volume could not do justice to such a varied field. I also have omitted philanthropic foundations, although many of the largest have strong social policy interests and a desire to influence the direction of public policy-making. Such foundations as Ford, Rockefeller, and Carnegie devote large sums of money to research, demonstrations, and action programs that are intended to influence new policy directions. Interestingly, institutions that bear the names of buccaneers of capitalism are often champions of new policies for the poor, the sick, the unemployed, the school dropout, and other disadvantaged groups. The foundations appear occasionally in these pages as sponsors of work at several think tanks reported here.

The final major exclusion is interest groups, advocacy organizations, and lobbies. These kinds of groups certainly give advice to government, and many of them do extensive analysis, such as the American Petroleum Institute, Ralph Nader's Public Citizen, the

Children's Defense Fund, and the National Association of Manufacturers. Their analysis is intended primarily to advance the cause of the association and to give them ammunition to use in the policy wars. It is extremely difficult to draw a line, however, between policy analysis that is done with an open mind, seeking to find the relative advantages and disadvantages of alternative policies, and policy analysis conducted when the final answer is already known. Even at their most objective and empirical, all analytic groups take certain parameters for granted. At the very least, academic training gives analysts a particular set of disciplinary blinders; for example, the economics profession, which provides the basis for much policy analysis, holds values of efficiency, benefits that exceed costs, and the virtues of the market. Further, the history and tradition of an analysis organization, and its own prior work, exert a powerful constricting force on the direction it takes. Savvy units may restrict their work to options that are seen as "feasible" and "politically acceptable." The known positions of bureaucratic superiors or organizational clients point in a particular policy direction. Above all, the prevailing political consensus, even when it impairs understanding and limits vision, comes to seem like objectivity—or even"truth."

The analytic endeavor itself can be suspect. At its most fruitful, analysis rarely grows out of a full-field open canvass of the terrain. Rather it is apt to start with an insight: This is how it must be. The analyst proceeds to check the insight against evidence and history. With the best will in the world, the analyst retains an attachment to the hypothesis and, if she or he notices contrary evidence, probably subjects it to stiffer scrutiny than the evidence she expects. Sometimes analysis starts with an end in view. Its charge is to find a mechanism for increasing user charges or reducing client claims. Not infrequently an analytic office takes upon itself the job of promoting a policy it believes to be effective. For a hundred reasons the line between analysis and advocacy blurs.

How then do we make a useful distinction between policy analysis organizations and advocacy groups that support analytic work to justify their stands? In most cases the difference is obvious from organizational history. For those cases in which the line is fuzzy, I suggest three clues. First, analytic organizations examine a range of empirical evidence. The evidence can be quantitative or qualitative, hard or soft. The point is that they look at whatever is available and do not sweep uncongenial information under the rug. Second, they handle evidence systematically. Whatever method they use, they apply it consistently and fairly. An organization with little regard for evenhanded methodical review may be on the side of the angels (or on the side of the angles, for that matter), but it hardly qualifies as analytic. Third, analysis should have the capacity to surprise. At least occasionally it should confront the organization with unexpected results. This is not to gainsay that many policy analysis organizations conduct some work for purposes of intellectual legitimation. They do some good analytic work to shore up a ready-made case. But if the organization engages only in this type of work, if the answer is always cut-and-dried before inquiry starts, it probably should be classed as an advocacy group.

In all events, with full recognition that the distinction may be almost impossible to make, I have sought to exclude organizations that put advocacy ahead of analysis. The institutions of policy advice in this collection are not devoted exclusively to advancing particular philosophical or political principles, and are probably open to unexpected ideas and arguments.

Carol H. Weiss

Notes

1. An early illustration of exemplary communication was the case of the RAND basing study. See Smith, 1966.

2. The popularity of the term *think tank* dates from the 1950s. It derives from military usage, where it referred to a secure place to plan strategy. But the phrase is ambiguous enough to suggest a variety of images: A military tank, mowing down all before it? A water tank high on the roof of a tall building, providing one of the necessities of life to the occupants? A tank of noxious chemicals polluting the atmosphere? A goldfish tank, with vivid multicolored fish on view, pretty to look at but basically useless? A receiving tank in a prison for accused and possibly dangerous violators? A scuba tank that enables divers to breathe deep down in even the murkiest of waters?

3. With the exception, as noted, of the Center for Policy Research in Education.

References

Blackstone, T., & Plowden, W. (1990). *Inside the think tank: Advising the Cabinet 1971-1983.* London: Mandarin.

Dror, Y. (1980). Think tanks: A new invention in government. In C. H. Weiss & A. H. Barton (Eds.), *Making bureaucracy work* (pp. 139-152). Beverly Hills, CA: Sage.

Dror, Y. (1987). Conclusions. In W. Plowden (Ed.), *Advising the Rulers* (pp. 185-215). Oxford, UK: Basil Blackwell.

Feldman, M. (1989). *Order without design: Information production & policy making.* Stanford, CA: Stanford University Press.

Lasswell, H. D. (1971). *A pre-view of policy sciences.* New York: American Elsevier.

Nelson, R. H. (1987). The economics profession and the making of public policy. *Journal of Economic Literature, 25*(1), 49-91.

Prince, M. J. (1983). *Policy advice and organizational survival.* Aldershot, Hampshire: Gower.

Pugliaresi, L., & Berliner, D. T. (1989). Policy analysis at the Department of State: The policy planning staff. *Journal of Policy Analysis and Management, 8*(3), 379-394.

Smith, B. L. R. (1966). *The Rand Corporation: A case study of a nonprofit advisory corporation.* Cambridge, MA: Harvard University Press.

Smith, J. A. (1989). Think tanks and the politics of ideas. In D. Colander & A. W. Coats (Eds.), *The spread of economic ideas* (pp. 175-194). Cambridge, UK: Cambridge University Press.

Weaver, R. K. (1989). The changing world of think tanks. *PS: Political Science and Politics, 22*(3), 563-578.

Willetts, D. (1987). The role of the Prime Minister's policy unit. *Public Administration, 65*(4), 443-454.

Acknowledgments

The papers on the congressional support agencies, and Verdier's comments on them, were given at the 1989 meeting of the Association of Public Policy Analysis and Management (APPAM) in Washington. Because of space limitations, I cut them from their original length, with the authors' permission. Rivlin's chapter on Brookings originated at a roundtable discussion in another panel at that meeting. She wrote up her remarks for this volume. The paper by Nelson on the Interior Department is reprinted from the *Journal of Policy Analysis and Management* with the permission of the author and John Wiley, publisher of the journal.

I would like to thank Kent Weaver of the Brookings Institution, author of a paper on think tanks (1989), who gave me his file of articles, and Charles Crothers of the University of Auckland for his comments. Jane Gerloff did her usual fine job of typing, keeping track of chapters and revisions, and picking up loose ends.

Helping Government Think: Functions and Consequences of Policy Analysis Organizations

Carol H. Weiss

In the 20th century a new organizational form emerged: the specialized analytic agency, staffed by experts, whose primary task was to provide policy information and advice. These analytic units were expected to mobilize intellectual resources in the service of social problem solving and, in effect, help government think.

The date of their emergence depends on the definition used. The Russell Sage Foundation was founded in 1907 through a grant from Margaret Olivia Sage to study social conditions as a means to improve them. In 1910 the Carnegie Endowment for International Peace was established through a gift from Andrew Carnegie, and the following year what was to become the Twentieth Century Fund was established with a gift from Edward A. Filene. Both went on to support public policy research.

In 1914 the Legislative Reference Service, the forerunner of the Congressional Research Service, was established, concerned primarily with the drafting of legislation. In 1916 the National Research Council was formed to serve as the staff operating arm of the National Academy of Sciences, a 19th-century arrangement to make scientific resources available to government. In 1921 the Department of Agriculture brought several research units together to form the Bureau of Agricultural Economics (Lyons, 1969). The Budget and Accounting Act of 1921 created both the Bureau of the Budget and the General Accounting Office, one to prepare a unified federal budget and the other to audit its expenditures. The Brookings Institution began work in 1927 with the amalgamation of three small earlier organizations. What was to become Columbia University's Bureau of Applied Social Research started in 1937 at Princeton University with a study of the impact of radio on American society (Barton, 1984).

The motives behind the creation of these and similar organizations were mixed. Their purposes were highly localized and largely pragmatic. But they arose against the background of the "good government" axioms of the Progressive Era, with its emphasis on fact gathering and rationality. The prevailing philosophy was to take the politics out of government administration and, in Rexford Tugwell's words as he boarded the train for Washington in 1933 to advise President Roosevelt, to speak truth to power.

World War II brought about enormous needs for planning not only in the military but also in the civilian economy, and the war stimulated the development and application of operations research and systems analysis. When the war ended, the RAND Corporation began existence to carry forward the kinds of work that operations researchers, scientists, and mathematicians had done for the Air Force. The postwar period saw a big spurt in policy-advising organizations of many kinds, as the American Enterprise Institute, the Bureau of Social Science Research, Resources for the Future, the Urban Institute, and dozens of other think tanks joined the scene.

Government, too, saw the growth of analytic units. In the Department of Defense, Secretary Robert McNamara, faced with the independence of the Army, Navy, and Air Force, and their interservice rivalries, used his team of analysts not only to improve the basis of decision making but also to help gain control over the unruly department. Styled the "Whiz Kids," they analyzed and rationalized decisions about force, deployment, and procurement and helped centralize authority in the office of the secretary. McNamara's staff introduced the Programming, Planning, Budgeting system (PPBS) to link decisions to budgetary allocations. President Johnson was so impressed with its effectiveness that in August 1965 he ordered the extension of PPBS to the other federal departments. Although PPBS did not survive long in the civilian agencies, at least partly because of its heavy demands for information and analytic capacity (Wildavsky, 1970), its coming strengthened the staffs of the analytic units that were already on the scene or developing in the departments, and its going hardly diminished the structures and staffs that carried on analysis functions.

Analytic units were set up in virtually every department. They went by various names—research and analysis, planning and evaluation, analysis and budget, and so on. The office in the Department of

Education is currently called the Office of Planning, Budget, and Evaluation. Within large departments, such as the then Department of Health, Education, and Welfare (now Health and Human Services), analytic units were attached not only to the Office of the Secretary but to component agencies three and sometimes even four layers down within the bureaucracy.

On university campuses, single-discipline and multidisciplinary research institutes, such as the University of Michigan's Institute of Social Research, were growing in the same period. Their growth was stimulated by the change of social science research from a solo-scholar to a large-scale enterprise. This development was due in part to the technology of the sample survey, which became a major source of data and required extensive field staff and advanced analytic capacity. As government funding for applied research began to increase in the 1960s, many academic research organizations sought a share of the action by addressing "applied" concerns, and new university institutes were formed with a focus on policy issues. In a few cases, government created and funded a university research center, as the Office of Economic Opportunity did with the University of Wisconsin's Institute for Research on Poverty.

At the same time, established for-profit consulting firms began to take on public policy analysis work, and new for-profit research and analysis organizations were begun to do analytic work for government. When government funding was at its peak in the 1970s, scores of such organizations (sometimes styled the Beltway Bandits, for the road around Washington on which many of them were located, as well as for the costs of their work) did research and analysis for government, much of it of higher quality than the soubriquet might suggest.

Reasons for Their Growth and Popularity

A recent count of U. S. policy analysis organizations *outside* of government, including those based in universities, came up with a figure of 1,000, about 100 of which were located in the Washington, DC, area (Smith, 1989). The criteria are inevitably a bit fuzzy, but whatever the figure, the surge in numbers inside and outside government is unmistakable. What accounts for the pervasiveness of analytic units?

1. They help policymakers understand and cope with complex problems. This is their official justification, and it is true and important. As the tasks taken on by government increase in number and complexity, more information is necessary to evaluate past performance, to consider future alternatives, and to try to foresee secondary effects and interactions with other policies and objectives. Someone has to take on the challenging job of amassing relevant information and—much harder—making sense of it in a policy framework.

2. Habermas has written of the "legitimacy crisis" of contemporary governments, and it is this environment that provides the backdrop for the turn to analysis. In a period of declining public confidence in governmental institutions, as opinion polls have regularly reported, political leaders seek to demonstrate the reason and rationality of their actions. Policy analysis provides a symbol that politicians and bureaucrats are going through the proper procedures to reach the proper outcomes. Internal policy analysis units offer immediate responsiveness to leaders' needs, and outside policy analysis units give the added fillip of independent review and confirmation.

3. Analytic units give officials at the top of a department sufficient understanding to exert greater control over subunits. The United States has a tradition of powerful, almost autonomous bureaus that pay little attention to the directives of the politically appointed secretary. The bureau chief, the chair of the cognizant congressional committee, and the leaders of the major interest groups formed an iron triangle that protected the bureau from incursions. With its formidable set of alliances, the bureau could outlast the initiatives that a relatively short-tenured secretary could try to introduce. Analysis is one tool that can help a secretary, as it helped McNamara, develop more effective mechanisms of control and tighten the reins on the component agencies.

4. Analytic units give central bureaucrats more knowledge of what is going on in the field. This knowledge is especially important since the federal government runs a large part of its business by giving funds to state and local governments and other corporate entities to administer—building roads, providing compensatory education to disadvantaged students, running national research laboratories, and so on. Policy analysis organizations can collect data and evaluate operations, giving officials in Washington as much or more information as officials in field offices routinely obtain. As a consequence, central officials and legislators can develop detailed procedures,

structures, and systems of incentives to constrain the manner in which policy is implemented. For better or worse, they can limit the procliv- ity of operating staffs to bend rules and to divert funds to the purposes they consider paramount and thus keep federal objectives high on the docket.

5. Because of the tendency of analytic units to increase centralized control, subagencies within the federal bureaucracies sought to develop their own analytic units. In large part, the purpose was to give them the knowledge and skill to make wiser decisions on issues within their purview and thus help improve their programs. In part, too, it was a move to protect the bureau from central surveillance. If information was going to be the currency with which the struggle for control was being waged, then the bureau wanted its own information source.

6. Outside analysis organizations increased in number partly because of the pulls of government demand. The government sought independent research and analysis under a variety of circumstances: if it did not have the requisite skills in-house, if large-scale work (such as survey research) would require hiring more staff than government ceilings would allow, if its need for certain kinds of work was spo- radic, if it wanted the imprimatur of outside authority, if it needed to impress skeptical congresspeople or citizens about the validity of its analytic work, if it wanted to ally itself with prestigious institutions. These kinds of conditions promoted the search for independent analy- sis, and old organizations expanded and new ones arose to accept federal grants and contracts.

7. Think tanks proliferated because of pushes on the supply side as well. Certain interests did not believe they were well represented in Washington. Thus, for example, the American Enterprise Institute (see chapter 2) began life because its founder believed that the values of free enterprise were going unheard in government councils. The Heritage Foundation was established to promote the cause of conser- vatism. The Center on Budget and Policy Priorities (see chapter 4) was founded to see what government policies might do for low-income families.

8. Perhaps it is well to note that some expectations for analysis units were out-of-left-field, pie-in-the-sky, and unreasonable. Some people hoped that analysis shops would "solve" policy problems. Others expected their arcane rites to dematerialize (or distract attention from) serious festering issues. Some decision makers believed that

patronizing the new analytic technologies would give them a reputation for being progressive and right thinking. Others used them to give an appearance of concern and activity (Prince, 1983). A host of self-serving and shallow, as well as responsible, motives sparked their growth and prosperity.

Why Policy Analysis Organizations Thrive in the United States

Policy analysis organizations exist in other countries, particularly in government agencies, and most particularly in those concerned with economic and fiscal matters. Nevertheless, it is the United States that has seen the greatest flowering of the species. They flourish in this country because they fill certain gaps in the American political structure.

1. The fragmentation of the governmental system creates a vacuum.
   a. The American system rests on separation of powers between the executive and the legislature. Unlike legislatures in parliamentary systems, Congress does not automatically adopt the president's program; it, too, initiates legislation. When Congress and the presidency are controlled by different parties, as they have been for most of the 1980s and into the 1990s, possibilities for independent action and conflict increase, creating multiple audiences for analysis.
   b. Executive-branch departments are themselves fragmented. Huge sprawling bureaucracies, like the Departments of Defense or Health and Human Services, are made up of strong component agencies, each with its own interests, clients, and policy preferences. The departments are balkanized and difficult for the secretary to control.
   c. Congress is fragmented. The House of Representatives and the Senate proceed quite independently, with negotiation largely limited to the period after the two chambers have passed differing versions of legislation. Within each chamber, power is dispersed over a large number of subcommittees. Congressional reforms in the 1970s reduced the power of the House and Senate leadership, reduced the importance of seniority in selection of committee chairs, and allowed committee members, and particularly subcommittee chairs, to have a greater say. While the number of committees was reduced, the number of subcommittees increased, and authority was more widely distributed.

      Each member of Congress is essentially an enterprise unto himself or herself. Each of the 535 separate congressional offices constructs its own priorities, commitments, and policy stands. Party discipline is exhibited mainly at the beginning of a new Congress in matters of organization of the chamber. Thereafter, each member is subject to the pressures of interest groups and constituents and decides on his or her own policy positions.

d. The United States is a federal system, with responsibilities dispersed between the federal government and the states. It is also a capitalist system, with division of responsibilities between private and public sectors, and a substantial nonprofit sector as well. The number of players in the policy game is legion.

2. Few bodies aggregate interests.

a. Political parties have not undertaken a serious effort at policy development. Even if they were to try, they have few resources to back it up. Campaign finance reforms have limited their ability to raise money for political campaigns, and thus they have limited resources to dispense to candidates and cannot call in past favors. In Congress they have few rewards or penalties to bring members into line.

b. The kinds of corporatist structures that aggregate interests in Scandinavia and elsewhere are weak or nonexistent. No effective peak associations exist that can negotiate for industry, labor, or other interests. Those bodies that do exist, such as the National Association of Manufacturers or the American Federation of Labor-Congress of Industrial Organizations (AFL-CIO), have declined in political influence and speak for only a fraction of their constituencies. No formal mechanisms bring them into negotiation with government over policy.

3. The problems of governing become increasingly complex. Problems have become entangled with other problems, such as the conflict between development and environmentalism, and trade-offs are difficult to foresee and comprehend. Even finding an appropriate expert or consultant has become difficult because problems do not present themselves in configurations that match the specializations of the academic disciplines. International interdependencies complicate the situation further.

4. The civil service, which in other countries takes up much of the slack, has become less influential. Some people believe that this loss of influence is due to the declining quality of recruits into public service, but no longitudinal data exist on the quality of public employees, and it remains a matter of conjecture. What is not in dispute is that since the Nixon presidency, more politically appointed officials have been brought into federal departments. While once appointees served only at the level of the office of the secretary, now they also serve in positions two and three levels lower in the departmental structure.

The increasing penetration of political appointments has weakened the standing of line civil servants and downgraded their influence—and perhaps their motivation. Officials at the secretarial level are more likely to turn for advice to other appointees than to career officials.

To some extent this is true in all political systems. Bureaucrats, in common lore and to some degree in actuality, tend to be preoccupied with internal concerns of the organization. They attend to issues of organizational survival and the preservation of the prerogatives, privileges, and power of the bureaucracy. Their allegiance to regulations can lead to ponderousness and elephantiasis, the elevation of procedure over substance. On some occasions and in some agencies—and perhaps particularly during the Reagan administration—they may be out of sympathy with the principles of the party in power. Finally, they often suffer from a shortage of fresh ideas; they are captives of the "this-is-how-we've-always-done-it" mentality[1] (compare Walter, 1986, on Australia). For all their knowledge and dedication, regular civil servants may be poorly suited to mobilizing and mediating interests, ideas, and agendas.

In sum, these characteristics of the political system create a void. Coordinative mechanisms are needed to overcome fragmentation, to aggregate interests, to cope with complexity, and to take longer and broader perspectives on issues. It is in this context that internal and external policy analysis organizations have flourished. They are filling a gap that few other mechanisms serve, and they are doing it with a philosophy of "rationality," "logic," "evidence," and "expertise" that is especially appealing to the American mind.

A final consideration is the American tradition of private philanthropy. From the days of Margaret Olivia Sage, wealthy individuals have established foundations with the express purpose of supporting research and action to bring about policy change. In no other country have the resources for independent think tanks been so richly available.

Recent Developments on the Analytic Scene

Organizations for policy analysis and advice have faced a changing world, and they have changed as well. Some of the most striking developments in the last dozen years or so are the following:

1. Independent think tanks continue to be established. A recent development is the appearance of regional and state organizations, particularly with conservative and free-market orientations, that offer advice on state and local policy (Andrews, 1989).

2. Policy analysis organizations are less likely to work for federal executive branch agencies. The Reagan cutbacks that began in 1981 affected not only programs but also research, evaluation, and analysis. Funding of research and analysis inside government was generally reduced. Funds available for contracting research and analysis to outside organizations declined. The initial cuts were steep, but funding gradually moved upward in the late 1980s. Still by the end of the decade, in most agencies it had not reached pre-1981 levels (General Accounting Office, 1987, discusses funding and staffing for evaluation).

3. Outside analytic organizations are directing more of their advice to Congress. They are disseminating analytic work to members of Congress and their staffs, through publications, speeches, testimony, hearings, and conferences. Reasons are several:

- President Reagan, whose rhetoric emphasized reducing government, showed little receptivity to new policy initiatives. As budget deficits increased, the press for retrenchment became more insistent. Continuing under President Bush, analysis and advice were rarely welcome unless they promised fiscal savings.
- Through the 1980s and early 1990s, Congress remained largely Democratic (although from 1981 through 1986 Republicans held a majority in the Senate). Democrats historically have been more receptive to extension of government programs and service to new publics.
- Congress represents a broader spectrum of opinion than does the executive branch, and analytic institutions of all political hues can find a likely listener there.
- Even more important, Congress has been playing a more active role in the making of federal policy. In taking the initiative on issue after issue, it needs information and advice. It wants analysis; it wants ideas.
- Congress traditionally has been unwilling to trust information emanating from executive agencies. It suspects them of biasing information to fit the administration's line, and never more so than when the administration is of a different ideological stamp. Democratic leaders were particularly suspicious that the Reagan administration would prevent honest information from reaching them.
- Unlike the large and specialized analytic staffs of the executive agencies, the analytic capabilities of Congress are limited. Although it increased the numbers of personal staff and committee and subcommittee staff during the 1970s, and it can draw on the four congressional support agencies—CRS, GAO, CBO, and OTA—these staffs cannot begin to match the executive departments in numbers or degree of specialization.

In sum, Congress is active in policy-making, has limited information, and distrusts much of what it has—not only from the administration but from interest groups as well. It is almost an ideal target for analytic communications.

4. A parallel development is an upswing in attention to the media. Policy analysis organizations devote increasing fractions of their time to getting their messages to the press, radio, and television. Of course, internal analytic units have less latitude than external units to go public with their work unless and until they receive official sanction. Still, their formal reports generally have to be accessible under the Freedom of Information Act, and it often has seemed sensible to make them publicly and widely known.

More press conferences are held, more press releases are distributed, more speeches are made, and readier responses are given to media reporters who are looking for an interesting point of view or a telling quote. Analysts try to place pithy articles on the op-ed pages of newspapers, or longer articles in journals of opinion. Some analysts have become standard entries in reporters' Rolodexes of sources and staples on television talk shows. Analysts from some of the Washington think tanks begin to complain about the amount of time they spend responding to reporters' questions rather than conveying the information that they believe important for the public to know (see chapter 1 on Brookings).

The main reason for the heightened attention to the media is the growing role that the media play in the policy-making process. In the situation of political fragmentation already mentioned, the media help bring a modicum of order. They, like policy analysis organizations, help focus attention and set the policy agenda. As communications researchers have long said, the media may not be successful in telling people what to think, but they are "stunningly successful" in telling them what to think about (Cohen, 1963, p. 13; Iyengar & Kinder, 1987). This maxim is as true for the president and Congress as it is for the general public. By flashing attention on a particular set of issues, the media help ensure that the issues will be processed. Further, the media often set the framework for discussion, the conceptual structure that will organize debate, and the terms of discourse used in argument.

Therefore, analytic organizations see the media as an efficient channel to reach not only the public but also the policy communities that cluster in and around government. Since opportunities for influence are greatest in the early stages of issue formation, before policy actors have taken stands and made commitments, analysis organizations like to get in early and help set the frame for discussion.

5. Another significant development is the growth of analytic organizations on the right. The Heritage Foundation is the most visible example in a host of others, such as the Cato Institute, the Hudson Institute, the Manhattan Institute for Policy Research, and such smaller ones as the Heartland Institute in Chicago and the Independence Institute in Colorado (Andrews, 1989; Rauch, 1988). Conservatives and libertarians, feeling besieged by liberal institutions and poorly represented in political debates, actively sought to redress the balance. They created new organizations to give voice to their perspectives.

In many ways, the development has been a useful one. Conservatives generally have been hostile to social science with its pragmatic, problem-solving orientation, and to such derivatives of social science as policy research and analysis. When Ronald Reagan was elected president in 1980, his first budget director, David Stockman, sought to decimate funding for basic and applied social science in all agencies of government. One interpretation of the move was that conservatives believed they had little need for research and analysis; their principles and values gave them the answers. Another reason may have been that social scientists traditionally have been more liberal than the population at large (Lipset & Ladd, 1972; Orlans, 1973); disproportionately few Reagan supporters would likely be found in their ranks. Further, the thrust of much policy analysis in the preceding decades had been, as Banfield (1980) noted, to locate new wrongs that could be righted only by increased government intrusion into the social fabric. For an administration whose proclaimed mission was "getting government off the backs of the American people," such prescriptions were anathema.

With the social and policy sciences tarred as the enemy, it seemed only time until all government support would fall under the axe. Instead, think tanks of the right made well-publicized efforts to beat liberals at their own game—to do policy analysis that rested on proper assumptions and proper models of the good society. In most strands of conservative thought, principles and ideals are the real stuff of history. Conservatives are more concerned about principled ends than technical means. Conservative and libertarian think tanks take as their starting point a core of values, which are "permanent lessons of history and experience" (Smith, 1989, p. 192). They tend to give priority to identifying the principles they should promote, whether the issue is Nicaragua, job training, or energy, and then go on to analyze the means by which those ends can be realized.

One result of the rise of think tanks on the right has been the legitimation of policy analysis and policy research. Almost unwittingly, they have protected policy science and social science from the knee-jerk antagonism of right-wing foes. Another result is that the new think tanks have brought fresh perspectives into the analytic community. Although some of the ideas they championed, such as deregulation and privatization, had long respectable pedigrees in academia, their forceful promotion in Washington and in the states enlivened debates. They pushed analysts who had taken welfare-state assumptions for granted to think again; they encouraged new appraisals of appropriate policy in a period of budget deficits and fiscal retrenchment. Even when their faith in markets seemed to sacrifice compassion, and their concern for defense and tax cuts helped to legitimate federal deficits, their presence stimulated more probing discussions and arguments. But to the extent that their stand on principles resists compromises, they have increased divisiveness in policy advice networks.

6. At the same time, policy analysis units within a number of government departments have suffered cuts in staffing and funds because of the budgetary crunch of the 1980s and early 1990s. While deficits are the immediate cause of cutbacks, a certain disillusion with the output of the units has contributed. In the view of some, policy analysis has failed to bring about the improvements in government policy that its promoters have promised.

7. Since the early 1970s, schools of public policy have been flourishing in American universities, both new schools and reorganized schools of public administration. Their mission has been to prepare students for positions in public management and policy analysis. In the last decade, more and more of their graduates have arrived in policy analysis organizations. They are generally well trained not only in analytic methods, with an emphasis on economic analysis, but also in the political and organizational environment in which government decisions are made and carried out. They are providing a new cohort of policy analysts both inside and outside government.

8. In some quarters sophisticated quantitative techniques have been deemphasized in favor of qualitative methods of information gather-

ing and analysis. Several analytic units, in a development parallel to some recent directions in academic social science, are giving explicit recognition to the importance of qualitative inquiry as a way to understand the perspectives of the people under study and the dynamics—the how and why—of change.

Consequences of Institutions That Think for Government

Have the internal and external analysis organizations made any difference in what government does? Have they had any effects? Inevitably, it is extraordinarily difficult to gauge the impact of a single input into the vast, complicated, and highly interactive processes of government action. Cynical observers note that government does not seem to have particularly increased in intelligence in the last decade or two. Still, I believe a few trends can be discerned.

1. Government policy-making is better informed. I do not think that much doubt exists on this score. More knowledge is available about social, economic, and political conditions; more and better data are collected and analyzed on trends in air quality, employment, recruits to the armed services, families moving in and out of poverty, educational achievement, and so on. More analysis is being done of the advantages and disadvantages of prospective policies; more evaluation is done of the effects of past policies and changes needed to increase their effectiveness. Analysts have looked at interrelationships among policies rather than limiting themselves to the one-agency-domain-at-a-time view of the not-so-distant past. More sophisticated understanding exists of the workings of bureaucracies, of the obstacles that policy implementation faces, of the likely responses to new initiatives from affected subgroups. In the current budget-constrained climate, much useful work has been done on cost containment strategies in field after field.

Of course, the nature of the "facts" that have been established depends on the assumptions and conceptual frameworks within which they are defined. Those who bring different values, perspectives, definitions, and analytic strategies can dispute much of the evidence and its interpretation. But within the prevailing frameworks, improvements in data have been made, not the least being the maintenance of longitudinal data series over extended periods of time.

Good analysis does not necessarily lead to better policy. Information is only one ingredient. What actually happens depends on the mix of interests, ideologies, and institutional procedures in the political domain (Weiss, 1983) and on the political will to make things happen. To the extent that policy analysis units were expected to link social knowledge directly to political action and lead to immediate policy improvements, the expectation has been fulfilled only intermittently and sporadically. Increased social knowledge remains one hand clapping. Others have to listen, to examine critically, to learn, to mobilize, and to act. Furthermore, much of what analysis has learned has turned out in practice to be incomplete, wrong, or rapidly obsolete.

Still, analysis has influenced understanding and interpretation of policy issues; in Rivlin's (1971) terms, it has raised the level of debate. Over time, many of the ideas derived from analysis have percolated into corridors of power. Although the route often has been circuitous and the speed of transmission slow, in a number of fields analytic information and insights have come into currency and changed the nature of policy discourse (Weiss 1977, 1980, 1986, 1989). Sometimes the ideas went underground for a time and surfaced years later under a different flag. Sometimes they managed to change the direction of policy. (For an interesting example, see Derthick & Quirk, 1985.)

2. Considerable discussion and negotiation occur within analytic communities. Members of inside and outside analysis organizations who work in the same subject area, particularly in Washington, often attend the same conferences, talk on the same panels, testify at the same hearings, and serve on the same commissions. Analysts of different persuasions spend sizable amounts of time in discussion. Even though much of the talk is confrontational, particularly if initiated by journalists who want to provoke debate, some of it winds up being a search for common agreement.

As analysts have served on interagency panels and external commissions to resolve technical perplexities, they have engaged in argument and negotiation and reached accommodations. By coming to something approaching consensus about the status of problems and likely strategies, they have made it easier for politicians to move to agreement. In this sense, they have served a mediation as well as an analytic function.

Some of the analytic units, including those serving Congress, also bring in representatives of alternative points of view during the study. The Office of Technology Assessment, for example, conducts its analysis with the participation of expert panels; a panel on medical technology might include specialists from universities, medical practice, manufacturers of equipment, and consumer groups. Many analysis organizations hold extensive series of conferences, inviting a wide array of participants to hear the latest analytic results. A major intent of these dissemination strategies is to create consensus and momentum for action; a by-product is the creation of intersectoral linkages to advance continuing conversation and discourse. (See Marsh, 1990, for the failure of Australian policy analysis organizations to attempt intermediation.)

3. On the other hand, as the variety of perspectives represented on the think tank scene increases and the advice they give diverges, a cacophony is rising on some issues. Sectarian analysis, done in the interests of advocacy, is used less for illumination than for ammunition in policy contests. Rather than helping overcome fragmentation, analysis may merely be changing the language in which the fragments contend. Each side now brandishes the latest analytic findings generated by its own unit. Debate degenerates into argument about the methodology that each group employed instead of centering directly on the goals and values of prospective policies (Malbin, 1980). So many ideas and arguments are in contention that chances for agreement on some issues appear to recede.

4. Some critics charge that the spread of analysis and analysis organizations has pernicious effects on the democratic process. It leads to an increasing technocratization of policy-making and, in consequence, the alienation of the general public from political participation. If problems are to be resolved in terms of benefit-cost ratios or predictions from abstruse models, the average citizen withdraws to the sidelines. The technocrat, with a mastery of esoteric ritual, reigns supreme (Fischer, 1990; Straussman, 1978).

Similarly, Fischer (1990) and others argue, administratively based cadres of policy experts outflank politicians and political parties. Hostile to politics and scornful of moral and ideological commitment, they seek to reduce all issues to matters of practical technical inquiry. As they seize greater control of the levers of government, policy decisions are better understood as learning processes among experts than as struggles among rival political forces. Their dominion is elitist; it leads to increasing centralization; at the extreme, it undermines democracy.

Assuredly, tendencies lean in this direction. Reliance on experts has always existed uneasily alongside basic beliefs in popular participation. The populist strand in American history has had its fair measure of anti-intellectualism (Hofstadter, 1963). On their side, some analysts tend to lay claim to objectivity and value-neutrality and try to position themselves above the fray. It can be assumed, in these postpositivist times, that they know (at some level of consciousness) that the claim to objectivity is at least partly self-serving. It validates their admission to the policy game and their status in the system. Yet the claim also represents an allegiance to standards of fairness, comprehensiveness, and appropriate method, and a rejection of what is often presented under the guise of analysis by lobbyists and advocacy groups: the biased one-sided amassing of confirmatory evidence suggestive more of adversarial proceedings in a law court than the canons of impartial investigation.

The critics of analysis and analytic organizations have rightly pointed out the elitist elements and the centralizing effects of much of the work being done. It is small rebuttal to cite the numbers of social and policy scientists who work for small policy centers on behalf of minority causes, who promote citizen participation and advocacy for underrepresented groups, and who in other ways work against the grain. They are there, but I doubt that they are an effective counter-weight to "establishment" analysis. More to the point, mainline analysts in increasing numbers are coming to recognize that their analyses incorporate values—values that are not necessarily univer-sally shared. For example, the prevailing analytic emphasis on effi-ciency may be outweighed in many other people's minds by concern with compassion or even self-interest. Majone (1989, p. xii) has writ-ten "it should not be left to policy analysts to fight the last battles of positivism," and many policy analysts are accepting the view that they speak for a particular set of values. They are likely to see them-selves less as technocratic experts seeking optimal solutions to policy problems and more as competent analysts applying system and rea-son to difficult issues and often engaging in advocacy for their pre-ferred policies.

Recognition of their value biases, however, leaves policy analysis organizations with an uncomfortable dilemma: If they sacrifice pre-tensions to neutral expertise, how do they maintain legitimacy? Nel-son, in chapter 7, offers a possible answer. In a democratic system that believes in the representation of diverse interests and conflicting opinions, the analytic unit can make a forceful case for one worldview. It may be a view out of favor with government, an underdog point of view, a view from the left or the right. It often happens to be what Schultze (1968, 1982) has called partisanship for efficiency, although analytic organizations have used other rallying cries to champion such other causes as school-based management, postmarketing sur-veillance of drugs, and energy self-sufficiency.

But if a policy analysis organization relinquishes the claim to neutrality, on what grounds does it speak? Who has anointed it as advocate? Lindblom (1990) suggests that too much has been ceded to experts; too much weight is given to analysis at the expense of human experience. More effort might well be put into civic education on policy issues for the public and participatory structures that allow their voices to be better heard.

In the meantime, a pragmatic response to fear of the reign of the technocrat is the fact that political leaders are still very much in control. In this volume, and wherever social scientists and policy analysts write, their common lament is that political actors rarely pay enough attention to the knowledge they have so laboriously acquired. Rather than running the world, they are sitting in their offices, struggling to devise better means of getting their message across and waiting for word that somebody has heard what they have been saying.

Nevertheless, the cumulative structure they have built in their collective enterprise—the organizations, networks, analyses, and people—continue to have important effects. For good and for ill, they help to shape the ways that government thinks.

Note

1. Bureaucratic offices of policy analysis can suffer from some of the same disabilities (Meltsner, 1976).

References

Andrews, J. K., Jr. (1989). So you want to start a think tank. *Policy Review, 49,* 62-65.
Banfield, E. C. (1980). Policy science as metaphysical madness. In R. A. Goldwin (Ed.), *Bureaucrats, policy analysts, statesmen: Who leads?* (pp. 1-19) Washington, DC: American Enterprise Institute.
Barton, J. S. (1984). *Guide to the Bureau of Applied Social Research.* New York: Clearwater.
Cohen, B. (1963). *The press and foreign policy.* Princeton, NJ: Princeton University Press.
Derthick, M., & Quirk, P. J. (1985). *The politics of deregulation.* Washington, DC: Brookings Institution.
Fischer, F. (1990). *Technology and the politics of expertise.* Newbury Park, CA: Sage.
General Accounting Office [GAO]. (1987). *Federal evaluation: Fewer units, reduced resources, different studies from 1980.* Washington, DC.
Hofstadter, R. (1963). *Anti-intellectualism in American life.* New York: Knopf.
Iyengar, S., & Kinder, D. R. (1987). *News that matters.* Chicago: University of Chicago Press.

18 ORGANIZATIONS FOR POLICY ANALYSIS

Lindblom, C. E. (1990). *Inquiry and change: the troubled attempt to understand and shape society*. New Haven, CT: Yale University Press.

Lipset, S. M., & Ladd, E. C., Jr. (1972). The politics of American sociologists. *American Journal of Sociology, 78*, 1485-1492.

Lyons, G. M. (1969). *The uneasy partnership: Social science and the federal government in the twentieth century*. New York: Russell Sage.

Majone, G. (1989). *Evidence, argument and persuasion*. New Haven, CT: Yale University Press.

Malbin, M. (1980). *Unelected representatives: Congressional staff and the future of representative government*. New York: Basic Books.

Marsh, I. (1990, May). *Globalisation, governance and think tanks*. Paper presented at the Third International Workshop on Governance in the Asia-Pacific Region organised by Canadian Institute for Research on Public Policy, Kuala Lumpur, Malaysia.

Meltsner, A. (1976). *Policy analysts in the bureaucracy*. Berkeley: University of California Press.

Orlans, H. (1973). *Contracting for knowledge*. San Francisco: Jossey-Bass.

Prince, M. J. (1983). *Policy advice and organizational survival*. Aldershot, Hampshire: Gower.

Rauch, J. (1988, October 22). Giving wings to ideas. *National Journal, 20*, 2655-2659.

Rivlin, A. M. (1971). *Systematic thinking for social action*. Washington, DC: Brookings Institution.

Schultze, C. L. (1968). *The politics and economics of public spending*. Washington, DC: Brookings Institution.

Schultze, C. L. (1982). The role and responsibilities of the economist in government. *American Economic Review, 72*(2), 62-66.

Smith, J. A. (1989). Think tanks and the politics of ideas. In D. Colander & A. W. Coats (Eds.), *The spread of economic ideas* (pp. 175-194). Cambridge: Cambridge University Press.

Straussman, J. D. (1978). *The limits of technocratic politics*. New Brunswick, NJ: Transaction Books.

Walter, J. (1986). *The ministers' minders: Personal advisers in national government*. Melbourne: Oxford University Press.

Weiss, C. H. (1977). Research for policy's sake: The enlightenment function of social science research. *Policy Analysis, 3*(4), 531-545.

Weiss, C. H., with Bucuvalas, M. J. (1980). *Social science research and decision-making*. New York: Columbia University Press.

Weiss, C. H. (1983). Ideology, interests, and information: The basis of policy positions. In D. Callahan & B. Jennings (Eds.), *Ethics, the social sciences, and policy analysis* (pp. 213-245). New York: Plenum.

Weiss, C. H. (1986). The circuity of enlightenment. *Knowledge: Creation, Diffusion, Utilization, 8*(2), 274-282.

Weiss, C. H. (1989). Congressional committees as users of analysis. *Journal of Policy Analysis and Management, 8*(3), 411-431.

Wildavsky, A. (1970). Rescuing policy analysis from PPBS. In R. H. Haveman & J. Margolis (Eds.), *Public expenditures and policy analysis* (pp. 461-481). Chicago: Rand McNally.

PART 1

External Think Tanks

1

Policy Analysis at the Brookings Institution

Alice M. Rivlin

This brief chapter is an insider's view of the Brookings Institution and its role in the Washington public policy community. My credentials for writing it are more than 30 years in the policy analysis trade, most of them on the staff at Brookings, with occasional forays into federal government service or academe. Some of these forays were quite long—I ran the Congressional Budget Office for more than eight years—but I always came back to Brookings like a homing pigeon.

I cannot pretend to give an objective outsider's evaluation, but I will try to answer some of the questions most asked about Brookings. How did Brookings get started, and what does it do? How does it view its role and gauge its impact? How is it funded? How has Brookings changed in recent years? I will close with a few comments on how Brookings and other policy analysis organizations might be more effective.

Purpose and Origin

The Brookings Institution is a nonprofit, nonpartisan organization located in Washington, DC, and is devoted to research and education on public policy issues. Its purpose is to analyze the choices facing government decision makers and to publish the results of these studies. It hopes to stimulate informed debate and to enhance public understanding of the difficult questions that face the nation.

We at Brookings used to disdain the faintly pejorative appellation "think tank," but we now use it as freely as everybody else. We even point out that Brookings, which celebrated its 75th anniversary in 1991, was the original Washington think tank. It was the model that subsequent entrants had in view when they started their own think tanks, whether their objective was to emulate Brookings or to differentiate themselves from it.

Its founding spirit was Robert S. Brookings, a successful St. Louis businessman who revered higher education and research although he had not been able to go to college himself. Partly as a result of serving in Washington with the War Industries Board during World War I, he became convinced of the importance of improving public understanding of policy problems. In the decade following the war, he devoted his energies and resources to nurturing three organizations, one of which was a graduate school, for the study of public policy. The three were consolidated into the Brookings Institution in 1927.

What Is Brookings Like?

The massive, undistinguished building on Massachusetts Avenue exudes an aura of solidity and cohesion. Inside, however, Brookings is anything but monolithic. Individual social scientists work separately on a wide variety of projects. Indeed, the Brookings research staff is much more like a graduate school faculty without a formal teaching program than like a bureaucracy. It is a collection of scholars whose allegiance is to their disciplines and whose common bond is that their work relates to public issues, usually to questions of federal government policy.

The organization is simple, and the atmosphere is collegial. President Bruce K. MacLaury presides over four major divisions plus administrative and fund-raising staffs. The three research divisions— Economic Studies, Government Studies, and Foreign Policy Studies— correspond roughly to departments of economics, political science and international relations in a good medium-sized university. Each is headed by a director, who would be called a department chair in a university.

The work atmosphere in the research divisions is like a university when the students are away and the professors are trying frantically to catch up on research. But differences do exist. One is the absence of pure theorists. Everyone works on applied research problems in public policy. Another difference is the absence of committees and, blessedly, academic politics.

The fourth division, called the Center for Public Policy Education, is Brookings's adult education arm. It holds conferences ranging in length from one day to a few weeks, in which businesspeople, government officials, and other interested citizens meet to learn about and discuss public issues. Many of these conferences are held in Washington; some are held in places as far away as Paris and Seoul. The center draws on the research staff for speakers, as well as on politicians, government officials, and non-Brookings scholars. It sometimes builds a "national issues forum" around a recent Brookings publication, bringing together critics, as well as supporters, of the policies suggested in the book. Sometimes it focuses on issues that none of the research staff happen to be working on.

The typical Brookings Institution research scholar is writing a book—about tax incidence or trade policy, relations with the Soviets or developments in Japan, trends in American politics or how to reform the public schools. The book originally was expected to be completed in two years but is usually behind schedule. The reason is that the prospective book, not to mention the scholar's last book, is designedly on a topic in which there is widespread interest. As a result, the scholar is being asked constantly to testify before congressional committees, to make speeches, to appear on talk shows, or to offer advice to public officials. The book is delayed constantly by the demands of the shorter term activities. The result is that Brookings scholars, including this one, work very hard and still feel guilty most of the time because they are behind schedule on The Book.

Ever since I have been at Brookings, I have heard periodic discussions of how to deemphasize books in favor of other products—journal articles, newspaper and magazine pieces, television programs—that may have more impact on public understanding of policy problems than do books. This discussion is partly an effort to assuage the guilt, since most of us spend more time on other types of presentations than we do on our books and would like our judgments about time-use vindicated. Nevertheless, the book remains the dominant Brookings product, the final output of most research projects. Foundations and other donors like to see books and researchers themselves, one suspects, like to feel that the fruits of their labors are enshrined forever between hard covers on a library shelf.

Brookings is an individualistic place. Its research scholars, like most social science professors, rarely work together. They lunch together, talk about the issues of the day, sometimes contribute chapters to an edited volume, and occasionally coauthor a book. Their usual way of working, however, is alone, not in joint projects. Moreover, there are no team leaders. Even senior researchers usually have no more staff than a junior research assistant without a graduate degree. This working style is undoubtedly inefficient. Most senior scholars would be more productive as leaders of teams of junior scholars than as writers of books by themselves, but the individualistic style is rooted deeply in the Brookings culture.

It follows that the visibility and public image of Brookings are primarily the visibility and image of the individuals who happen to be there. Whether Brookings is in the news and considered influential depends on whether its scholars have chosen to work on subjects that the nation and the media currently are concerned about.

The influence on public policy of scholars at Brookings, like that of a public policy faculty, is indirect and hard to measure. None of us draft legislation, sit in committee markups, or even talk more than sporadically to those who do. Presidents do not call to ask What should we do in the Middle East? or How can we balance the budget? Cabinet officers or subcabinet officers also do not call—at least not very often. Rather, we write books and articles that are read by students, other public policy professionals and, we hope, the press and opinion leaders. We participate in policy conferences in which, unfortunately, public policy academics mostly talk to each other but that also involve public officials. We try to help politicians and their staffs understand the issues before them through testimony, briefings, and informal conversations. We try to reach a wider public, at least the reading and listening public, through speeches and media appearances.

Our main hope is that we raise the level of public debate in and out of Washington. If decision makers are better informed about the consequences of their acts or understand a little better the choices they have to make because they have read or heard about some research done at Brookings, the institution is succeeding. Unfortunately, it is hard to know how often these successes occur.

The Ideology Question

The press, apparently believing that every organization needs a label, frequently calls Brookings a "liberal think tank." Most Brookings researchers, however, do not fit easily into either "liberal" or "conservative" cubby holes. They tend to be middle-of-the-road pragmatists, technocrats rather than ideologues, and debunkers of the zealots who offer simplistic solutions. Indeed, if a recurrent theme exists in Brookings policy analysis, it is that public choices are really hard, that there are no easy answers, only difficult trade-offs. Brookings's all-time best seller, Arthur Okun's *Equality and Efficiency: The Big Tradeoff* (1975), is an eloquent statement of this theme.

Occasionally, a Republican politician will refer to Brookings as the "Democratic government in exile," a phrase coined in the Nixon administration, which does not hold up under scrutiny. Undoubtedly, more registered Democrats than registered Republicans are at Brookings, despite some effort to find more Republicans. A small number of Brookings senior fellows, most notably Charles L. Schultze, have held prominent positions in government. Hardly any, however, are involved actively in partisan politics. Brookings is not a temporary haven for people whose more permanent job is running the government. In fact, exactly the opposite is the case. Brookings scholars who have served in government generally think of that service as an exciting but difficult interlude in a more permanent career of research and analysis.

Where the Money Comes From

Unfortunately, the Brookings fortune was not of Carnegie or Rockefeller proportions. From the beginning, the Brookings Institution depended on a variety of funding sources, including foundation, corporate, and individual gifts, both to endowment and to operating expenses.

Brookings does not do contract research and makes a big effort to ensure that its independence and integrity are not compromised by taking money from sources with an interest in the outcome of research. It occasionally undertakes projects funded by the government but has never become dependent on government money. In recent years, government funds have been an extremely small portion of total funding.

How Has Brookings Changed?

I am frequently asked how Brookings has changed over the several decades that I have been associated with it. My perception is that Brookings has not changed as much as the Washington world around it. The institution has adapted to the new ways in which policy is made and discussed.

First, we have more interaction with Congress. Congress has become an increasingly important consumer of policy analysis. The growth of congressional staffs and the increasing analytical sophistication of Congresspeople and Senators themselves has increased steadily the appetite of Congress for testimony, briefings, and conversations about policy issues.

Second, we have much more interaction with the media. Indeed, press attention has become overwhelming. Brookings researchers with expertise on front-line issues—from the savings and loan crisis to Middle Eastern politics—sometimes have to hide from the press to get any work done at all. Where a handful of national newspapers and wire services and three major networks used to be, now are many dozens of print, television, and radio reporters who want quick quotes, sound bites, or background insights and information. Their calls create a dilemma. One wants to be responsive, to contribute to public understanding of the issue in question, but responding is time-consuming and further delays The Book.

Third, we interact more with other Washington think tanks. Brookings is now one of a whole group of somewhat similar organizations. Brookings scholars are frequently in meetings and on panels with their counterparts in other organizations. Mostly the scholars enjoy the interaction, while administrators worry about competing for the same sources of funds.

How Could Public Policy Organizations
Do Their Job Better?

In closing, let me offer a few thoughts about how Brookings and organizations like Brookings might do a better job of elucidating public policy issues, contributing to informed debate, and ultimately to a better governed country.

First, I believe more sustained attention should be paid to a given subject. I do not mean that we should write longer books, but that research should build more on prior research. Scholars with expertise on different aspects of a complex subject should have more sense than they do now of contributing to a growing body of knowledge and insight. Complicated and recurring questions—controlling health costs, increasing political participation or deescalating conflicts in the Middle East—cannot be solved by an individual scholar working alone. Sustained efforts of different kinds of people working together, accumulating data, and reacting to each other's work ultimately would be more productive. The tradition of solo research, however, is deeply ingrained both in academic social science and at places like Brookings. Moreover, think tanks, like universities, feel they have to cover a wide range of subjects and cannot afford more than one or two experts on each.

Second, Brookings, like many similar institutions, should be training more young people in policy analysis and applied research. Not all of these people should stay in think tanks, of course. Many, indeed most, eventually should pursue careers in government or universities. The dilemma is that able young scholars on the tenure track in universities and rising young stars in government or business cannot usually afford to take time out to do policy analysis. Moreover, policy-relevant work is not currently the best ticket to tenure in our leading universities.

Some of these problems might be alleviated by closer links between academic institutions, especially public policy schools, and Washington think tanks. Exchanges of faculty and graduate students would enrich both kinds of institutions. One can imagine sustained cooperative projects, with subprojects being carried out both in think tanks and universities by researchers who were sharing information and critiquing each other's work.

Third, research organizations like Brookings need to find better ways of involving wider groups of people in thinking more than superficially about issues facing the nation. We need to find some middle ground between the scholarly book and the 30-second sound bite. Those who bemoan the level of public understanding of the issues they research might spend some time preparing teaching materials for adults and young people or informative background material for citizen forums.

Fourth, we all need to find more effective ways of working with the press than simply fielding questions. What do we think people should understand about policy issues? How can we help the press get these messages across in ways that are more informative than the nightly news and less boring than the average talk show?

Finally, it would be useful if policy experts spent more time working out compromise solutions with people of differing views. We should not try to substitute for the political process, of course. But the evolution of constructive policy would be advanced by more efforts to simulate the political process. Currently the politicians call in an array of experts that give differing advice and then try to make sense of it themselves. If the experts sat down and negotiated with each other, recording not just the outcome but the elements of process, they might come up with some new solutions, as well as a new sensitivity to the problems faced by the politicians.

Reference

Okun, A. (1975, May). *Equality and efficiency: The big tradeoff.* Washington, DC: The Brookings Institute.

2

American Enterprise Institute for Public Policy Research

Patrick Ford

The American Enterprise Institute for Public Policy Research (AEI) burst into national prominence in the 1970s, when the best and brightest of the outgoing Ford administration, including the former president himself, joined AEI and began pumping out hundreds of studies and essays on energy policy, government regulation, inflation, stagflation, and a wide range of other domestic and international issues. AEI was hailed as the first right-leaning think tank to challenge the supremacy of the Brookings Institution. It was credited with laying a good part of the intellectual foundation for the regulatory reform efforts that began under President Carter and took a strong hold under President Reagan. Numerous think tanks have sprung up on the right and left during the intervening period, and AEI had to endure a cataclysmic financial and management crisis in the mid-1980s that almost drove it out of business, but it continues to house an elite faculty of scholars and to build on a solid reputation for credible, high-quality research and writing.

To understand what makes AEI prestigious and how it developed its basic character, one must go back to the beginning. It is important to focus on three aspects of AEI's history: its relationship to the leaders of American enterprise; its perpetually rocky financial situation, which causes it to have to "go to market" every year to support itself; and the relationship of its development with that of the so-called conservative agenda.

Getting Started

The American Enterprise Institute's precursor came to life at a time when America's most important enterprise was self-preservation. It was 1943 and the world was preoccupied with war. American business—indeed, the economic system at large—was focusing on little beyond wartime production. A small group of business leaders recognized that serious thought needed to be given to the postwar economy; in the wake of extensive wartime controls, the economy would have to be geared toward free enterprise again. It would be easy, they reckoned, for the nation to lapse into a centrally planned and controlled economy. The need to deal with the Great Depression and World War II had strengthened the federal government enormously. The Democrats had controlled the executive branch for 10 years, giving them pervasive control over policy-making and judicial appointments. Few alternatives to the New Deal agenda existed.

President Roosevelt had his Brain Trust, but the Republicans and the business sector had few intellectual resources on which they could rely. The leading independent source of ideas on public policy, the Brookings Institution, could hardly be counted on in those days for probusiness ideas. To fill this void, the group of business executives, led by Lewis Brown of the Johns Manville Corporation, formed the American Enterprise Association (AEA). During the first decade of its life, the AEA operated much more like today's business associations (such as the Business Roundtable) than today's think tanks. It had only a few full-time staff members, using lawyers and economists on a free-lance basis to analyze proposed legislation. The founders seemed to have little interest in growing the organization; in 1954 it had only five staff members and an annual budget of $80,000.

Top Priority: Legislative Analysis

In those early years the AEA saw its mission to be as almost an independent "staff" for members of Congress, especially Republicans. Its most widely read publications were legislative analyses, which were written most often by lawyers and followed a set format: a straightforward description of the legislation and what it would do, then the pro and con arguments to let decision makers consider the merits and pitfalls. The legislative analyses series lasted into the 1980s and was one of the organization's most popular programs.

In 1954 the organization almost went out of business because many of the corporate executives on its board believed that its mandate no longer existed. The economy has prospered, they said. The Democrats no longer controlled the government. Staff sizes in both the executive and legislative branches were growing. The kind of basic "staff" work that the AEA had performed so ably seemed superfluous.

Some AEA members, however, saw the need for a continuing voice in Washington on behalf of free-market principles. They urged that the organization be kept alive and that its mandate be broadened to a more proactive role in developing public policy options.

The latter forces prevailed, and the AEA board reaffirmed its commitment to the organization. It also recruited a new executive director, a little-known executive named William J. Baroody, Sr., at the U.S. Chamber of Commerce. They teamed him with a respected director of research named Glenn Campbell. These two men worked closely together until the end of the decade, when Campbell was recruited to take over the Hoover Institution at Stanford University.

Baroody as Builder

Baroody and Campbell quickly set about changing the character of the AEA. They sought out the finest scholars in the country and enlisted them to write studies for the AEA, which Baroody and Campbell circulated much more widely than in the past. Among these academics were Milton Friedman, the future Nobel laureate; Gottfried Haberler, the renowned international trade professor at Harvard; Paul W. McCracken of the University of Michigan's School of Business; and G. Warren Nutter of the University of Virginia. These and other leading thinkers were recruited to serve on AEA's academic advisory board (later called the Council of Academic Advisers), which would be a companion body to its board of trustees and would be charged with maintaining a high level of academic credibility in AEA's research programs.

By the 1960s the AEA had broadened its research into foreign policy, legal studies, and a wider range of domestic issues. Its reputation continued to improve, and despite the election of John F. Kennedy to the White House, it seemed that the "conservative" agenda was gaining popularity, particularly among Republicans.

"Why I Am Not a Conservative"

To be clear in explaining AEI's role in the development of the so-called "conservative movement" from Barry Goldwater through the present day, one must establish what the term means. Great irony has been found in the increasing use of *conservative* to describe free-market advocates and *liberal* to describe those who favor government solutions to economic and social problems. Friedrich von Hayek wrote an essay on this in 1960, "Why I Am Not a Conservative," in which he explained how the truly liberal point of view—which cherishes liberty and economic freedom—is vastly different from the conservative point of view, which opposes change of any kind.

The confusion over these labels is acutely evident today. In the Soviet Union, people who favor free-market reforms are rightly called liberals, and the hard-line Communists who staunchly resist *perestroika* are rightly called conservatives. Americans say that the Hungarian economy is liberalizing itself when it introduces free-market systems. Yet we continue to call Ronald Reagan—a staunch advocate of free-market policies—a conservative.

By now, George Bush has thoroughly discredited the label "liberal," and in any event most people who qualify as classical liberals have long since given in and taken to the conservative label. Thus, in this discussion common usage will apply and liberals will be called conservatives.

The Goldwater Connection

As the 1960s got under way, many conservatives held out high hopes for the presidential prospects of Barry Goldwater. Not the least was William J. Baroody, Sr., who was active behind the scenes on Goldwater's behalf. This involvement created great opportunities and eventually great problems for AEI in the decade ahead.

On the one hand, Baroody, already an acknowledged master as an "idea broker," gained stature in Washington and became familiar with many of the best conservative minds in the country. He would later help place many of these individuals in important jobs in the Nixon administration and enhance his and the organization's influence substantially. On the other hand, his involvement raised suspicions at the Internal Revenue Service about the organization's status as a nonpartisan educational and research institution under Section 501(c)3 of the Internal Revenue Code, and the IRS conducted an exhaustive audit that threatened the organization's existence as well as its future tax exemption.

Although the institute survived the audit, repercussions were so strong that the organization seemed obsessed with maintaining a totally nonpartisan image for years to come. Right into the late 1980s AEI kept a full-time lawyer on staff who had to clear every publication, press release, and other public document to watch for partisanship.

A Guiding Vision

This was the vision that guided AEI for many years:

Competition of ideas is fundamental to a free society. A free society, if it is to remain free, cannot permit itself to be dominated by one strain of thought. Public policy derives from the ideas, speculation, and theories of thoughtful men and women. Policy makers themselves rarely originate the concepts underlying the laws by which people are governed. They choose among practical options to formulate legislation, governmental directives, regulations, and programs. If there is no testing of ideas by competition, public policy decisions may undermine rather than bolster the foundations of a free society.

This brilliantly crafted statement expressed the purpose of a policy research institute while making a point that was crucial in the late 1960s and 1970s: Public policy was too heavily dominated by the New Deal/New Frontier/Great Society elite and by the Brookings Institution. Ideas needed to be subjected to more competition—a concept that was compelling for business executives, a key constituency.

By the mid-1980s this notion had evolved in a different way. Some in AEI's faculty and many on its staff believed that such competition needed to exist *within* the institute, not only *between* AEI and other institutions with different points of view. Fed by AEI's aversion to giving the appearance of partisanship, the tendency toward completion of ideas led some on the right to become impatient with AEI and to turn to the more activist Heritage Foundation to carry the conservative flame.

Internal competition of ideas was not necessarily bad for AEI. It gave the institute the opportunity to do what Bill Baroody, Sr., had been so good at: advance the conservative agenda while upholding the image of independent nonpartisanship. This image gave it great credibility in Washington among journalists and other opinion leaders, and nationally among business leaders.

New Name

Baroody engineered an important institutional change in 1962. He received approval from the board of trustees to change the name of the organization to the American Enterprise Institute for Public Policy Research. He believed it had to be seen by policymakers, journalists, and intellectuals as an independent research institution rather than as one of many Washington associations. The board insisted on retaining the American Enterprise part of the name but agreed to call it an institute and accepted Baroody's strong recommendation that "for Public Policy Research" be added. At the same time, Baroody's status was changed from executive director to president. He kept that title until 1978, when he passed it on to his son, William, Jr.

After Goldwater's defeat, Baroody set about building AEI's network. He developed lists of scholars in various fields and worked the Washington policy community like a master politician. He developed close relationships with members of Congress, such as Gerald Ford and Melvin Laird. Baroody, Jr., worked on Laird's staff along with Edwin Feulner, who would later head the Heritage Foundation, and David Abshire, who later joined AEI and then started the Center for Strategic and International Studies (CSIS) at Georgetown. Baroody, Sr., served on CSIS's board and both Baroodys later chaired the board of the prestigious Wilson Center at the Smithsonian.

The elder Baroody also cultivated such Washington insiders as Bryce Harlow, one of Washington's influential wise men and a champion of the corporate Washington representative community. The business community has its own network in Washington, thanks in part to Harlow's leadership. Through groups like the Business-Government Relations Council, Washington representatives keep in touch and share information on public policy trends. In Baroody, they found an ally and a great resource for information and analysis. They embraced him almost as one of their own, which proved extremely helpful in the 1970s, when AEI sought to build its corporate support by getting CEOs to solicit funds from other CEOs. Many CEOs have said that the funds would never have come if not for strong approval among those companies' Washington representatives.

Seeking Critical Mass

Richard Nixon's election in 1968 marked a major step forward in AEI's drive toward national prominence. Close Baroody allies, such as Laird and McCracken, assumed top positions in the administration, and they needed talented intellectuals to staff the agencies. Baroody's influence continued to grow, and AEI's stature gained with it.

By 1971, Baroody and AEI's board made a strategic decision to build a resident "faculty" in Washington, to reach critical mass, as Baroody described it. Until this point, the institute's full-time staff had remained small; Baroody and his director of research, Thomas F. Johnson, commissioned studies and held conferences, using professors from universities throughout the country. They would continue to maintain relationships with leading academics, but from that point on they also recruited talented scholars from universities and from government, as officials completed service in the Nixon and Ford administrations.

They started with two leading economists, Gottfried Haberler of Harvard and William Fellner of Yale. Each was about to retire from academic rigors and agreed to relocate to Washington. Shortly thereafter, Fellner started what would become an important tradition at AEI—going *from* the institute to government—as he joined President Nixon's Council of Economic Advisers. Eventually he returned to AEI and remained there until his death in 1985. Haberler, at age 90 in 1990, continues his affiliation with AEI and his work as one of the world's most respected international trade economists. He comes to work every day and joins his colleagues at the "economists' table" in AEI's dining room. The spirited policy debates that take place each day at tables in the dining room are an essential part of the organization's culture.

A brief digression: Food is essential to a successful think tank. In addition to the daily luncheons in the dining room, AEI serves meals

or refreshments at hundreds of events each year. Think tank luncheons, dinners, and breakfasts provide the Washington equivalent
of the traditional American dinner table—where discussions are lively
and it is okay (even preferable) to disagree. AEI Resident Scholar
Robert Goldwin once said, only half in jest, "AEI is 50 percent scholar-
ship and 50 percent catering."

Once set in motion, the revolving door among AEI, government,
and academia produced a steady stream of scholars and fellows, some
of whom came for 6 to 12 months, some who came to stay. One of the
most striking things about such think tanks as AEI (especially AEI) is
what a good professional environment it provides for intellectuals.
Few leave under normal circumstances. It is a stimulating environment; it places few demands on scholars' time, other than that they
try to be the best in their field; it allows them to pursue outside income
from writing and speaking; and it requires no teaching. Resident
Scholar John Makin, who directs tax and budget research, marvelled
about it after arriving in 1984.

> If I want to discuss some technical point on tax policy, I can go down the
> hall to see Willie Fellner or Herb Stein, two of the most knowledgeable
> economists in the country. If I have a practical question, I can go to the next
> office to ask Barber Conable [the former congressman and World Bank
> president, who was then at AEI]. If I have a political question, Austin
> Ranney or Norm Ornstein are just around the corner. It is a remarkable
> atmosphere, one you can't find in a university.

Baroody recruited a small core of resident scholars and built the
staff slowly through the 1970s. By 1980 the resident staff of scholars,
fellows, and support staff neared 150 and the annual budget, $10
million, had increased tenfold over 1970. Baroody also recruited
scholars and experts to serve on advisory councils for individual
research programs, which allowed him to bring other influential
intellectuals and politicians into AEI's circle. Among the former or
future cabinet members who served on advisory councils during the
1970s were Gerald Ford, George Bush, George Shultz, David Stockman, James Lynn, William Simon, Nicholas Brady, Melvin Laird,
Clark Clifford, and Jack Kemp. They also included members of Congress, former or future subcabinet officials, future Supreme Court
Justice Antonin Scalia, and members of the Joint Chiefs of Staff.

With the new resident staff, Baroody expanded AEI's research
agenda with programs on government regulation; social security and

retirement policy; and health, legal, tax, energy, defense, and foreign policies.

Regulatory studies were a special focus. Following a Weidenbeam study on the costs of regulation, a team of regulatory specialists came directly from the Ford administration and carried on the work they started in government. Paul MacAvoy, who had started a series of regulatory studies while in government, completed the project at AEI with cost/benefit analyses of various forms of regulation. James C. Miller III and Marvin Kosters came from government and formed the Center for the Study of Government Regulation at AEI. The institute launched a highly influential magazine, *Regulation*, edited by Antonin Scalia (now a Supreme Court justice), Murray Weidenbaum (later chair of the President's Council of Economic Advisers), and Anne Brunsdale, now chair of the International Trade Commission. Christopher DeMuth, who would later become president of AEI, was a frequent contributor.

Baroody brought in two respected political scientists—Austin Ranney and Howard Penniman—to start a program on political and social processes that would help set AEI apart from its competitors. Until that point, most think tanks focused on issues analysis; AEI paid great attention to processes and institutions. In the late 1970s Baroody went even further by recruiting Michael Novak, a theologian from Syracuse University.

Ideas of the 1970s

A theologian at a public policy think tank? This turned out to be one of the Baroodys' most brilliant moves. Novak wrote one of the most important books ever published under AEI's auspices, *The Spirit of Democratic Capitalism*. After years of denigration of capitalism, here was a scholar who made a compelling case for the *moral*, as well as economic and political, superiority of democratic capitalism. This seminal work had a profound impact on national debate, and the promotion of these ideas in the late 1970s by Novak and fellow neoconservatives Irving Kristol and Ben Wattenberg pleased AEI's sponsors. Here were intellectuals—former leftists at that—telling us that it is okay to be a capitalist!

It is no small tribute to these scholars and their like that it seems almost absurd to make a big deal of this in 1990; in the 1970s, however, socialists still enjoyed the high ground. For many, especially young idealistic students, the idea of "from each according to his means and to each according to his needs" sounded compelling and compassionate. Novak cut through to show that socialism was really only a one-dimension system, an economic one. Democratic capitalism, Novak asserted, was really three systems in one—economic, political, and moral/cultural—and they were interdependent. Democratic capitalism also meshed with basic human nature. Novak was fond of pulling out a dollar bill and reading the words "In God we trust." This means, he would point out, "nobody else." The key is to allow everyone to pursue his or her self-interest and to channel this basic human drive into productive efforts that benefit everyone.

Socialism, on the other hand, tried to deny this fact of human nature and to pretend that everyone's will could be bent toward some central agenda formulated by supposedly public-spirited government leaders. This notion collapsed under the weight of empirical evidence, not without intellectual help from the Novaks and Kristols of the world. Novak, Kristol, and Wattenberg are still part of AEI's core staff.

The relationship between Baroody, the son of an immigrant Lebanese stone-cutter, and Kristol, a great neoconservative intellectual and himself a master idea broker, was a key to AEI's growth. Kristol was a leader of the neoconservative movement and gave the quintessential definition of a neocon: "a liberal who has been mugged by reality." Kristol not only helped Baroody build AEI's "critical mass" in research talent, he also teamed with Willard Butcher, then president of the Chase Manhattan Bank, and other scholars to harangue business leaders into building their support for AEI. A crucial war of ideas is going on in Washington, they told CEOs back in the late 1970s, and you are not being heard. It is not enough to have a corporate office or an association working directly on your behalf; you must support credible third parties that favor market-oriented policies yet maintain their independence.

Butcher, who would later pluck AEI from the jaws of oblivion during its financial disaster of 1986, took Kristol, Novak, Wattenberg, and other scholars on barnstorming tours around the country to enlist corporate support. AEI's corporate contributions increased nearly fourfold in the latter half of the 1970s, and the work they did then continues to bear fruit. No other think tank came close to AEI's corporate support level in the 1980s.

Major Works

AEI's research gained increasing attention during the 1970s, particularly its work on government regulation. Many major books were written at the institute during the decade, including the following:

Government Mandated Price Increases (1975) by Murray Weidenbaum was a seminal study on the costs of government regulation. It compiled for the first time an estimate of what regulatory policies cost the U.S. economy.

The Antitrust Paradox (1978) by Robert Bork, then as now a resident scholar at the institute, changed the way many people thought about antitrust laws.

Modern Times (1983), the best-selling historical volume by British historian Paul Johnson, was written during a one-year fellowship at AEI.

While many major works, such as the Bork and Johnson volumes, were published by commercial publishers, AEI itself published hundreds of titles each year during the 1970s, many of them monographs or short special analyses on critical issues. On some issues, AEI commissioned a team of scholars to produce books covering various aspects of the problem. Examples: regulatory issues, social security, minimum wage, and something called "mediating structures."

The mediating structures project was a special pet of Baroody, Jr., who joined AEI as executive vice president in 1977 after serving as director of the Office of Public Liaison in President Ford's White House. The mediating structures project got started with a short monograph by sociologists Peter Berger and Richard Neuhaus, *To Empower People* (1976). They said that increased attention should be paid to structures, such as family, church, neighborhood, voluntary associations, and ethnic subgroups, that stand between the individual and the large institutions in society, such as big government or big business. They urged that government empower these structures rather than try to solve social problems directly. AEI committed considerable resources to this idea, which led indirectly to a strategic decision in 1981 that seemed to backfire on AEI.

In 1981, President Reagan asked Baroody, Jr., to conduct a major study on private sector initiatives that could deal with social problems while allowing some reduction in federal spending. Since AEI clearly had been leading the way in this area for nearly five years, Baroody, Jr., committed $1 million on a 1-year project that would incorporate the work of 17 authors. He made it the institute's top priority from June 1981 through the summer of 1982. The resulting volume, *Meeting Human Needs*, combined essays by recognized policy experts (many of them AEI scholars) with examples of private sector initiatives already undertaken by major corporations and communities. With so many contributors on such a short timetable, however, the volume lacked focus and failed to lay out a blueprint for reform of social policy. Although individual pieces of it received media attention, the overall project was ignored by the major media and, even worse, by President Reagan and his staff. This was a major setback for an organization that was facing financial difficulties, and it may have been the genesis of a slow slide that almost led to the end of AEI.

New Emphasis on Outreach

In the 1970s, in addition to the research and staff expansions, the Baroodys—especially the younger Baroody—made enormous strides in promoting AEI's work and getting it into the hands of decision makers. The institute began a regular "town hall meeting" program in the early 1970s that evolved into the monthly television series "Public Policy Forums." The institute produced this series itself and set up a national distribution system that placed it on more than 600 commercial, public, and cable television systems across the country. The shows were highly successful precursors of the network public affairs talk shows of the 1980s, featuring a panel of four experts who usually were renowned in their field. The panels were balanced ideologically; one show, for example, had Ronald Reagan on one side and Ralph Nader on the other. AEI also produced a weekly half-hour radio program that was carried over the Mutual Radio Network and later AP Radio. These broadcast series fell victim to budget constraints in the mid-1980s.

AEI also launched several periodicals in the late 1970s. *Public Opinion*, a lively bimonthly magazine, combined political essays with a wide range of data on public attitudes. *Regulation* presented clear, leading-edge thinking on regulatory issues. *The AEI Economist* was a monthly newsletter edited by Herbert Stein, a senior fellow at AEI and former chair of the President's Council of Economic Advisers. In 1989 AEI folded these three into one publication, *The American Enterprise*, edited by Karlyn Keene, the widely respected editor of *Public Opinion*.

The new magazine covers a broad terrain and is quoted frequently in the media.

AEI actively courted the Washington media and took advantage of the growing trend in newspapers across the country to open up their op-ed pages to outside columns. The institute packaged hundreds of articles drawn from its books, magazines, and forums and distributed them to op-ed editors. Before this practice spread, leaving op-ed editors swamped with unsolicited manuscripts, AEI columns received widespread use. Most popular were pro-con packages edited from the televised forums; they offered newspapers the best thinking on each side of an issue by recognized authorities.

Changing of the Guard

In 1978 the elder Baroody's health deteriorated. Seeing the need to build a financial base or endowment under the institute, he passed AEI's presidency to his son and took the title senior counselor. His role was to head a special campaign to seek endowment grants and long-term contributions. He was just beginning to succeed (having secured several grants or long-term commitments to establish university-style named chairs) when he died in July 1980.

Baroody, Jr., faced his first major challenge at the end of that year, when Ronald Reagan became president and took with him some 30 staff members from AEI. In a short time, Arthur Burns, Jeane Kirkpatrick, Murray Weidenbaum, James Miller, David Gergen, and Richard Erb, among others, left to join the administration. While this migration enhanced the institute's perceived clout, it depleted the research staff at a time when Baroody wanted to expand AEI's reach. Such talent would be hard to replace under any circumstances, but especially when AEI was holding their places for them (they were listed as on leave, not as former staff members).

Contrary to what most people thought at the time, the Republicans' rise to power also had a latent negative impact on AEI. During the Carter years, especially in the election year of 1980, AEI led the loyal opposition. As in its early years, AEI filled a void. It kept influential, respected former officials in Washington and active on policy issues and served as a counterpoint to the Democrat-controlled executive and legislative branches. With the advent of the Reagan administration, AEI was suddenly no longer in opposition. If you wanted the definitive conservative viewpoint, you got it from government or from the more activist Heritage Foundation, and then perhaps from AEI.

Intellectuals like nothing better than being in opposition. They love the fight as much as—perhaps more than—any glory that comes from winning. One could speculate that a Democratic victory in either 1980 or 1984 would have been more beneficial to AEI, though few of its scholars would have wished for such an outcome.

The Reagan election and the appointment of so many AEI scholars led to renewed attention, and in many respects the institute prospered intellectually in the ensuing years. Novak's *The Spirit of Democratic Capitalism*, Kirkpatrick's *Dictatorships and Double Standards*, Wattenberg's *The Good News Is the Bad News Is Wrong*, and major new books by Austin Ranney, Norman Ornstein and Thomas Mann, and Herbert Stein, among others, gained widespread attention.

AEI's annual Public Policy Week anchored an extensive conference schedule. More and more of AEI's conferences were broadcast on the Cable-Satellite Public Affairs Network (C-SPAN), which resulted in an exponential gain in attention for the institute. That AEI's scholars were ubiquitous in the media during this period is evident from a quote in *Newsweek*, describing the growing use of think tank scholars by news organizations: "Still, the impression conveyed (in the media) is of a world that contains only a handful of knowledgeable people, half of whom seem to come from someplace called the American Enterprise Institute." (3/25/89, p. 69)

Financial Setback

In 1985, following several years of what seemed to almost everyone (including one of the big eight public accounting firms, which conducted annual audits) to be prosperity for AEI, Baroody announced plans for a lavish new headquarters. Amid great fanfare about a $3 million project to expand AEI's space and build state-of-the-art conference and media facilities, AEI's staff spent much of the year planning for the move.

By the end of the year, the new headquarters plans were scrapped by AEI's board, and Baroody was pressed to cut back sharply on spending. Willard Butcher, then vice chair of AEI's board, discovered that inappropriate (though apparently legal) accounting practices had hidden a growing deficit. During the Christmas holidays, more than two dozen AEI employees were told their jobs had been eliminated. Another two dozen jobs were eliminated in April 1986.

In June 1986, with finances still a mess and support from the scholars waning, Baroody was convinced to resign. Paul McCracken, the renowned professor emeritus of the University of Michigan, served as interim president for the latter half of the year and helped Butcher search for a permanent president.

The biggest problem, and the greatest lesson for future think tank leaders, was that Baroody tried to accomplish too much and was unwilling to say no to scholars who came to him with good ideas. Instead of tackling the financial problem when it first arose in 1981, he tried to give the impression the financial situation was healthy and then constantly scrambled behind the scenes to make ends meet. When new ideas were proposed, he approved them in the hope that potential donors would fund them later. In the meantime, funds were used as they came in, regardless of their stated purpose, and more and more obligations were accumulated.

After Baroody left, the board brought in James Hicks, a financial manager from the Dow Chemical Company, which provided him on executive loan for two years. He completely revised the financial management system and applied business-style discipline to AEI. Meanwhile, the board members, many of them chief executive officers of major corporations, gave special supplemental contributions to help AEI through the short-term cash problem. Butcher took McCracken and then Christopher DeMuth on whirlwind tours to hold meetings around the country with AEI contributors in order to reassure them of the continued commitment to AEI's mission.

Meanwhile, the effects of the crunch were felt in every aspect of AEI's work. Annual spending dropped from a peak of $12.7 million in 1985 to $7.5 million in 1986.

Renewed Spirit

Butcher talked the brilliant young lawyer/economist, Christopher DeMuth, into giving up a lucrative consulting practice in Washington to take the reins at AEI. DeMuth, a proven intellectual (he had taught at Harvard's John F. Kennedy School in the late 1970s), a former government official (he served as administrator of the Office of Information and Regulatory Affairs at the Office of Management and Budget under President Reagan and thus led the administration's deregulation efforts from 1981 through 1984), and a business-oriented lawyer/economist from the University of Chicago school of thought, brought a renewed excitement to AEI. While the financial problems required a long-term repair program that still continues, DeMuth reestablished the intellectual dynamism that AEI had enjoyed in the 1970s.

He worked with Jeane Kirkpatrick to attract a major grant from the Bradley Foundation to fund an entirely new foreign policy program (most of the scholars working on foreign policy issues had been laid off in the earlier cutbacks). This grant allowed Kirkpatrick to recruit a small cadre of bright young scholars such as Joshua Muravchik and Alan Keyes to the institute. Irving Kristol, who had become virtually inactive and was based at New York University, moved to Washington and took up residence in one of two John M. Olin Chairs at AEI. The other was filled by Robert Bork, who joined AEI shortly after being rejected by the Senate for the Supreme Court.

Using the advice of these and other scholars, DeMuth set out in a style reminiscent of the elder Baroody to recruit such prominent intellectuals as the economist Allan Meltzer and the defense specialist Richard Perle and to strengthen AEI's ties to influential outside intellectuals. AEI's research agenda became more sharply focused on issues that affected business, such as international trade, intellectual property rights, and (again) regulation.

Two research projects stand out as examples of AEI's work in the late 1980s and as illustrations of the forward-looking nature of research at AEI and similar organizations.

In 1984, Resident Fellow Claude Barfield organized a team of academics for a series of books on international trade in services. They were advised by a blue-ribbon advisory council chaired by Laird and including two future U.S. Trade Representatives—Clayton Yeutter and Carla Hills. This issue was barely on the public agenda at the time, but by the time the books were published in 1987, this was a central issue in the Uruguay Round of the General Agreement on Tariffs and Trade (GATT) multilateral negotiations. AEI's books were the first such studies prepared in this way and served as useful background for U.S. officials, scholars, and journalists.

In 1988, well before the savings and loan debacle, AEI recruited economist William Haraf from the White House staff to direct a project on financial deregulation. He also enlisted prominent academics, policymakers, and financial executives to advise a team of scholars with a series of books on various aspects of financial regulation. The books proved invaluable to lawmakers and regulators as they tried to address savings and loan and banking problems later in the decade.

Contradictions

Through the years, AEI has been an interesting study in contradiction, both in fact and in public perceptions. Consider the following:

Finances

AEI carved out a niche as an elite think tank, recruiting top names who had already achieved great reputations and enlisting trustees from among the chief executive officers of America's leading corporations, but it has been in fact one of the poorest such organizations.

Among its leading competitors are Brookings and the Hoover Institution, each of which sits atop enormous endowments that provide both security and usable revenues each year. AEI actually has a *negative* endowment: The small endowment it had in the early 1980s was spent (in some cases with the consent of the donors) but AEI continues to fulfill the commitments made to the donors. This commitment means that several named chairs and other activities are maintained even though no endowment funds the activities. They are, therefore, financed out of general funds.

Lacking an endowment, AEI operated for years on a month-to-month basis while maintaining a well-to-do image. This situation has turned around under AEI's current president. AEI has had four consecutive years in which it raised more than $1 million above expenditures, and in mid-1990 it reached a positive net worth for the first time in perhaps a decade. But it still lacks an endowment.

Ideology

When AEI attained prominence in the late 1970s, it was often portrayed as the conservative counterweight to the liberal Brookings Institution. When it encountered financial problems in the mid-1980s, many people cited "ideological drift" as the cause. Those of us who saw the books had to chuckle over those reports; in fact, the funds were still coming in but financial management was the problem. The rise of the aggressive Heritage Foundation was described often in zero-sum terms: If Heritage gained, it must have meant that AEI lost. The reality is much more complicated than the speculation over conservative and liberal labels. The political infighting among various factions on the right during the 1980s (neoconservatives versus paleo-conservatives versus libertarians, etc.) should illustrate how obsolete the broad labels are. In any case, AEI's ideological underpinnings remained strongly on the side of limited government and strong defense throughout the 1980s, as it had in the 1970s. It may be that AEI became more centrist, but the center itself moved—the center of gravity moved to the right. AEI's publications and conferences reflected its new place at the center of the mainstream.

AEI and Brookings were and remain in the ideological mainstream. The public perception to the contrary was always off the mark. This mainstream position is appropriate for institutions that count American business among their most important constituencies (especially AEI, which derives half its income from corporate contributions). And it is appropriate because one of the most important roles these organizations play is that of stepping stones for senior government officials on the way into or out of government service.

Research Style

Articles on think tanks often describe AEI as stodgy, inclined toward lengthy books as opposed to the Heritage Foundation and other feisty upstarts who specialize in brief, punchy backgrounders and position papers. In fact, AEI's book production fell off drastically during the 1980s, and as the decade ended, its staff was geared more to op-ed articles and television panels than to lengthy books. In 1989, AEI's scholars and fellows had more than 400 articles published in newspaper opinion pages, intellectual magazines, and scholarly journals. Scholars such as Norman Ornstein, William Schneider, Ben Wattenberg, Jeane Kirkpatrick, and Robert Bork appeared frequently on television programs such as "Nightline" and "McNeil/Lehrer NewsHour."

AEI's is a lively, fertile environment in which current affairs are not only discussed and debated internally but also discussed with hundreds of news organizations, public officials, business leaders, and academics on a continuing basis. With its financial problems under control if not entirely eliminated, AEI has reemerged to a position among the leading public policy research institutions. With its depth of talent and mix of research on international, economic, and political issues, AEI is well suited for the public policy problems likely to dominate the 1990s.

References

Alter, J. (1985, March 25). Round up the usual suspects. *Newsweek*, p. 69.
American Enterprise Institute. (1979). *AEI Handbook*. Washington, DC: Author.
American Enterprise Institute. (1982). *Meeting human needs*. Washington, DC: Author.
Berger, P., & Neuhaus, R. (1976). *To empower people*. Washington, DC: American Enterprise Institute.
Bork, R. (1978). *The antitrust paradox*. New York: Basic Books.
Internal Revenue Code, Section 501(c)3.
Johnson, P. (1983). *Modern times*. New York: Harper & Row.
Kirkpatrick, J. (1982). *Dictatorships and double standards*. New York: Simon & Schuster.
Meyer, J. (Ed.). (1982). *Meeting human needs*. Washington, DC: American Enterprise Institute.
Novak, M. (1982). *The spirit of democratic capitalism*. New York: Simon & Schuster.
von Hayak, F. A. (1960). Why I am not a conservative. Publisher unknown.
Wattenberg, B. (1984). *The good news is the bad news is wrong*. New York: Simon & Schuster.
Weidenbaum, M. (1975). *Government mandated price increases*. Washington, DC: American Enterprise Institute.

3

The RAND Corporation

Barbara R. Williams
Malcolm A. Palmatier

The RAND Corporation is a private, independent, nonprofit institution engaged in research on matters affecting national security and the public welfare. RAND conducts its work with support from federal, state, and local—and on occasion from foreign—governments; from foundations and other private philanthropic sources; and from its own funds drawn from fees earned and from endowment income. It also operates the RAND Graduate School, an accredited doctoral institution offering a Ph.D. degree in public policy analysis.

RAND is located near the beach in Santa Monica, California. With an annual operating budget in 1989 of $94 million, it employs more than 1,100 persons and draws on the services of some 300 consultants. RAND, now in its 42nd year, had its birth in the institutional baby boom that followed World War II. The father was General H. H. "Hap" Arnold, Commander of the U.S. Army Air Forces, who saw a need to retain the talents of operations researchers, mathematicians, and defense strategists who had done so much to bring the war to a victorious conclusion. Such individuals were understandably anxious to leave government service and to return to their campuses and corporate headquarters.

Arnold turned to a special consultant, Edward L. Bowles of the War Department, who had close connections with the Office of Scientific Research and Development, the home base for wartime operations researchers. Ideas were being traded about at the time for "procuring" brainpower in the same manner that one would acquire aircraft components or maintenance services. In the words of Bruce L. R. Smith, an early historian of nonprofit advisory corporations:

In this general atmosphere, the idea emerged of a contract with a private organization to assist in military planning, and particularly in coordinating planning with research and development decisions. Thus, the concept of Project RAND [an acronym formed from the expression "Research and Development"] began to emerge in nascent form in mid-summer 1945. (Smith, 1966, p. 39)

In the fall of 1945, Franklin R. Collbohm, an aide to the chief engineer at the Douglas Aircraft Company, proposed the creation of a civilian group within Douglas to help the Army Air Forces in planning future weapons development. Impressed with the Collbohm proposal, Arnold convened a group of "founding fathers," including Bowles, Collbohm, and Donald Douglas, among others. There the initial decisions were made that would create a special "Project RAND" within the Douglas Company, give it start-up funding of $10 million, and set it to work on a project about intercontinental air techniques of the future.

Project RAND (while still managed by Douglas Aircraft) produced its first report in May 1946 on a subject that outstripped in scope even intercontinental air warfare: *Preliminary Design of an Experimental World-Circling Spaceship*. This forward-looking, multiauthored piece started from a firm base of engineering analysis and proceeded straight into thoughtful speculation on future space operations and even "man-in-space."

The confining atmosphere of research efforts within the strictures necessary to an airframe company, as well as fears of conflict of interest, led to the separation of the project from Douglas in 1948 and the founding of The RAND Corporation. In its articles of incorporation, RAND described itself as "a nonprofit corporation formed to further and promote scientific, educational, and charitable purposes, all for the public welfare and security of the United States of America." Franklin Collbohm was named its director, and in 1956 its first president. He was succeeded in 1967 by Henry S. Rowen, in 1972 by Donald B. Rice, and in 1989 by James A. Thomson. RAND continues to site its corporate headquarters in Santa Monica, at a significant and deliberate remove from seats of government power (the Defense and State departments, especially) in Washington, DC, although it maintains a small research/liaison office in the nation's capital.

RAND projects today are managed under four broad research divisions: Project AIR FORCE, National Security Research, Army Research, and Domestic Research. The divisional substructure with an array of programs and projects cuts across and draws personnel from a vertical array of six discipline-oriented research departments: Behavioral Sciences, Economics and Statistics, Engineering and Applied Sciences, Information Sciences, Political Science, and System Sciences. Research products are reported to RAND'S sponsors and (with the exception of classified material) to the public through reports, notes, papers, and books, as well as through briefings. A broad system of subscription deposits places RAND titles in libraries around the world.

The RAND Corporation is sometimes called "Mother RAND" in recognition of its status as an early think tank and as parent, over the years, of a varied progeny of smaller think tanks. It stands apart from the community of such institutions, however, in its stubborn independence and refusal to accept a constricting label such as "conservative" or "liberal." This quality of free expression pervaded the RAND staff in the early years and still is seen, although it has yielded somewhat to stricter controls in recent times. RAND professionals were encouraged to spend 20% of their work week on personal research efforts. The RAND building never closed (still true); office lights burned at all hours; some analysts never went home at all, but slept on their study tables. Staff members traveling by air (with briefing charts rolled in long tubes) always flew first class. (This practice stopped in the mid-1960s.) Employees were not asked to account overtly for their time; records were kept, discreetly out of sight, by secretaries. Badges were regarded as *infra dignitatem*; security guards were obliged to memorize the full names of every member of the research and support staff and to speak them, on sight, into a tape recorder as employees arrived each morning (still true). Support persons mingled easily with the research staff, even joining their projects and sometimes claiming a place for themselves on the technical roster. (At least three former editors became nationally known analysts.)

No outreach was made to the media; a small "public relations" office in New York was tasked with keeping RAND's name *out of* the newspapers. (This isolation was reversed in the late 1960s.)

Inverse status symbols were common: plain offices, wooden desks, short-sleeved Hawaiian shirts. High-ranking visitors (John von Neumann, the mathematician; Enoch Powell, the British MP; Charles Lindbergh, the celebrated aviator) mingled easily with numerical savants and Soviet specialists. The leading author one year was not a member of the technical staff at all, but one of the guards.

RAND, in sum, began its corporate life in equipoise between the scientists of the Academy of Lagado, in the third part of Jonathan Swift's *Gulliver's Travels,* and those of Francis Bacon's *New Atlantis.* It was a community of intellectuals—young, brilliant, untiring, totally committed—that could hardly be matched anywhere in the world.

The Formative Years: 1948-1967

The early and middle years of RAND's history saw an intensification of its technology- and national-defense-centered beginnings. They can be bracketed by the tenure of RAND's founding director and president, Franklin R. Collbohm. These formative years began with hands-on, hard-science projects, proceeding over time from engineering studies affecting the U.S. Air Force, RAND's original sole sponsor; to deep "systems analyses" of the vulnerability of U.S. overseas air bases and the feasibility of communications satellites; to analyses leading to the crucial national decisions of the mid-1950s on hydrogen weapons and ballistic-missile delivery systems; to work under the vexed budgetary problems and mixed signals of the post-Sputnik days; to the manifold productions of economists, political scientists, and other "defense intellectuals" of the McNamara period; to counterinsurgency studies during the start-up years of the Vietnam War.

Diversification and Growth

The 1950s were the hot years of the Cold War, and the Air Force was an indulgent RAND "client." As one of RAND's early specialists in computer theory phrases it: "The Air Force, in effect, handed us a bag of money and said 'Spend it in our best interests.'" But RAND's sponsorship was already diversifying, a circumstance accepted by the Air Force. In 1950 a research contract was let by the Atomic Energy Commission (AEC), followed 8 years later by contracts (with the Air Force's blessing) with the National Aeronautics and Space Administration (NASA) and the Advanced Research Projects Agency (ARPA).

The early 1960s were marked by the acquisition of sponsors from other corners of the Pentagon and from the Department of State. By the mid-1960s the distribution of sponsorship was U.S. Air Force (chiefly Project RAND), 68%; Department of Defense (including ARPA), 17%; NASA, 6%; AEC, 2%; research sponsored by RAND using its own funds, 2%; U.S. Agency for International Development, Department of State, 2%, the National Institutes of Health, 1%, and others, 2%.

In this period, RAND's organizational structure evolved from (a) its original, decentralized inverted-T form—a small front office with line authority descending straight down to a row of semiautonomous research departments—to (b) a cluster form in the mid-1950s—loose aggregations of related departments ("divisions") under a policy of partial centralization—and return to (c) a modified inverted-T form in the early 1960s, with the divisional aggregations split back into research departments, and with the addition of a Research Council in a general planning role. In the late 1950s the System Development Division, which had been formed earlier to study how groups of men operating complex machines function together under stress, ballooned to nearly twice the size of the rest of RAND and was spun off ultimately as a separate company (the System Development Corporation).

The Addition of the Social Sciences

Even before RAND's incorporation, the extension of its research agenda beyond the borders of the physical and engineering sciences was being discussed. In late 1946 John Williams, a mathematician (later to head the Mathematics Department), discussed with General Curtis LeMay, then Air Force Deputy Chief of Staff for Research and Development, the possibility of adding social scientists to the RAND staff. LeMay agreed. A follow-on conference of social scientists was assembled in New York in September 1947 at which the aims and programs of Project RAND were explained. Two subsequent recruits from the social sciences were later to become heads of RAND departments: Charles J. Hitch (Economics) and Hans Speier (Social Science). Bruce Smith summarizes the peculiar advantage of expanding into the "soft" sciences:

> The addition of the social sciences was necessary sooner or later because the broad systems-analysis work that RAND sought to do could not be done effectively without social science skills. While the bulk of RAND's work consisted of simple operations-research problems of the World War II variety, the social sciences were not so necessary. But as the problems RAND dealt with became more complex, the social science input became vital. (Smith, 1966, p. 65)

RAND's Classic Systems Analysis: Overseas Basing

The "broad systems-analysis work" referred to by Smith was to lead to remarkable successes. (The expression "systems analysis" is said to have been invented by Ed Paxson of RAND.) Operations research of the traditional World War II variety addressed quantifiable tactical problems in a precise way. It could, for example, examine and set forth graphically and in supporting tabulations the "mission profile" of an aircraft (a) flying a certain distance with an ever diminishing load of fuel, (b) dropping to low-level penetration, (c) releasing its bombs, and (d) returning "at altitude" to its base. Systems analysis, however, is less quantitative and far broader; it addresses wide-ranging strategic and policy questions, seeking to clarify choice under conditions of uncertainty. Application of economic principles is central to this analytical method, which also draws upon and integrates skills from many other disciplines.

RAND's work through the early years was marked by several broad and influential systems analyses, as well as by individual efforts in basic scientific methods and in economics and historiography. The classic example of in-depth systems analysis at RAND is the "basing study" led by Albert Wohlstetter in 1951-1953. RAND was tasked with what appeared to be a routine study of the most effective ways to acquire, construct, and use air bases overseas. Wohlstetter, after spending some months trying to formulate the problem, concluded that the wrong questions were being asked. They should center, he felt, on vulnerability—that is, on what would happen to U.S. overseas bases if an enemy struck first. In historian Smith's words:

> The [ensuing] analysis pointed toward the shattering conclusion that in the last half of the 1950s the Strategic Air Command [SAC] . . . faced the danger of obliteration from enemy surprise attack under the then-programmed strategic basing system. (Smith, 1966, p. 208)

Wohlstetter assembled a small team and went to work. With his colleagues, he analyzed four alternative basing schemes in detail. One was shown to be clearly preferable: operating bases in the United States with refueling bases overseas. Wohlstetter then prepared a briefing that he took to SAC and the Pentagon in a saturation round of 92 presentations. Finally, the study was published, after some delay, as RAND Report R-266, *Selection and Use of Strategic Air Bases*, 1954, declassified in 1962.

In the end, many of RAND's suggestions were adopted by the Air Force. As a friendly critic and outsider/adviser, RAND was able to reach straight through to top decision makers with few impediments. And within RAND, with its climate of independence and freedom of maneuver, a single researcher was able—and was given the time and the go-ahead—to redefine and find answers to a question of vital national policy.

Vietnam

RAND's analytical contributions to the force engagements in Vietnam spanned a period from the early 1960s to the late 1970s. They opened with a symposium in 1962 on the subject of counter-insurgency. The resulting report (still not officially cleared for public release) took a pragmatic approach to the issue, collecting the views of Australian, British, French, Philippine, and U.S. experts on such topics as the aims and tactics of counterinsurgency, intelligence, political action, and psychological warfare.

In the middle years of the decade, RAND teams mounted a broad study of "motivation and morale" among cadres of the Viet Cong, the force opposed to the South Vietnam government. Some 2,000 interviews were conducted with Viet Cong prisoners and defectors. From an examination of captured documents, RAND published its influential *Viet Cong Repression and Its Implications for the Future* (Hosmer, 1970), identifying repression as a vital part of the overall enemy effort to erode South Vietnam government strength.

RAND staffers, like the general U.S. population, were divided over the course of the U.S. involvement in Vietnam. In late 1969, six members of the staff collaborated on a letter to the *New York Times* and the *Washington Post,* calling for an end to U.S. participation in the conflict. It was in this atmosphere of sharp debate that Daniel Ellsberg of RAND's Economics Department leaked part of a highly classified DoD-commissioned history of U.S. involvement in Indochina to the news media (the Pentagon Papers).

The Vietnam controversy continued to divide RAND staff members throughout the 1970s. The differences that surfaced then, and linger still, mirror larger societal divisions over the allocation of resources between national defense and domestic concerns.

Basic Research and Publications

Contributions of another kind were made by several RAND investigators in this early period. These were studies of basic methodologies in the fields of mathematics and cost analysis: linear programming (Dantzig), dynamic programming (Bellman), and planning-programming-budgeting (Novick). Other fundamental work was done in materials and structural theory (Shanley), computer theory (Newell, Shaw, Simon), the theory of games (Shapley), and Soviet national accounts (Bergson, Hoeffding). Roberta Wohlstetter published her pathbreaking study *Pearl Harbor: Warning and Decision* in 1962, five years after its issuance as a classified RAND report.

The corporate policy for reporting RAND research was established early and has varied little in its fundamentals. Publications go first to the client that funded the research. Individual authors are credited; the publications bear the RAND imprint; and the corporation, after client review, handles all initial, and much subsequent, distribution. A private series of internal working papers creates a forum for free expression of ideas throughout the corporation. The premier product is the RAND Report (R), supported in the early decades by the utility Research Memorandum (RM) and currently by the Note (N). All are subject to a rigorous peer-review system managed by the department heads; reviews are signed and submitted in writing. Contract reports are strongly seconded by formal briefings to top decision makers. Discussion papers fall in the Paper (P) series. A little-known letter series of this period, the "Recommendation to the Air Staff," was reserved for subjects of unusual urgency.

A strong book program evolved in the Collbohm period, featuring parallel publishers' acceptance reviews (at both commercial and university presses) against strict deadlines imposed by RAND. A sales program was begun in the mid-1960s, and soon thereafter a "subscription depository" arrangement was established that has placed open-literature RAND publications into hundreds of libraries around the world.

In Sum

The period 1948-1967 marks the formative years of RAND's corporate history. Nothing was quite the same afterward, as congressional oversight grew more insistent, client relations more formal and restrictive and less close, the analytical competition more intense, and funding more constrained.

The Rise of Domestic Programs: 1967-1980

After the retirement of President Collbohm in 1967, the presidency changed hands twice. Henry S. Rowen, who had participated in the overseas basing study with Wohlstetter, assumed office in 1967. In his five-year tenure, RAND experienced the tribulations of defense budget constraints and the Pentagon Papers (1971). At the same time, RAND initiated a dynamic new program of domestic research; opened a policy research institute in New York City; launched the first of several influential social experiments; and founded the RAND Graduate School, a unique, accredited doctorate-granting institution for policy studies.

Rowen was succeeded in 1972 by an engineer/economist, Donald B. Rice, whose 17-year administration was to see the swift rise of RAND's domestic programs to the level of parity with its defense work; the establishment of an Institute for Civil Justice; an in-depth engineering study for the Netherlands government of a storm surge barrier against the North Sea; and research into criminal justice and regulatory issues. In this period, RAND's core contract (Project RAND) was placed under a new funding structure—that of a Federal Contract Research Center—and was renamed Project AIR FORCE.

The New York City-RAND Institute

In mid-1969 RAND established what was designed to be a long-term relationship with the City of New York intended "primarily to conduct programs of scientific research and study, and to provide reports and recommendations relevant to the operations, planning, or administration of the City of New York."[1] The New York City-RAND Institute signaled a dramatic new policy focus and organizational self-image for the corporation. Defense- and aerospace-related work was to be augmented and partly supplemented by research on issues of domestic (i.e., civil) interest.

Unfortunately, the City's budgetary crisis of the mid-1970s did not permit a continuation of the New York/Institute relationship. The institute was dissolved in 1976 after an estimated savings to the city of tens of millions of dollars, with fundamental research accomplished on water resources, law enforcement, fire protection, health, housing, welfare, regulatory matters, and urban issues.

While the institute in New York lasted only seven years, a new Domestic Research Division at RAND in Santa Monica took root during the 1970s, making up half the corporation's revenues by 1976.

Social Experiments

RAND tried hard, in its domestic programs, to retain the "big picture" questions, the close client relationships, and the contractual qualities that it had always valued in its work for the Air Force. The effort was relatively successful in the beginning. The major social experiments carried out by RAND during the 1970s in health, housing, and education were launched to aid decisions about social policies being considered by the (then) Departments of Health, Education, and Welfare and of Housing and Urban Development, and by the National Institute of Education. The projects themselves, designed collaboratively (if not always with full agreement) by RAND and the sponsoring governmental agencies, were large, interdisciplinary, multiyear efforts.

The Health Insurance Experiment was, of the three, the flagship study. Rarely have government-funded domestic studies offered such long-term, adequately funded, "hands-off" conditions for policy research. A 15-year, $100 million effort, it enrolled over 2,700 families at various sites around the country in health insurance plans ranging from free care to 95% co-insurance. The purpose was to observe the effects of various methods of financing health care on the use of health care and on personal health. RAND's Health Insurance Experiment showed that when families enjoyed free health plans, they used 50% more health services than families who joined cost-sharing plans or belonged to health maintenance organizations (HMOs). Yet, on the average, personal health outcomes were much the same. Between 1982 and 1984, the period immediately following publication of the experiment's findings, the number of major employer health plans with deductibles for hospitalization increased from 30 to 62%, and those with deductibles of $200 or more increased from 4 to 21%. Corporations and unions used the study results to support claims that cutting medical fringe benefits would not necessarily undermine health.

Adjusting to the Marketplace

RAND's domestic research followed the path of grant (instead of open contract) proposals and of proposals for sole-source contracts. As domestic policy agencies developed their own research programs during the 1970s, however, and as other research organizations positioned themselves to work on the same programs, the RAND staff had to learn to respond competitively to grant solicitations and Requests for Proposals (RFPs). RAND established a respectable track record in competitive awards from federal domestic agencies in critical policy areas. Still, the organization has never abandoned its preference for control of the research approach and for the close relationship with a sponsor that RFPs do not foster. In the mid-1970s, when competitive awarding of research projects was the norm, only about a third of RAND's domestic revenues were earned by responding to RFPs.

The RAND Graduate School

The RAND Graduate School of Policy Studies was founded in 1970 to provide advanced graduate training leading to the doctorate in policy analysis. This field is defined as "the application of scientific methods to problems of public policy and choice in domestic, national, and international security." Students spend half their time in coursework, taught mostly by members of RAND's senior staff, and half their time working on RAND research projects. Today, the school collaborates with UCLA in two specialized programs: Soviet studies and health policy studies.

As of 1990, the school had 66 graduate fellows, including 22 women and 11 foreign students. By the spring of 1990, some 72 students had received the PhD degree—a greater number of public-policy doctorates than from any other academic institution—and have taken positions within government, in academe, and in industry.

The POLANO Study

An international dimension was added to RAND's domestic program in 1975, when the corporation entered into a joint research project with the Rijkswaterstaat, the Netherlands government agency responsible for water control and public works, to explore alternative means of protecting the large Oosterschelde estuary from destructive floods from the North Sea. This project took the name Policy Analysis of the Oosterschelde (POLANO). A year later, RAND briefed its findings on three alternative approaches (closed case, storm-surge barriers, and open case) from the point of view of cost, security, ecology, and economic/social impacts. After some debate within the Dutch government, a decision was taken to install a storm surge barrier (Goeller et al., 1977). Installation was accomplished, and the barrier has since functioned successfully (it reportedly was deployed three times during the hurricanes of 1989-1990).

The Institute for Civil Justice

RAND's Institute for Civil Justice (ICJ) was established in 1979 to bring objective, empirical, and systematic analysis to the discussion of civil justice issues. The ICJ has a broad charter: to develop a better understanding of how the system works, to measure its outcomes, to examine its problems, and to explore alternative courses of action.

For the first time, RAND accepted substantial support from the private sector—in this case, insurance companies. The change was debated actively among the staff and condemned by many for several years. To maintain both the reality and the appearance of its cherished independence, RAND solicited private-sector money for support of the institute as a whole, never for specific projects; sought and gained support, as well, from its traditional foundation and government sources; and included every major interest group in the policy area on the institute's Board of Overseers. A decade of ICJ research has yielded a stream of "firsts" in objective, empirically based findings on civil justice issues. This fact has gone far to reduce apprehensions of control by special interests.

The institute has focused on three key aspects of the civil justice system: its process, costs, and outcomes. Studies to date include analyses of arbitration programs, medical malpractice tort reforms, remedies for civil trial delay, aviation accident liability litigation, and comparative jury verdict awards in personal injury cases. Work under way touches on automobile no-fault insurance and procedures for handling mass toxic tort cases.

Changes in Structure and Culture

The changing mix of national security and domestic research in this period stimulated internal shifts both in organization and in culture. The management structure evolved into a two-dimensional matrix, with the research departments (as columns) offering a disciplinary home base to the professional staff, and with the research programs (as rows) assembled within broad divisions, offering work opportunities to the staff. In theory, the two elements of the matrix were equal in power, but in truth, program managers soon outdistanced the long-powerful research department heads. The reason was simple: Department heads no longer had contract budgets to allocate; program managers now controlled the resources, even in the national security divisions.

But it was time sheets, introduced in response to government accountability requirements in 1972, that most changed the atmosphere of RAND. To acquire a charge number ("coverage") for eight hours of every day for five working days each week was a new and unpleasant chore. Time sheets seemed peculiarly inappropriate to people who worked in an organization open 24 hours a day, seven days a week, and who measured their achievements by output, not by input. The days of leisured, forward thinking without time pressures were at an end.

The Conduct of Domestic Research

The introduction of domestic research brought to the corporation not only new areas of expertise—demography, education, health, criminal justice, and urban policy were among the first research programs in the new division—but also very different client relations. For the first time in RAND's experience, the entity that funded the research was not necessarily the entity that would wrestle with its findings. For example, while research to inform the education policy area is most often funded by a federal education establishment (the

National Institute of Education, the Office of Education, and the National Center for Education Statistics), most education policy actually is made by state and local governments. Criminal justice policy is similar: The National Institute of Justice must devote its resources to research that will be useful mainly to state and local enforcement agencies. But the latter agencies ultimately may reject, or simply ignore, the fruits of such research.

RAND's influence on federal domestic agencies, then, mainly concerns research *direction*. Research findings that federal agencies find challenging or provocative simply may irritate the real decision makers. In the view of some states and communities, a meddling federal agency has given money to an outside organization to do research on a topic that they would not have chosen, with results that they do not believe.

A classic example of this sort of dissatisfaction can be found in the RAND detective study. In the mid-1970s the National Institute of Justice (NIJ) underwrote a nationwide study of the investigative process. The results suggested that the information provided by patrol officers from their preliminary investigations is an extremely important determinant of whether a follow-up investigation (by detectives) will result in an arrest. This finding, which challenged the mystique of the all-powerful fictional detective, set off stormy debates at local levels. Not until the early 1980s was it fully accepted and motivated local police departments to change procedures (Petersilia, 1987).

Few federal domestic research projects are funded at a level that allows continued contact with local policy audiences after termination of the research, although this is the very time when findings exist to be put to use. The accompanying tendency for domestic agencies to fund one-shot, short-term projects makes realistic policy options difficult to craft; on such projects, RAND's (or any other research organization's) influence is at best indirect. Under this more erratic domestic funding environment, RAND has been forced to rely more heavily on its published and widely distributed reports than on briefings and personal encounters to stimulate change.[1] In several policy areas (education is the most notable example), staff members who have had little opportunity to see their research translated into practice have become instead students of the implementation process.

RAND's "change agent" study (Berman & McLaughlin, 1975), a powerful critique of federal efforts to influence local decision makers, established RAND's strength in implementation research. Federal folklore had held that models of institutional change shown to be successful in one setting could be transferred to other settings and perform similar transformations. The change-agent study found this model to be seriously flawed in changing educational institutions. The RAND authors showed instead that local institutions have an almost infinite ability to resist changes and to manufacture their own. Models of change must themselves be transformed by local institutions to be effective.

RAND staff members have grown increasingly adept over the years at addressing the problems of state and local decision makers. For example, research projects involving the cities of St. Paul and Cleveland in the 1980s draw on the lessons from RAND's work a decade earlier in New York, in Green Bay and South Bend (sites of the Housing Allowance Supply Experiment), and in St. Louis, Seattle, and San Jose (sites of early work on urban policy).

The Evolution of Two Cultures

RAND management during the 1970s and beyond watched two cultures develop within the staff—one culture strongly committed to national security concerns and clients, the other to domestic ones. Some corridors were peopled by older males, whose office doors sported pin-up photographs of aircraft and missiles, while other corridors housed younger men and women whose doors displayed pictures of school children and civil rights marches. Management resisted any official recognition of the duality. RAND continues to insist, for example, that most full-time staff members receive clearances at the Secret level—even when they have no immediate intention of working on a classified project. The presumption is that RAND researchers have a "need to know" about work at that clearance level and should be able to serve as technical reviewers wherever their skills are appropriate.

The two cultures coexist to the present time, their ideological divisiveness moderated considerably. Over time, as government funding has ebbed and flowed between national security and domestic concerns, an increasing fraction of the staff is experienced in both cultures.

The Reassertion of Defense Priorities: 1981-1989

The 50/50 balance that was struck in the mid-1970s between national security research and domestic research at RAND was tipped in the 1980s to approximately 80/20. These were the Reagan years of the "evil empire," promulgation of the Strategic Defense Initiative, and U.S. defense buildup. Plowshares were once again being beaten into swords.

Formation of Federally Funded Research and Development Centers

Federally Funded Research and Development Center (FFRDC) is a term applied to nonprofit organizations that provide specialized technical and scientific support to government. Such advisory institutions, RAND included, were looked on with suspicion in the 1970s, particularly by Congress, which tended to see them as interlopers in the federal decision-making process—a shadow government, if you will, supporting high-salaried consultants unconstrained by the marketplace or by civil service regulations. In the 1980s suspicions eased toward FFRDCs that displayed strict responsibilities to the public trust.

Project RAND had been placed in the category of FFRDC in 1976 and renamed Project AIR FORCE. Defense work at RAND that fell outside Air Force interests was assembled in 1984 under an umbrella FFRDC named the National Defense Research Institute (NDRI) and placed organizationally within RAND's National Security Research Division. In the following year the Arroyo Center, a U.S. Army policy analysis research activity housed at the California Institute of Technology Jet Propulsion Laboratory, was transferred to RAND, where it formed the core of a new Army Research Division—and thus became RAND's third FFRDC.

These entities held out, to an organization that had weathered national recessions and budgetary cutbacks, the promise of continuity of research, recruitment of a staff of high quality, a privileged relationship with a sponsor, and fund-raising stability—in short, something like the climate of research vis-à-vis the U.S. Air Force that had marked RAND's formative years.

Research Agenda

By the 1980s RAND's defense research ran chiefly to practical military problems: the survivability and utility of tactical air forces, military enlistment bonuses, uncertainty in Army logistics, U.S. basing in the Philippines, improving the military acquisition process, advanced technologies for defense, and arms control in Europe.

Uncomfortable messages still found their way to the client. For example, a 1988 Arroyo Center study addressed the problem of improving the combat availability of high-tech subsystems for major weapon systems such as the Abrams (M-1) tank (Berman, McIver, Robbins, & Schank, 1989). The analysis showed that if the Army were to change the location of its repair facilities, re-allocate special test equipment, and improve its distribution and depot management, it could dramatically increase the availability of combat-ready tanks. Such complex changes, however, fly in the face of a venerable tenet of Army command—that each battle unit be capable of repairing its own equipment. Messages of this sort are more palatable when the bearer understands the client and has time for explanation, discussion, and resolution of doubts. An FFRDC allows, even encourages, those very processes.

The domestic research agenda at RAND followed certain governmental priorities of the time and eschewed others. For example, as HUD's research dollars declined, housing and urban policy research ended. But in the policy areas of health, education, and criminal justice, RAND sought support from private foundations to bolster its substantially reduced federal dollars. Studies of the appropriateness of various medical procedures, a major social experiment on reducing adolescent drug abuse, and establishment of the Center for the Study of the Teaching Profession—were sponsored by foundations. By the end of the decade, 40% of RAND's $20 million domestic research funding came from foundations and other private sources. Transnational issues were added to the agenda, including creation of the Center for U.S.-Japan Relations to study economic issues of mutual interest.

Changing Priorities

In the early 1980s RAND experienced a decline in growth as the social experiments ended and military budgets faced uncertainty under a new federal administration. By 1983 the RAND staff had been reduced by about 23%. The second half of the decade reversed this trend as defense priorities were reasserted. The achievement of strategic parity by the Soviet Union was the single most important factor in this reversal. At RAND the defense component grew with the advent of the Army's Arroyo Center and with an expansion of the research programs of the other two national security FFRDCs to annual revenues of nearly $75 million.

Rand in the 1990s

As it enters the 1990s, RAND is deeply conscious of the social and political earthquakes that have reduced communism from a belief system posing a major international security threat to so much ideological rubble. The United States and its allies must now work out strategies of national and international security as new and profound as those developed after World War II. For its part, RAND must rethink and restructure its national security research agenda; indeed, it is already heavily involved with its sponsors in that process. The domestic research agenda is sure to be altered as well, giving close attention to studies of the environment, of investment in the infrastructure, and of strengthening U.S. economic competitiveness.

Total revenues in 1989 were about $94 million; the endowment fund was just over $40 million. The professional staff numbered an all-time high of 606 (nearly 40% are female, 11% minorities) with an additional 318 consultants at work. Another 526 staff members provide research support to the professional staff. The divisional distribution of research effort was Project AIR FORCE, 26%; national security research, 29%; Army research, 22%; and domestic research, 22%. Research sponsored by the corporation using its own funds amounted to $2.5 million. Over 130 sponsors currently fund RAND projects at the $100,000-or-greater annual level.

At least four features of the RAND culture have persisted over the 42 years of RAND's corporate history. First, high marks are still given to intellectual playfulness and imagination—oxygen-like qualities that permeated the working environment of the early RANDites. Second, the RAND briefing has evolved almost into an art form. It offers the audience a clear, concise, articulate summary, with supporting graphics, of major research findings and policy conclusions. Most briefings are subject to tough, intense peer review before they are taken on the road. If they are intended for top decision makers, RAND briefings receive more management attention than any other form of documentation. Third, RAND continues its fierce attachment to independence of research conclusions, including open publication of its research studies. (Roughly 80% of RAND's publications are in the open literature.) Finally, RAND appreciates and rewards good technical reviewers who combine tough criticism with constructive suggestions for report improvement. One of the best indicators that new staff members will do well in the RAND environment is their ability to benefit from no-holds-barred reviews by their peers.

RAND's research today falls into 13 major areas whose diversity and intellectual scope match those of the universities. Scientists at RAND do photogrammetry and photoanalysis of the moon and planets or lead conferences to develop an agenda for breakthroughs in antimatter research. Social scientists severally analyze the Soviet agenda in the Third World, predict attrition rates among first-term enlistees in the military, and develop evidence about improving telephone rate structures. An engineer heads a group that works to improve weapons reliability and maintainability; an information scientist heads a group to develop task sequencing for a computer algebra tutor for high school students; and a behavioral scientist heads a group to evaluate the national medical consensus development program.

The year 1990 marks the first full year in the tenure of James Thomson as RAND's fourth president. Before moving up, Thomson, a physicist and an insider, held the position of executive vice president; earlier still, he was head of the Project AIR FORCE Division. He had served on the National Security Council in the Carter administration. His aim is to establish a research and funding environment similar to that of an FFRDC for the Domestic Research Division. It is possible that research centers funded by foundations, private associations, and federal agencies will be the best domestic equivalent for FFRDCs that RAND can achieve. Today, RAND has 14 separate institutes and centers, ranging from the Center for Aging Studies to the Institute for Civil Justice to the RAND/UCLA Center for Soviet Studies and to the recent Drug Policy Research Center. Some reside more or less easily within research programs; others report directly to a divisional vice-president.

Many of RAND's institutes and centers are broader in scope and larger in funding base than the programs that spawned them. They generate conferences, workshops, and new client or decision-maker contacts. They permit the development of fresh ideas and the pursuit of lines of research not feasible with the project-by-project funding under which most domestic research programs labor. From RAND's point of view, the institutes and centers take domestic research in a valued direction. Thus far, however, the corporation is not structured to take full advantage of their existence.

The uneasy coexistence of narrowly based research programs and the broader-based centers and institutes well illustrates the changing policy and funding environment that RAND faces. Historically, its research programs have developed within a problem/policy area claimed as the specific province of a small set of agencies within one or two cabinet-level departments of government. But a growing number of problem/policy areas today not only involve many more policy-making bodies, but extend beyond the national boundaries as well. As that happens, domestic and national security concerns become more difficult to disentangle. Immigration policy, drug policy, and economic policy all manifest transnational characteristics. All are recent additions to RAND's research agenda. All rely heavily on foundation and private funding sources that cut across the more confined, territorial concerns of established federal departments. How rapidly the government will want or even be able to respond to these broader global policy problems is not answerable today. The answer will certainly affect RAND's future.

The 1990s are a watershed period for U.S. policy. As alliances and economic fortunes shift, as old threats diminish and new players emerge, both international and domestic policy will be challenged to respond with new paradigms. RAND aspires to be at the leading edge of those changes. To that end, its new president has launched an internal effort to set future directions for RAND and to identify research areas that warrant continued support. Two policy issues are sure to receive priority: U.S. national security after the collapse of the communist system, and the development of a more competitive workforce through education and training, so critical to U.S. prosperity and national security in the 1990s.

Notes

1. New York City–RAND Institutue, First Annual Report, October 1970.

2. In discussing the "knowledge utilization" aspects of RAND's criminal justice research, Joan Petersilia, who directs RAND's work in this field, comments that "implementation is the weakest link in the criminal justice research-to-practice process" (Petersilia, 1987, p. xiii).

References

Berman, M. B., McIver, D. W., Robbins, M. L., & Schank, J. F. (1988, October). *Evaluating the combat pay-off of alternative logistics structures for high-technology subsystems* (Report No. R-3673-A). Santa Monica, CA: RAND.

Berman, P., & McLaughlin, M. W. (1975, April). *Federal programs supporting educational changes: The findings in review* (Report No. R-1589-HEW). Santa Monica, CA: RAND.

Douglas Aircraft Company, Inc. (1946, May 2). *Preliminary design of an experimental world-circling spaceship* (Report No. SM-11827).

Goeller, B. F., Abrahamse, A. F., Bigelow, J. H., Bolten, J. G., DeFerranti, D. M., Dettaven, J. C., Kirkwood, T. F., & Petruschell, R. L. (1977, December). *Protecting an estuary from floods—A policy analysis of the Oosterschelde: Vol. 1, Summary Report* (Report No. R-2121/1-NETH). Santa Monica, CA: RAND.

Hosmer, S. (1970). *Viet Cong repression and its implications for the future* (Report No. R-475/1-ARPA). Santa Monica, CA: RAND.

Petersilia, J. (1987, June). *The influence of criminal justice research* (Report No. R-3516-NIJ). Santa Monica, CA: RAND.

Smith, B. L. R. (1966). *The RAND corporation: Case study of a nonprofit advisory corporation.* Cambridge, MA: Harvard University Press.

Wohlstetter, A. (1954). *Selection and use of strategic air bases* (Report No. R-266). Santa Monica, CA: RAND.

Wohlstetter, R. (1962). *Pearl Harbor: Warning and decision.* Stanford, CA: Stanford University Press.

4

The Center on Budget and Policy Priorities

Isaac Shapiro

Kathryn H. Porter

Robert Greenstein

In 1981, when extremely large federal budget reductions were enacted in programs serving low-income people, most of the media coverage and public understanding focused on such rhetorical images as a "safety net" for the "truly needy." Analysis of these terms or of the effects of these cuts on low-income households was meager. Moreover, most of the limited data available on the likely effects of these changes came from the Office of Management and Budget, the federal agency primarily responsible for proposing the reductions. The dearth of widely usable, nontechnical information on low-income programs, the composition of the poverty population, poverty trends, and potential impacts of the proposed budget cuts on low-income families handicapped the efforts of nonprofit and advocacy organizations, public officials, and journalists to participate in the debate on the administration's budget proposals.

The Center on Budget and Policy Priorities was founded in this climate in December 1981. The organization was formed to prepare policy analyses and research reports on issues affecting low- and moderate-income households. These analyses and reports were to be made available not only to the research community but also to policymakers, the general public (through the news media), and national, state, and local organizations. One of the center's founding goals was to improve public understanding and debate on budget issues affecting low-income families.

In the past decade the center has attempted to fulfill this primary function, while expanding its work to include a broad range of poverty and income distribution issues. Moreover, the center now examines these issues at state and local levels, as well as at the national level. The center's analyses of policies and economic trends affecting low- and moderate-income people typically reflect the belief that the government should play a larger role in assisting these people and that in recent years it often has neglected that role.

The center is a nonpartisan organization, and its analyses are used by policymakers of all political persuasions, as well as by program managers, journalists, and interested members of the public. It takes an empirical approach to the issues, presenting the best available data on the poor and policies that affect them.

Issues Addressed by the Center

As examples of its work, the center is producing an ongoing series of reports on how state tax codes affect low-income households, along with analyses presenting and assessing various targeted policy options for providing state tax relief to poor households. In addition, the center is issuing a series of reports on low-income housing conditions, both nationally and in a number of metropolitan areas. The center also examines issues related to food stamps and other federal food assistance programs, the minimum wage, the unemployment insurance system, welfare employment and training programs, and other policy matters. Somewhat detailed descriptions of the center's work in three key areas—the federal budget, poverty and income trends, and federal tax issues—are presented below.

Although most of the center's work is not tied to the legislative process, this chapter includes several examples of legislatively oriented work in order to illustrate the relationship of the center's research to the policy process.

Federal Budget Issues

At the heart of the center's work is its analysis of the impact of federal budget policies on low-income households. The center tries to ensure that the effects of budget proposals on different income groups are considered seriously by policymakers and other policy analysts and that organizations focusing on low-income people have the information and analysis they need to work effectively on budget issues. Center budget reports are used frequently by journalists as well. The center pays particular attention to analyzing the distributional impact of competing options for reducing the deficit. For example, when the congressional leadership and the administration held summit negotiations in the fall of 1987 on deficit reduction measures, the center issued several analyses on budget trends and various deficit reduction options under consideration. One such analysis (*Low Income Programs*, 1987) found that total appropriations for nonentitlement programs for low-income people (other than appropriations for subsidized housing programs) had declined nearly 30% in real terms from 1981 to 1987. Summit negotiators cited this analysis during the negotiations and later credited it with having played a role in helping avert cuts in programs with a major low-income component.

Similarly, a 1985 analysis (*Gramm-Rudman, 1985*) of the effects of the original version of the Gramm-Rudman-Hollings bill on poor households sparked intense interest. The analysis was credited with helping ignite a successful drive to exempt most major low-income benefit entitlement programs from the across-the-board spending reductions mandated under the legislation when deficit targets are missed.

Poverty and Income Issues

Every year, the center issues an analysis of the Census Bureau's annual poverty and income report. The analysis is issued on the same day as the census report and usually receives coverage in the newspaper and television stories on the census report.

In addition, much of the center's analytic work focuses on poverty trends and their contributing factors. A recent example of such work is the center's 1989 report on the rural working poor—a detailed examination of census, Labor Department, and other data on rural working poor households (Shapiro, 1989). Moreover, a 1988 center report (*Shortchanged*, 1988) on Hispanic poverty, income, and employment trends has been used widely by researchers with an interest in Hispanic issues.

Federal Tax Issues

The center has prepared a series of analyses and reports on low-income tax issues. One analysis in 1984 (*Taxing the Poor*, 1984) found that the combined income and payroll tax burden on working families at the poverty level had quadrupled since 1978. This report attracted media attention and stimulated interest among organizations and analysts that had not previously focused on this development. Center analyses also played a role in shaping the low-income provisions of the Tax Reform Act of 1986. For example, in May 1986 Senate Finance Committee Chairman Bob Packwood unveiled a major tax reform proposal to close loopholes and flatten tax rates. A Center analysis (*New Tax Plan*, 1986) found that several little-noticed provisions of the plan would reduce tax relief for working poor families, but that two changes in the earned income tax credit (a credit for working poor families with children) could address this problem without unraveling the basic structure of the Packwood plan. Senator Bill Bradley circulated the analysis and secured the adoption in the Senate Finance Committee of the earned income credit recommendations reflected in the analysis. These recommendations ultimately became law.

Since 1986 the center has issued additional analyses on the earned income tax credit. One series concluded that the work incentive effects of the credit were being weakened because the credit was counted as income in determining eligibility for AFDC, Medicaid, food stamps, and housing benefits, and so led to a reduction in these other benefits. These analyses were read and discussed by both policymakers and tax poverty program experts and have helped lead to a shift in federal policy in this area (e.g., *Disregard of EITC*, 1986).

The center has issued a series of analyses assessing the desirability of adjusting the earned income credit by family size so that it rises (up to a limit) with the number of children in a family. These analyses have found that if working poor families are to be raised to the poverty line, an expanded earned income credit adjusted by family size is an essential policy tool. (e.g., *Working Poor Families*, 1986).

The Nature of the Center's Work

Much of the center's work attempts to fill the gaps that often exist between research institutions and various sources of data on the one hand, and policymakers, advocacy groups, program managers, and journalists on the other hand. Part of the center's purpose is to make the results of research and analysis accessible to people concerned about issues affecting low- and moderate-income people but who do not ordinarily have research findings available to them in a form they can use easily.

Presentation of Information

Center analyses often are based on data from such government agencies as the Bureau of the Census, the Bureau of Labor Statistics, and the Congressional Budget Office. All these agencies produce large quantities of high-quality statistical information that is potentially very useful to policymakers, program managers, and advocacy organizations. The primary focus of many of these agencies, however, is not the accessibility of the information to the nontechnical user.

The center attempts to analyze these statistics, to relate them to current policy issues, and to present the information in a manner accessible to the average reader. This goal leads to some basic stylistic approaches that characterize the center's products.

At the center a substantial emphasis is placed on writing clear, nontechnical prose. When particularly technical subjects are addressed, the main body of the report typically is written for the general reader. Technical explanations requiring a deeper grasp of statistics are left often to footnotes or an appendix. Writing for those with an interest in policy issues also demands that close attention be paid to format. Executive summaries are a must if the reports are to be used by policymakers, journalists, and program managers, among others. Often, a good executive summary can interest such individuals in proceeding to read the full report. Liberal use is made of graphs and tables that can catch the attention of readers and lead them to delve deeper into the reports.

While the center's prose may be less technical than that in most academic research reports, center reports attempt to achieve the same standard of accuracy and reliability. Washington is awash with papers and reports; to read any one report, readers must be able to trust the accuracy of the analyses. The impact of any particular piece, moreover, is often determined by the general reputation of the organization.

Research Approach

The center often synthesizes and disseminates relevant research findings that ordinarily would not be noticed by those outside academic and research institutions but that can illuminate policy deliberations and public understanding of poverty issues. For example, Center reports have highlighted the results of academic studies of the effects of the WIC program on the healthy development of children, as well as studies of the relationship between the minimum wage and job loss (e.g., Shapiro, 1988). In addition, a report in the spring of 1990 (Porter, 1990) synthesized the recent research on welfare-to-employment programs and discussed how this research could be used by state and local administrators responsible for planning the employment programs required by federal welfare reform legislation.

Occasionally, the center collects data or conducts surveys on its own. As one example, in conducting an analysis of state poverty policies, the center discovered that information on state general assistance programs was lacking and so subsequently conducted a nationwide survey of these programs. The results of the survey were published as part of a series of reports, one for each state, entitled *Holes in the Safety Net: Poverty Programs and Policies in the States* (Shapiro & Greenstein, 1988).

The center also undertakes analyses of areas that other researchers have not fully explored. Until quite recently, for instance, little analytic work had been undertaken on the effects of the federal earned income tax credit. As previously indicated, center researchers have taken the lead in examining the effects of this credit on low-income households and the credit's relationship to other policies and programs aimed at these households.

Range of Reports

Much of the center's research results in medium to long background reports and policy analyses. The reports usually are not tied to immediate policy issues, but tend rather to be broader analyses of income, poverty, and policy developments.

These backgrounders are in many respects similar to descriptive and analytic reports done by traditional research organizations. Center reports, however, are more likely to synthesize existing data or research findings and are written for the wider and more varied audience the center attempts to reach.

Other center reports differ more sharply from those typically produced by traditional research organizations. Some are short pieces that respond quickly to breaking developments. For example, on the day the administration releases its federal budget proposals each year, the center prepares and distributes an analysis of the effects of the proposals on programs for low-income people. This same-day distribution requires that center staff digest quickly the voluminous data in the budget and prepare an analysis within a period of one day. The total preparation time for this report is, of course, much more than one day. The center spends weeks of advance work preparing background data and analyzing the issues likely to be raised by the new budget. Ongoing analytic work on other, longer budget reports facilitates this ability to digest the new information quickly.

On occasion, the center analyzes particular pieces of legislation as they are dancing their way through the Congressional process. In 1990, the center prepared a variety of short reports on the effects of particular provisions of competing House and Senate low-income tax credit provisions. Such reports are distributed to other researchers, members of Congress, the media, and interest groups while the policy issues are still being debated.

The center's interest in the policy and public education process leads its researchers to place an emphasis on short pieces intended for broad public consumption. Accordingly, center staff members sometimes write spin-offs of longer center reports as articles for newspapers or feature pieces for magazines. As mentioned, in 1988 the center published a series of reports on state safety nets, including a 70-page national overview report (Shapiro & Greenstein, 1988) and a 15- to 20-page report for each of the 50 states and the District of Columbia. Based on these reports, center staff then wrote articles for several magazines whose primary audiences are state and local administrators of poverty programs and other state public officials.

The Dissemination Process

The center tries to ensure that its reports are disseminated to a broad audience. Accordingly, the compilation of up-to-date and comprehensive mailing lists is an important center activity. The center maintains a list of nearly 2,000 people who subscribe to center reports, as well as lists of members of Congress and their staffs, and selected journalists both in Washington and across the country. Depending on the report, the center may also develop new lists. To provide a current example, the center is in the midst of issuing a series of reports on rural poverty. An essential element of this project is the development of a list of media contacts interested in rural issues.

For certain center reports an attempt is made to obtain maximum media coverage, often the best means of reaching the American public. Media coverage tends to increase the level of interest in a report, as well as its potential policy impact. Because the number of reports competing for the attention of those interested in policy questions is much greater than they can possibly read, media coverage is a good way to set one report apart from the rest.

For these reasons, the center attempts to think through its media release strategy carefully. Sometimes a press conference is the best approach to releasing a report, as in the example of a series of reports on housing conditions in particular metropolitan areas. The most effective release strategy is to hold a press conference in the metropolitan area covered by the report, in conjunction with local officials and community organizations who have a direct involvement in housing issues. Center staff members also set up local meetings with officials and organizations, as well as other press events, on the day of the press conference.

Audiences for the Center's Work

Most center analyses are designed for one or more of the following audiences:

- National, state, and local advocacy organizations
- Journalists
- Federal and state policymakers
- Federal, state, and local managers of poverty programs
- The academic and "think tank" research community

Advocacy organizations that use center reports include such national groups as the U.S. Catholic Conference, the Children's Defense Fund, and the Food Research and Action Center. State and local users include groups such as the Southern Regional Council, the Kentucky Task Force on Hunger, the State Communities Aid Association (in New York), and the Western Center on Law and Poverty.

The center is concerned about making the information in many of its reports accessible to journalists. Since the center is known for expertise in various areas and for a willingness to translate research for general usage, it receives several inquiries daily from reporters or editorial writers. Most of these inquiries seek background information, guidance on how to make sense of the data, or advice on which sources of data to use and which researchers to contact in doing a story. Providing this information presents opportunities for center staff members to discuss their analyses of the issues at hand.

The Center distributes its reports to elected officials. Legislators and other officials at the federal and state levels are often glad to have material that helps them make sense of government poverty data. Moreover, distributing certain reports to elected official helps ensure that the effects of particular policies on low-income people are not overlooked, as they sometimes have been in the past.

The center's work also is used extensively by state and local program managers. For example, the center issued a series of reports on state practices in requiring AFDC and food stamp recipients to report monthly on their incomes (Greenstein & Nichols, 1988a, 1988b). The analyses presented the results of a national survey of state procedures for "monthly reporting" and synthesized other research that found that monthly reporting neither reduces errors nor is cost-effective. The analyses led several state welfare agencies to reduce their use of monthly reporting.

Center reports are being used increasingly by traditional research organizations and academic researchers. Members of the center's staff work closely with researchers at such organizations as the Urban Institute, the Manpower Demonstration Research Corporation, the Aspen Institute Rural Economic Policy Program, and public policy schools and university-based research institutes. In the summer, the Center operates an internship program that typically includes students from graduate public policy programs.

Other Activities Related to the Policy-Making Process

While the primary focus of center activity is the preparation of policy analyses and research reports, the Center also undertakes a mixture of activities not typically associated with a research organization. For example, a small fraction of the staff's time involves direct legislative activity.

In some instances, the center has operated what amount to outreach programs. The most notable example is the center's leading role in

encouraging low-income working families who do not owe federal
income taxes to file a tax return in order to receive a refundable earned
income tax credit. Collaboration between the center, public interest
groups, local and state officials, and the IRS has characterized this
outreach campaign, which was launched in 1989.

Staff who are primarily analysts spend a significant fraction of their
time on public education. They frequently make presentations, lead
workshops and panel discussions, and provide technical assistance to
advocacy groups and government policymakers and program administrators.

Organization of the Center

The center is a nonprofit organization, with foundations providing
most of its funding. The current budget is about $1.5 million, with a
significant portion devoted to the costs of publishing and disseminating the center's reports and analyses.

The staff has grown considerably from its first few years, when the
center consisted of fewer than 10 people; it now includes 23 members.
The staff consists mainly of analysts with backgrounds in public
policy analysis, experience in the programs they study, or both. The
most common advanced degree is a master of public policy from a
school such as Harvard's John F. Kennedy School of Government.

The founder of the center, and its executive director since its
inception, is Robert Greenstein. In 1979 and 1980, Greenstein was the
administrator of the Food and Nutrition Service at the U.S. Department of Agriculture, the agency that operates the federal food assistance programs.

Although a deputy director has been hired to help strengthen
internal management, the organizational structure of the center is
mostly horizontal. Individual researchers and other key personnel
operate for the most part outside of a hierarchical environment. In
addition to the center's expertise in budget issues and general poverty
and income trends, many staff members have established their own
niche as "Washington experts" on welfare reform, the working poor,
federal and state tax policies, or housing.

Ongoing Challenges

The ongoing strength of the center largely depends on meeting two challenges. First, the center's analyses must be presented in clear, nontechnical language that is readily accessible to the general reader while meeting high standards of analytic quality. Second, the work must be fair and evenhanded.

To meet these challenges, the center continues to use the best and most recent government data available. As Greenstein was quoted in a September 8, 1986, article in the *Washington Post*, "We do our analyses with technical accuracy. We get it out quickly. We work very hard to make it simple and clear and smooth and readable" (Rich, 1986, p. A13).

References

Center on Budget and Policy Priorities. (1984, April). *Taxing the poor.* Washington, DC: Author.

Center on Budget and Policy Priorities. (1985, October). *The Gramm-Rudman proposal* (rev.). Washington, DC: Author.

Center on Budget and Policy Priorities. (1986, March). *Working poor families with children have been falling behind. Tax reform offers what may be the best opportunity of the decade to assist them, by expanding the earned income tax credit (EITC) and adding a family size adjustor.* Washington, DC: Author.

Center on Budget and Policy Priorities. (1986, May). *New tax plan reduces tax relief for working poor—but this problem can be remedied through a modest adjustment in the earned income tax credit.* Washington, DC: Author.

Center on Budget and Policy Priorities. (1986, July). *Disregard of EITC for public assistance programs.* Washington, DC: Author

Center on Budget and Policy Priorities. (1987, November). *Low income programs already sharply reduced.* Washington, DC: Author.

Center on Budget and Policy Priorities. (1988, November). *Shortchanged: Recent developments in Hispanic poverty, income and employment.* Washington, DC: Author.

Greenstein, R., & Nichols, M. (1988a, September). *Monthly reporting in the AFDC program.* Washington, DC: Center on Budget and Policy Priorities.

Greenstein, R., & Nichols, M. (1988b, September). *Monthly reporting in the food stamp program.* Washington, DC: Center on Budget and Policy Priorities.

Porter, K. (1990, March). *Making JOBS work: What the research says about effective employment programs for AFDC recipients.* Washington, DC: Center on Budget and Policy Priorities.

Rich, S. (1986, September 8). Robert Greenstein: Legislative impact by the numbers. *The Washington Post*, pp. p. A13.

Shapiro, I. (1988, July). *The minimum wage and job loss*. Washington, DC: Center on Budget and Policy Priorities.

Shapiro, I. (1989, October). *Laboring for less: Working but poor in rural America*. Washington, DC: Center on Budget and Policy Priorities.

Shapiro, I., & Greenstein, R. (1988, May). *Holes in the safety net: Poverty programs and policies in the states* (national overview report). Washington, DC: Center on Budget and Policy Priorities.

Shapiro, I., & Greenstein, R. (1990, March). *Fulfilling work's promise: Policies to increase incomes of the rural working poor*. Washington, DC: Center on Budget and Policy Priorities.

5

The Center for Policy Research in Education: An Overview

Susan H. Fuhrman

The Center for Policy Research in Education (CPRE) was established in 1985 as a result of a 5-year grant from the Office of Educational Research and Improvement (OERI) of the U.S. Department of Education.[1] Its mission is to study state and local policies to improve schooling. Although CPRE focuses exclusively on education, several aspects of its mission and operation make it more akin to policy research agencies discussed in other chapters of this book than to most other education research centers.

CPRE's overarching goal is to provide research that is useful to state and local education policymakers—research that meets their needs for information and is readily accessible to them. While some of the center's research is intended to make theoretical contributions, all of it is intended to provide advice about policy options to enhance learning. Unlike many policy advice institutions discussed in this book, CPRE's research is not directly supported by the clients it serves; state and local policymakers do not provide for our support, except in their roles as U.S. taxpayers. Federal policymakers appear to welcome advice on the implications for federal policy of state and local experience, but the center specifically does not focus on federal policy efforts. Therefore, CPRE is supported by one level of government to study policy developments at other levels of government. Such an arrangement exists in other areas of domestic policy, but it seems particularly well suited to education. Historically, the federal policy role has been limited in comparison with local districts and states, and the one constant in the rather fluid and shifting federal interest in education has been its responsibility for research and information-gathering.

This chapter discusses CPRE's provision of policy advice by focusing on its distinguishing features: a research agenda built around client concerns; a national consortium structure that unites education policy researchers at various institutions and facilitates contact with state and local policymakers in diverse regions; and an emphasis on creating a dialogue between the producers and users of research.

Building a Research Agenda Around Client Concerns

As is the case with each of the 21 research and development centers OERI supports, CPRE's mission is defined broadly by the federal government. Both OERI and CPRE researchers, however, desire that the work of the center be responsive to the needs of its primary constituents—state and local policymakers. Therefore, from the center's inception its role has been to provide a research capacity around issues of interest to state and local policymakers rather than to embark on studies defined by federal officials.

The federal government has been supporting research centers in education since 1965, but few if any of them have dealt directly with policy issues. In 1985 the Department of Education held a new competition, redefining the missions of research centers and opening the competition to new applicants. The new mission statements grew out of an extensive consultation process with researchers, educational organizations, professional associations, and public interest groups over a 2-year period.

Fearing that "policy" would not appear on the final list of missions to be competed, several organizations representing key state and local educational policymakers lobbied hard on its behalf. The National Association of State Boards of Education, the National Conference of State Legislatures, the National Governors' Association, and the National School Boards Association urged then Secretary of Education Terrell Bell to establish a research center on state and local policy, arguing the importance of research built around policymakers' needs. As the executive director of the National School Boards Association has written:

> Our concern at that time was two-fold. First, the educational research which
> had been developed until that time had been designed to meet the needs

of the professional educator and was quite often incomprehensible to public officials who had to make decisions on programs or policies to improve the quality of education. Our second related concern was that the existing research was not designed to implement policy decisions but rather designed to assist in developing classroom practices. (T. A. Shannon, personal communication, May 24, 1990)

OERI approved a policy center and defined its mission broadly to center on the effects of state educational reform, which by 1985 had become the most salient policy activity in education at the state level. CPRE's proposal for the policy center stressed responsiveness to clients. Early in our planning process, we met with staff of national policymaker associations individually; at a later stage we convened them as a group to react to our developing agenda. As a result, our research plans called for focus on aspects of reform, particularly higher standards for high school students and changes in teacher certification and compensation, that were attracting the most attention from policymakers. At the specific urging of the clients we consulted, we also proposed to provide flexibility to respond to policymaker information needs over time. Called Emerging Strategies and Structures, this program of research included commissioned and occasional papers on new educational problems and developing policy solutions. While any number of factors might have contributed to CPRE's success in the competition, the emphasis on meeting the information needs of clients was undoubtedly important to the peer reviewers who selected our proposal for funding.

Suggestions about which new problems and emerging solutions to study were to come from our clients through a governance structure designed to give them input. The multitiered structure—consisting of an Executive Board, Research and Dissemination Advisory Committees, affiliated organizations, and a Management Committee—that we proposed in 1985 has served us as intended over time.

The Executive Board, or national advisory panel, is the primary mechanism for sensing the information needs of the policy community. The board comprises elected and appointed policymakers (governors, legislators, chief state school officers, state and local board members, public and private school administrators) and other participants in the policy process, including teachers, parents, and business leaders. Other members are scholars with significant research experience in education policy. At an annual meeting and through informal communications throughout the year, board members advise us about framing our research so that it is most useful to policymakers.

The Research Advisory Committee, composed of outside scholars from state and local research agencies, as well as universities, is a mechanism for ensuring the integrity, quality, and coherence of center research. By including researcher members not otherwise associated with CPRE, the center gains the perspective of users of its research—in both the academic and practitioner communities—and benefits from the expertise of colleagues who perform similar work. The six-member Dissemination Advisory Committee is composed of outside scholars who specialize in knowledge utilization, journalists, and experts in public relations. The committee provides advice on the basis of its assessment of dissemination performance and prospects. It is a mechanism for ensuring integration of dissemination strategies across projects and responsiveness to the needs and usage patterns of policymakers.

The 19 national associations that are formally affiliated with CPRE represent the range of center constituents—key policymakers, practitioners, and interested participants who compose the education policy community. The associations, which range from the American Federation of Teachers and the National Education Association to the Council of Chief State School Officers, National Governors' Association, and the National Alliance for Business, provide important advice about information needs. At regular meetings and through frequent consultation, their staffs advise on CPRE's research agenda, dissemination plans, and progress. The associations also assist in the dissemination of CPRE products.

The CPRE Management Committee, composed of representatives of consortium institutions, uses the advice of such client representatives to make final determination of research topics. The research projects we have proposed to OERI in yearly continuation applications and outlined in 1990 in a major proposal for a new 5-year grant are justified on the basis of client interest.

Although CPRE researchers enter these consultations with our own strong notions about future avenues of research, we consistently learn from our advisors. Over the years, the interaction around research themes has taken three primary forms. First, at formal meetings of our board, advisory committees, or affiliated organizations, we present overviews and emerging findings of research in progress with the purpose of encouraging debate about further questions raised by current research. For example, early in our research on the impact of stricter high school graduation requirements, we realized that these policies could not be studied in isolation from related policies, including university entrance requirements, curriculum frameworks, and student testing. When we suggested broadening our studies of graduation standards, our constituents helped us think through the entire range of policies whose interactions we should explore. As a result, we made sure to include textbook adoption policies and professional development policies.

Second, consultation about our research agenda at advisory meetings occurs when we ask advisors to reflect on emerging policy issues and problems. In this fashion, we learned that our constituents were concerned about moving beyond a factory model of schooling to organizational forms more supportive of teaching and learning. This concern reinforced our own interest in conducting studies on policy links to organizational, curricular, and pedagogical improvements suggested by new research on the ways students learn. Subsequent discussions led to a major research focus on how policy can encourage new roles and responsibilities for teachers and administrators in designing schools around ambitious notions of learning.

Third, any time we are presenting research findings to advisors or policymakers we encounter through dissemination activities, questions and discussion may suggest interesting research angles. For example, while we had determined that new roles and responsibilities were emerging for school personnel, constituents helped us see that new forms of school organization posed changes in roles across all levels of the public school system. At regional meetings we hosted in 1986 and 1987, we learned that school board members felt bypassed by school reform and uncertain about their roles, given new standards emerging from states and demands from school-level educators for more discretion over their own operations. We broadened our notions of new roles and responsibilities to include a focus on district-school and state-district interaction.

The responsiveness of our research agenda can be judged by its evolution over time. In 1985, two years into an extensive state education reform movement that stressed state-level policy solutions to problems of school improvement, our agenda focused heavily on new state standards for students and teachers and ways of measuring progress that resulted from such standards. Of our 12 initial research projects, 8 reflected the growing prevalence of state mandates around such core education issues as who should teach and what should be taught. In 1990, a few years into a so-called "second wave" of education reform that stressed school-based change and de-emphasized state mandates, 7 of 13 research projects focused on the changing roles and responsibilities of teachers, administrators, and policymakers around school-designed improvement.

CPRE's National Consortium Structure

A second distinguishing feature of CPRE is our structure as a consortium. The national consortium structure has been a critical aspect of our operation and is worth discussing.

Research centers are intended to conduct systematic, programmatic research. They provide a mechanism for addressing major educational issues, such as the relationship between educational policy and student learning, with a program of integrated research that draws on the perspectives of varied disciplines. Because centers have a relatively long life (5 years for current OERI centers), they can develop research that is longitudinal in nature, as well as design studies that build on one another in a way that progressively narrows in on key research questions. Because centers are designated hubs of research activity around particular problems, they can attract the sustained participation of senior researchers and provide national leadership in both substantive and methodological areas. Centers also have mechanisms for disseminating findings and creating long-term interaction with practitioners and researchers.

Because we believed no single institution could fulfill the broad mission of a center focused on educational policy, we created an organization comprising several core institutions. CPRE was housed at four institutions: Rutgers University, Michigan State University, Stanford University and the University of Wisconsin-Madison.[2] As a result of the 1990 competition for an additional 5-year grant, Harvard University and the University of Southern California joined the consortium. Each institution is a full partner in all research and dissemination activities; each is represented on all governance and management structures.

CPRE's operation is greatly enhanced by this consortium structure. First, the location of the six institutions in different geographical regions facilitates dissemination and collaboration with regional, state, and local actors; it also lowers the cost of conducting national research. For example, for five years CPRE has conducted a major project that studies reform development, implementation, and effects of state education in six states—Arizona, California, Florida, Georgia, Minnesota, and Pennsylvania. Project design, instrumentation, and analysis are jointly conducted by researchers at various CPRE member institutions, dividing data collection responsibilities to capitalize on the proximity of CPRE's institutional members to sample states. Furthermore, as CPRE researchers had extensive prior experience in education policy analysis, they brought to CPRE well-developed contacts in their state and regional policy communities. Our national consortium structure enables us to build on, expand, and unite localized networks. In fact, one may argue that a national education policy center should be a consortium rather than a single institution because regional dispersion enhances understanding of and access to various policy contexts.

Second, CPRE can draw on many of the most talented education policy researchers in the country. No one institution has the wealth of education policy expertise of CPRE's partners. Most importantly, these researchers have chosen to work together. Although they represent many disciplines (current staff have backgrounds in economics, education, history, law, political science, psychology, and sociology), they share an interest in improving schooling through policy research. Unlike individuals who collaborate because they happen to work at the same institution, CPRE staff choose to work together because they enjoy learning from one another.

The collegial interaction fostered by the consortium is probably at the core of CPRE's success. The opportunity for intellectually rewarding collaboration is the primary reason CPRE researchers participate in the center. The structure permits interaction of classroom-based researchers with social scientist policy experts—interchange that is rare in other settings—as well as sustained, extensive collaboration among policy researchers who had long admired each other's work and sought opportunities to work together.

At the top of the list of factors that make CPRE researchers so compatible is our strong belief in using good research to improve policy and schooling. Clearly, the center is a means for achieving the professional goals we hold as individuals. We would not be able to exert the impact on policy we desire, however, without the collaborative research made possible by the consortium.

Third, the consortium structure means that several institutions are strongly committed to the center and provide it with resources and experience that a single institution cannot match. Rutgers's interest in policy-making, political leadership, and change processes; the University of Southern California's interest in educational finance; Michigan State's interest in policy built around challenging conceptions of teaching and learning; Stanford's interest in national policy and schools as productive work sites; Wisconsin's concern with curriculum policy, effective schools, and the law; and Harvard's interest in school organization and policy together provide a balanced and sound foundation for center research. These consortium partners provide CPRE with extensive resources, including renowned faculty, excellent support services, and alliances with important related efforts in research, dissemination, development, and school-university collaboration.

Finally, a consortium structure takes advantage of technological advances that overcome many of the drawbacks of geographic dispersion. CPRE's institutional bases have compatible microcomputing equipment for communication purposes, including disc drives, modems, and printers available for each staff member. Mail and document transmittal among institutions is carried out through the electronic network BITNET. Each institution has a FAX machine for use when computerized data transmission is not feasible. Express mail services and extensive teleconferencing complete the complement of communication options for rapid interaction. CPRE researchers probably communicate with one another more frequently than researchers located at the same institution. Because communication is so simple, consortia are becoming more popular structures for national research centers, at least within education. In 1985 CPRE was unique among OERI supported centers in its consortium structure. In the 1990 competition, a majority of the proposals came from institutional consortia.

Constructing and operating a successful consortium is much more than a matter of electronic linkages among interested researchers. Consortium institutions must be compatible on a number of dimensions to sustain a collaborative research endeavor; these include beliefs about governance, the priority of centerwide concerns, appropriate division of labor, and shared institutional support. Compatibility on these dimensions may be maximized in alliances among institutions of the same type—for example, among universities, among contract research centers, and among government research agencies. Universities, contract research associations, and government agencies may have very different approaches to a number of issues (e.g., cost-sharing or the extent to which research staff can commit the institution on fiscal or structural matters), posing challenges to consortia composed of different types of organizations.

With regard to the first dimension of center governance, the partners need to develop decision-making mechanisms for the center that reflect shared beliefs about how the center should be run. Partners must agree on fundamental issues, for example: which and how much of the center's activities are subject to democratic governance; how institutional partners are represented; whether institutional partners are equally represented; and how center governance may be modified, if necessary, over time.

CPRE's Management Committee includes a representative of each consortium institution. That representative serves as the responsible principal investigator for the projects and activities conducted at his or her institutional base. Together, through consensual decision-making procedures, the Management Committee members develop policies and procedures for centerwide day-to-day operations, safeguard quality control through internal review of projects and products and oversight of external review, and form the hub of the planning process for research and dissemination. While center plans are informed by CPRE's Executive Board and other advisors and are subject to periodic review by OERI and its external reviewers, final determination of the research and dissemination program rests with the Management Committee. Hence, partners share equally in governing the center. University officials treat CPRE work the same as any such endeavor taking place entirely on their own campuses, delegating complete authority for CPRE's operation to the relevant Management Committee member, within the context of university guidelines governing externally funded research.

As a second dimension, consortium members need to be compatible on the relative priority placed on centerwide, as opposed to institutional, concerns. In CPRE, decisions about the nature of the research and dissemination program take center needs into account first. The Management Committee considers responsiveness to constituent concerns and the contribution of each project and activity to CPRE's overall mission. Individual members, with the support of their institutions, apply such criteria even though specific decisions may direct research projects and funds to other partners and away from their own institutions. It is possible that such cooperative attitudes prevail only because general understandings exist about approximate institutional shares of the total OERI grant—understandings that date back to the start of each institution's participation in CPRE. Each institution has been willing, however, to accept more than marginal differences in dollar amounts from year to year, depending on the institutional division of labor dictated by the nature of the research program.

A third area in which institutional partners must reach agreement is the issue of division of labor. Some consortia prefer strict institutional division of authority, perhaps by substantive area of research, predominant research methodology, or other such criteria; other consortia may prefer to share all activities across institutions to promote unity. In CPRE we have reached agreement, albeit tacitly, to be flexible on this dimension. We have some functional division of responsibilities; all publications are produced and all CPRE-sponsored meetings are organized at Rutgers, the lead institution. We also have had from time to time some substantive division of labor; for several years all research on curriculum-related policy took place at Wisconsin. The substantive allocations have shifted, however, as the research agenda has evolved.

A fourth characteristic of a successful consortium is shared institutional support. The support of the universities for CPRE indicate that they all value policy research, that they accord priority to applied research and public service. CPRE's institutional partners express their support in a variety of ways, including generous cost-sharing of faculty time and donation of facilities and equipment. The lead institution, Rutgers, has created three tenure-track faculty lines to augment CPRE's capacity; all partners have encouraged graduate students and faculty to participate in CPRE research and have subsidized, at least in part, their efforts to do so. The important point is that the partners share a commitment to CPRE and that each feels the others express that commitment in equally generous ways.

Though not without potential difficulties, a consortium is a sensible and cost-effective arrangement for a national policy research center focused on state and local issues. In CPRE's case, the consortium provides a primary incentive for individual researchers to participate, enabling collaboration with colleagues that would otherwise not occur. Collaboration with constituents is encouraged also by the national consortium structure.

Creating a Dialogue Between Producers and Users of Research

In order for policy research to be useful, researchers must account for the variety of ways in which research is used. While acknowledging that social science research has few direct effects on policy (for example, Lindblom & Cohen, 1979; Lynn, 1977; Weiss, 1978; Weiss & Vickers, 1990), at CPRE we expect that from time to time our research will be instrumentally useful to policymakers as they make their decisions. More often, we expect that CPRE research will influence policy by forming the backdrop of policy deliberations, shaping debates, and spurring public discussion (McDonnell, 1988; Weiss, 1979). We contribute to policy deliberations by identifying the conceptual issues underlying policy problems and clarifying the assumptions of alternative policy solutions.

An example about the development and use of our research on state differential treatment of districts illustrates how our work has influenced policy deliberations. As is the case with most of our projects, the research had its genesis in both our own analyses and in consultations with constituents. Through our efforts to track reform in six states, we learned that state and local relationships in education were changing but not necessarily in ways predicted by reform critics who feared that new state reforms would signal the end of local control of education. We found that state education agencies lacked the capacity to enforce reform requirements; reform brought no break with the past tendency for states to rely more on influence strategies than compliance strategies (Fuhrman, Clune, & Elmore, 1988; Fuhrman & Elmore, 1990). Also, gaining momentum from the proliferation of testing student performance during the reform years, was a trend toward state differential treatment of districts. State agencies simply could not pay equal attention to all districts, and performance measures gave them objective means by which to discriminate among districts. States were beginning to vary regulatory strategies, providing regulatory waivers and less oversight to some districts and more intensive oversight, including the severest sanction of state takeover, to others. Our observance of this trend coincided with our constituents' interest in the topic of changing roles of state and local policymakers. We therefore pursued a study of new forms of state-local regulatory relationships.

Our work on state differential treatment of districts began with a telephone survey of state department of education personnel in 25 states. We reported our findings in a paper that explored the conceptual underpinnings of various strategies. *Diversity Amidst Standardization: State Differential Treatment of Districts* (Fuhrman, 1989) was circulated to key constituents, including our Executive Board and affiliates, in draft form. Board member Terry Peterson distributed copies to the South Carolina reform oversight group he staffs as background for their discussions on providing regulatory flexibility to local schools. According to reports we have received, the paper was important in influencing South Carolina policy leaders as they developed the Flexibility Through Deregulation Program. For example, the program was designed, as the paper recommends, to provide regulatory free zones for participating schools rather than rule-by-rule waivers on school request. Subsequently, we consulted with the committee in its review of state regulations to identify areas of exemption.

We have continued our research on differential treatment with field-based research in four states. We distributed the final version of *Diversity Amidst Standardization* and spoke on the subject to policymakers from many states. It is clear that our initial work in the area had very tangible effects in South Carolina and is informing discussions in other states.

Other such examples are found. Based on CPRE research on how to measure educational progress (Kaagan & Coley, 1989; Oakes, 1986; Williams, 1987), CPRE and the Educational Testing Service staff designed an indicator system for the state of Missouri that is now being implemented. Our work on early childhood education, choice, school-based management, improving the math and science curriculum, and student retention-in-grade has assisted policymakers to structure debates by illuminating the major dimensions of policy issues and the assumptions underlying various options (Clune & White, 1988; CPRE, 1990; Elmore, 1986; Grubb, 1987; Raizen, 1988; Romberg, 1988). We have worked also with print and television journalists to enhance understanding about these complex issues. We have consulted with several task forces active in education reform, such as the Kentucky Task Force on Education Reform, which redesigned the entire school system in the state in response to a court decision. The National Governors' Association Task Force on National Education Goals, established after the Charlottesville Education Summit of 1989, drew on a number of reports and studies in which we participated (Clune, 1989; David, 1989; David, Cohen, Honetschlager,

& Traiman, 1990; Elmore, 1988; Smith & O'Day, 1988). The national goals activity also drew on our emerging understanding, shaped by our own research and that of others, of necessary future directions for education policy: greater focus on ambitious notions of student learning; greater coherence within and across levels and sectors of educational policy; and more sensitivity to variation among students, schools, districts, and states. (National Governors' Association, 1990; Smith & O'Day, 1991).

Acknowledging the variety of ways in which research can influence policy suggests a dissemination strategy built on the following principles:

Dissemination is continuous. We do not wait for the results of research we undertake but instead select, translate, and deliver knowledge that already has been produced. We see as part of our mission the identification of policy implications suggested by more basic educational research and the translation of other educational research to policymakers.

Dissemination is an integrated endeavor. It is not separate from other activities. We believe that involving users in the planning and production of information encourages their use of it. A sense of ownership is valuable, and such a sense can be engendered through the dissemination process, as well as through the advisory process discussed above. Much of CPRE's dissemination activity is designed to solicit ideas for research from policymakers; dissemination activities supplement the meetings of our advisory structures. Our dissemination activities are also occasions for examining how our constituents use research to inform policy-making. Finally, at CPRE the same individuals who conduct the research deliver it to practitioners. This procedure is important for two reasons: It ensures that researchers are exposed to ideas and suggestions from people in the field, and it helps prevent distortion of information in the passage from researcher through intermediaries to policymakers.

Dissemination relies on existing channels to the extent possible. The primary channels for disseminating policy research are the national organizations to which policymakers and participants belong. These organizations bear the continuing responsibility for providing information, technical assistance, and other services to their members. Evidence suggests that, in large part, education policymakers look to their own professional associations for information (Nelson & Kirst, 1981). For example, an OERI-funded study of five national organizations found that policymaker members of these organizations rely on the state education agency as the major in-state source of information and on the Education Commission of the States and their membership organizations as the major national sources (Cohen, 1985; Fuhrman & McDonnell, 1985).

We explicitly recognized the special standing of these organizations in the structure of an affiliated organization, discussed previously. CPRE provides affiliates with materials to disseminate; we write articles for their newsletters and present panels at their meetings. From the beginning of 1986 to spring 1990, we participated in approximately 480 meetings of policymakers and practitioners, reaching a total audience of almost 40,000. We also enhance the clearinghouse activities of affiliated organizations, providing multistate information when we have gathered it, suggesting topics of interest, and referring information requests to them on a regular basis.

Working with the organizations brings many benefits. CPRE is able to capitalize on the major channels of information flow to policymakers, while minimizing information overload for busy clients. Since our constituents receive at least one regular newsletter from their associations, we do not publish our own. Instead, we place articles in their periodicals, summarizing our reports or highlighting the policy implications of our research. Thus, we significantly multiply our audience. For example, our own mailing list for policy briefs is approximately 5,000 individuals; when the National Association of Secondary School Principals reprinted two of our briefs in its *Bulletin*, we reached an audience of 45,000. Affiliation with the associations also creates visibility for CPRE. We have become more widely known as a result of our participation in association meetings and activities. Finally, we hope that interaction with CPRE strengthens the capacity of association staff to provide policy advice.

Dissemination is multifaceted. Often dissemination relies on only a few ways of communicating with policymakers, and typically most of the communications are in written form. Recognizing that different audiences are receptive to different communication forms, CPRE uses multiple information activities, both written and person-to-person. Written materials range from reports to policy briefs and press releases. Literature on research utilization has found "translation" to be a major problem (Caplan, Morrison, Stambourgh, 1975; Weiss,

1978). Unless research products are short, free of jargon, and placed in proper context, they will not receive practitioners' attention (Bellavita, 1981; Van Horn & Hetrick, 1987). Hence, we place great emphasis on succinctness and clarity. We have learned also that policymakers create files by topic (e.g., dropouts, retention in grade, restructuring schools). Therefore, rather than highlighting the variety of research areas we pursue, each of our policy briefs concerns a single issue, making it easy to store for future reference.

Our face-to-face activities range from tailored technical assistance to meetings of several hundred policymakers. One dissemination activity we believe to be unique is the Regional Policy Workshop. The workshops convene approximately 15 state and local policymakers in different roles from each of four to six states for a 2-day meeting. The workshops emphasize discussion and exchange of ideas among policymakers—including state and local board of education members, legislators and their staffs, governors' aides, state agency leadership, and local superintendents—who rarely have opportunities for informal, in-depth discussion of important policy issues. Key features of the workshops are agendas built around critical policy issues as identified by a planning team of policymakers from the region, small-group discussion and interchange among researcher-facilitators and participants, and structured opportunities for substantive discussions among participants from the same state. One of the most challenging aspects of workshop design is balancing the opportunity for discussion among participants and the presentation of research findings. At first, we erred in the direction of providing too much time for participant interchange and too little for research presentations. Participants wondered why we had convened them and why they had traveled a significant distance only to go away without new research findings. It took extensive discussion among CPRE staff, puzzling over why learning from fellow policymakers was accorded less value as a substantive experience than learning from researchers. Our workshops may be the only setting where such a phenomenon ever occurred, and a period of trial-and-error was needed until we struck the right balance.

It is fortunate that our corrective action did not diminish the opportunity for informal dialogue among participants from the same state. That opportunity was so appreciated, and apparently otherwise so rare, that groups from several of the 28 states that have participated in CPRE's workshops have continued to meet in the period since the workshop.[3] Clearly, the cross-state nature of the workshop provides a context and comparative framework that is useful in spurring within-state discussions; it provides a starting point for those discussions. Also, a cross-state meeting provides the kind of neutralized, "out of the heat of politics" atmosphere that promotes candid interchange. Some of the participant groups from specific states continue to meet to provide a forum for sharing perspectives on key policy issues; their agendas change from meeting to meeting and reflect important developments in the state. Other state groups that have continued to function have taken on a theme (for example, restructuring in Nebraska and school readiness in Missouri) with the expectation that exploring the theme will suggest policy options for the state.

Conclusion

CPRE is a national center, yet it is focused on state and local policy. It is strongly tied to the needs of its clients, yet receives no direct financial support from them. It is focused just on education, but differs in orientation from other education research centers that place lower priority on client needs and dialogue. In some sense, CPRE is unique. What we have learned about producing and disseminating research for education policymakers may be useful to participants in the 18 university-based state education policy centers that have developed over the past 5 years. These efforts are quite different from CPRE in some respects; for example, they involve direct support from state policymaker clients, through contracts for research projects or through state university support of center services, and most are not consortia but programs at individual universities. We share, however, a fundamental interest in improving education through policy research. It is our hope to undertake collaborative research with the state policy centers in the future. Collaboratively designed, comparable studies involving many states would enhance greatly the research base for policy advice to state and local education policymakers within those states and throughout the nation.

Notes

1. The Center for Policy Research in Education (CPRE) is a consortium of Rutgers, the State University of New Jersey; the University of Southern California; Harvard University; Michigan State University; Stanford University; and the University of

Wisconsin-Madison, supported by the Office of Educational Research and Improvement, U.S. Department of Education, through grant number OERI-R-117G10007. The opinions expressed in this article are those of the author and are not necessarily shared by the U.S. Department of Education, CPRE, or its institutional partners.

2. Prior to 1987, the RAND Corporation participated in the CPRE consortium, along with two of the current university partners.

3. The Danforth Foundation has underwritten the expenses of Regional Workshops in 1989 and 1990 with the explicit purpose of encouraging continued meetings within states. Federally supported regional laboratories, and particularly the Mid-Continent Regional Lab, have assisted in hosting and supporting the continued meetings.

References

Bellavita, C., Kirst, M., Meltsner, A., & Nelson, L. (1981). *Policy research and educational policy making: Toward a better connection.* (Final report to NIE, under a grant to the Institute for Research on Education Finance and Government). Palo Alto, CA: Stanford University.

Caplan, N., Morrison, A., & Stambaugh, R. (1975). *The use of social science knowledge in policy decisions at the national level.* Ann Arbor, MI: Institute for Social Research.

Center for Policy Research in Education. (1990). Repeating grades in school: Current practice and research evidence. *CPRE Policy Briefs.* New Brunswick, NJ: Author.

Clune, W. H. (with P. A. White & J. H. Patterson). (1989). *The implementation and effects of high school graduation requirements: First steps toward curriculum reform.* New Brunswick, NJ: Rutgers University, Center for Policy Research in Education.

Clune, W. H., & White, P. A. (1988). *School-based management: Institutional variation, implementation and issues for further research.* New Brunswick, NJ: Rutgers University, Center for Policy Research in Education.

Cohen, M. (1985). *Meeting the information needs of state education policymakers.* Washington, DC: State Education Policy Consortium, National Association of State Boards of Education.

David, J. L. (with S. Purkey & P. White). (1989). *Restructuring in progress: Lessons from pioneering districts.* Washington, DC: National Governors' Association.

David, J. L., Cohen, M. K., Honetschlager, D., & Traiman, S. (1990). *State actions to restructure schools: First steps.* Washington, DC: National Governors' Association.

Elmore, R. F. (1986). *Choice in public education* (Report No. JRE-03). Prepared for the Center for Policy Research in Education. Santa Monica, CA: RAND.

Elmore, R. F. (1988). *Early experience in restructuring schools: Voices from the field.* Washington, DC: National Governors' Association.

Fuhrman, S. H. (with P. Fry). (1989). *Diversity amidst standardization: State differential treatment of districts.* New Brunswick, NJ: Rutgers University, Center For Policy Research in Education.

Fuhrman, S. H., Clune, W. H., & Elmore, R. F. (1988). Research on education reform: Lessons on the implementation of policy. *Teachers College Record, 90*(2, Winter), 237-257.

Fuhrman, S. H., & Elmore, R. F. (1990). Understanding local control in the wake of state education reform. *Educational Evaluation and Policy Analysis, 12*(1), 82-96.

Fuhrman, S. H., & McDonnell, L. M. (1985). *Meeting education policymakers' information needs: The role of the national organizations.* Washington, DC: State Education Policy Consortium, National Association of State Boards of Education.

Grubb, N. W. (1987). *Young children face the states: Issues and options for early childhood programs.* New Brunswick, NJ: Rutgers University, Center for Policy Research in Education.

Kaagan, S. S., & Coley, R. J. (1989). *State education indicators: Measured strides, missing steps.* Princeton, NJ: Center for Policy Research in Education and Educational Testing Service (ETS). (Available from ETS Publications Order Service, Princeton)

Lindblom, C. E., & Cohen, D. K. (1979). *Usable knowledge.* New Haven, CT: Yale University Press.

Lynn, L. E., Jr. (1977). Implementation: Will the hedgehog be outfoxed? *Policy Analysis, 3,* 277-280.

McDonnell, L. M. (1988). Can education research speak to state policy? *Theory into Practice, 27*(2), 91-97.

National Governors' Association. (1990). *Educating America: State strategies for achieving the national education goals.* Washington, DC: Author.

Oakes, J. (1986). *Educational indicators: A guide for policymakers* (Report No. OPE-01). Prepared for the Center for Policy Research in Education. Santa Monica, CA: RAND.

Raizen, S. A. (1988). *Increasing educational productivity through improving the science curriculum.* New Brunswick, NJ: Rutgers University, Center for Policy Research in Education.

Romberg, T. A. (1988). *Changes in school mathematics: Curricular changes, instructional changes and indicators of change.* New Brunswick, NJ: Rutgers University, Center for Policy Research in Education.

Smith, M. S., & O'Day, J. (1988). *Teaching policy and research on teaching.* Unpublished manuscript, Rutgers University, Center for Policy Research in Education, New Brunswick, NJ.

Smith, M. S., & O'Day, J. (1991). Systemic school reform. In S. H. Fuhrman & B. Malen (Eds.), *The politics of curriculum and testing,* 1990 Yearbook of the Politics of Education Association. Philadelphia: Falmer.

Van Horn, C. E., & Hetrick, B. (1987). *Buyers and brokers: Information flow in education policy communities.* Unpublished manuscript, Rutgers University, Center for Policy Research in Education, New Brunswick, NJ.

Weiss, C. H. (1978). Improving the linkage between social research and public policy. In L. E. Lynn, Jr. (Ed.), *Knowledge and policy: The uncertain connection* (pp. 23-81). Washington, DC: National Academy of Sciences.

Weiss, C. H. (1979). The many meanings of research utilization. *Public Administration Review, 39,* 531-45.

Weiss, C. H., & Vickers, M. (1990, in press). The impact of research on educational policy. In M. C. Alkin (Ed.), *Encyclopedia of educational research* (6th Ed.). New York: Macmillan.

Williams, P. A. (1987). *Standardizing school dropout measures.* New Brunswick, NJ: Rutgers University, Center for Policy Research in Education.

PART 2

Executive Government Units

6

White House Domestic Policy Analysis

Walter Williams

Domestic policy analysis, distinct from economic and national security analysis, had precursors but started in a concerted way in the federal government with the development in 1964 of the Office of Economic Opportunity (OEO) analytic staff.[1] In 1965 several domestic analytic units were established at the top of the executive agencies under the Planning-Programming-Budgeting System promulgated by the Bureau of the Budget (BOB). Although BOB on occasion performed domestic policy analysis, it was mainly a traditional budget shop. Domestic policy advisers Clark Clifford (Truman), Theodore Sorenson (Kennedy), and Joseph Califano (Johnson) had real power, and the latter had great authority after Vietnam consumed LBJ, and headed a highly visible generalist staff. But White House policy analysis began in earnest in 1970 with the creation of the Domestic Council staff.

In looking at domestic policy analysis in the Executive Office of the President (EOP) over the last two decades from Richard Nixon through Ronald Reagan, three factors stand out. First, none of the domestic policy units in the White House gained the high level of analytic competence that once marked the National Security Council (NSC) staff. Most of the time policy generalists were on top, and what passed for policy analysis was far inferior to that performed in the good agency analytic offices and outside think tanks. Second, the Office of Management and Budget (OMB), with its great depth of talent, usually surpassed the domestic policy units in analytic competence and policy clout. Third, the ties between the president and the institutional policy analysis structure of the EOP and the executive agencies often have been weak. The president's top domestic policy advisers seldom have been policy analysts, and many have had limited analytic literacy, as was the case in the Reagan era with Edwin Meese and Donald Regan. The president often has been linked inadequately to the ongoing institutional policy process. Moreover, in the Reagan years, executive branch institutional analysis showed clear deterioration in both the quality of underlying policy information and the competence and status of analytic office staffs.

Presidential Policy Analysis in the Nixon-Ford Years, 1969-1976

Presidential policy analysis in the domestic policy areas flourished during the Nixon-Ford years. First, OEO's Office of Planning, Research, and Evaluation (PR&E) represents a transition situation in which an *agency* analytic staff served the White House through the OEO director who was also a presidential assistant. Second came the Domestic Council staff, which was not an outright success but rather a failure or a near miss, depending on different accounts.

A Presidential Think Tank

In the Nixon administration, OEO underwent major changes in functions. Much to everyone's surprise, President Nixon, who had attacked OEO in his campaign, continued the agency. Donald Rumsfeld, appointed both OEO director and assistant to the president, had a policy role at the White House level. The research effort in support of policy increased materially, and at full strength PR&E had a staff of over 50 professionals, compared with 20 professionals in the Johnson years. The total research budget increased from slightly over $7 million in the last year of the Johnson administration (fiscal year 1968) to $23 million in fiscal year 1971, with roughly two thirds of the funds allocated for major field experiments such as the New Jersey negative income tax.

Almost immediately, PR&E's policy analysis efforts moved from direct concerns of the agency to those of the White House and the newly created Domestic Council. The office through Rumsfeld provided the White House a flow of analysis. PR&E engaged in a number of large research efforts, including a continuation of the New Jersey experiment, the funding of a companion rural negative income tax experiment, a performance contracting experiment in the field of education, and planning for a major health insurance experiment. None of these studies concerned OEO's direct operating programs. In its brief life PR&E, with a highly competent analytic staff, was close to being a think tank for overall federal poverty policy.

The Domestic National Security Council

President Nixon, in a March 1970 message to Congress, stated: "The Domestic Council will be primarily concerned with *what* we do; the Office of Management and Budget will be primarily concerned with *how* we do it and how *well* we do it." Domestic Council staff head John Ehrlichman was to occupy a position for domestic policy analysis similar to that of Henry Kissinger at the National Security Council (NSC) for foreign policy. OMB was to be downgraded or removed from major analytic activities, concentrating instead on management and assessment.

Raymond Waldmann, who served on the Domestic Council staff, claimed that the unit was a successful analytic office. During 1971-1972, which Waldmann called the heyday of the Domestic Council, he argued that the Domestic Council staff "succeeded to a degree never before attempted in gaining centralized political control over the Executive Branch for the president. . . . It kept information, analysis, and proposals flowing to the Oval Office and reactions, decision, and presidential priorities flowing to the agencies" (Waldmann, 1976, p. 266). The Domestic Council staff's "success" has another side. The staff, at least on the drawing board, had the main function of serving the cabinet members who made up the council. As Cronin observed: "[T]he Domestic Council staff at the White House became, at least under Nixon, a kind of operating center. . . . Some of the Domestic Council staff soon became more prominent in policy decisions than the members of the Council—the cabinet officials—whom they were supposed to assist" (Cronin, 1976, p. 127).

Where the Domestic Council staff ran into problems, even in its heyday, was with OMB. First was a pure power question. The proposed split between the Domestic Council and OMB was not fully implemented, in part because of the power of OMB Director George Shultz, who was at least a coequal to Ehrlichman in the presidential policy process. Further, the Domestic Council staff suffered because of its lack of established institutional channels to information such as those that existed in budgeting. Third was the matter of competence. Cronin's question is especially apt: "But is it now enough to have a small band of staff lawyers or former public relations specialists manage the nation's domestic policy?" (Cronin, 1976, p. 89). As Heclo has observed: "It was an ill-starred division of tasks [between the Domestic Council staff and OMB]. Thinking about what to do turned out to be difficult without having the people around who could tell you how to do it. Since they had a great deal of the necessary experience and expertise, OMB staff were increasingly drafted into Domestic Council operations. . . ." (Heclo, 1976, p. 89). But whatever the bureaucratic difficulties, it should be underscored that in Nixon's analytically oriented presidency, sound policy information and analysis had a critical place in the institutional process.

The politicization of OMB is crucial to an understanding of presidential policy analysis in domestic policy. OMB (then, the Bureau of the Budget) prior to the Nixon reorganization had few political appointees; until the Eisenhower administration, only two appointees were political (*The Executive Presidency*, 1988). The office relied heavily on its career, professional staff that unquestionably was the elite career staff in the federal government. Career staff held most of the top spots, were at the center of power, and were viewed as the ultimate nonpartisan analysts. The career division chiefs were the most powerful GS-18s (then the highest civil service grade) in the government. With all its flaws, including the typical lack of imagination of budgeters, BOB was a place "to look for [budget] analysis with a minimum of political body English" (Heclo, 1976, p. 89). This type of analysis—referred to as "neutral competence"—was not apolitical in the sense that it avoided the political and bureaucratic political issues that were central to policy. What it avoided was a partisan spin with the "answer" fudged to suit the predilections of a particular president or political ideology. Further, when undertaken by high-level career staff who had worked their way up in BOB, the analysis was marked by a strong dose of institutional memory.

The politicization of the central budget agency came about mainly because of Nixon's unceasing effort to gain control over the permanent staff in the EOP and the agencies. The changes placed a new layer of political appointees between the career staff and the OMB director and hence the president. A panel of the National Academy of Public Administration (NAPA) has observed: "The emergence of a powerful White House staff which has progressively assumed the role of speaking for the president has seriously diminished the responsibilities of the career, professional staff of OMB and its capacity to provide the kind of objective and expert counsel to the president which characterized earlier operations" (*Watergate*, 1974, p. 43). The politicization of OMB became an even larger question with Ronald Reagan and David Stockman.

Carter's Domestic Policy Staff, 1977-1980

The Domestic Policy Staff (DPS) under Stuart Eizenstat vividly illustrates the strengths and weaknesses of a White House domestic policy unit in its service to a president deeply concerned with policy and information. Carter himself was extremely intelligent and thought much like a narrow analyst, albeit based on an engineering, not a policy analysis, framework. At the same time, Carter did not think strategically, as captured by the statement repeated by a former OMB political executive: "Secretary of Defense Harold Brown looks at the trees; the president himself looks at the leaves; National Security Adviser Zbigniew Brzezinski looks at the biosphere; and the forest goes unnoticed." A member of that administration told me that Carter had a first-rate analytic mind and had the capacity to master complex issues. Indeed, Carter often looked very much like the classic policy analyst qua engineer/operations researcher who seeks some pristine optimum solution without concern for political, institutional, or bureaucratic reality. Perplexingly, however, he did not demand a high level of domestic policy analysis or see the value in building a strong analytic staff in support of the domestic presidency.

A central factor in understanding Carter and Eizenstat's rise to power was the forced resignation of OMB Director Bert Lance, who was Carter's peer, best friend, and top adviser—his number one policy generalist. "Lance was the administration's free-floating adviser drawing on the OMB's analytic staff when needed but standing apart as the president's man, not the Bureau's man. Lance may have been a Georgian but he was different from Hamilton Jordan, Jody Powell . . . and Stuart Eizenstat. . . . These young men were not peers. . . . After Lance left, it was 'Carter & Sons' with all the connotations of a small family business" (Williams, 1986, p. 33-34). Also important, OMB Deputy Director James McIntyre was not expected to get the number one job and remained an acting director in limbo for several months with OMB. Although McIntyre was finally made director, he and OMB never recovered in status.

Eizenstat and Domestic Policy Staff Operations

After Lance left, Eizenstat became Carter's most important generalist policy adviser and the only member of the inner circle consistently looked to for advice on domestic policy. Eizenstat's rise is intriguing and important for an appreciation of the dynamics of a policy office. Eizenstat himself is an appealing figure—hardworking, fair-minded, extremely intelligent and seemingly without the desire for power that often characterizes a young White House insider. One interviewee told me that Eizenstat never really understood how much power he had and "at times seemed not to understand that he had much power at all."

Eizenstat grew tremendously in his job, and at the end had most of the traits needed by a generalist policy adviser. His long on-the-job training at the top, however, was a costly endeavor. A Carter administration subcabinet member told me after reading an earlier version of this chapter, "You are far too nice to Stu. He is a super person—of the highest quality. But you should not judge Eizenstat by how he acted at the end of the Carter administration. By that time, Stu was much more sophisticated. But he had messed things up for two years getting to that point." Further, while the Eizenstat staff and the other two lawyers at the top were bright, competent policy analysts were few, and none were at the top. The policy analysis framework did not guide the DPS efforts.

DPS roughly doubled in size over time, finally numbering 55-60 members, of whom about half were professionals, and took on more and more policy development responsibilities. The staff continued to work with the agencies that did the major analyses and with their counterparts in OMB. One high DPS official stressed the good working relationships at lower levels with OMB and said that "OMB was involved at all stages." From its earliest days in the Carter administration, DPS produced a covering memorandum for the president that summarized the agency positions and offered DPS's own recommendations on domestic policy decisions. Over time DPS recommendations became more important. In the pecking order, DPS moved to the top.

In 1979 the *Congressional Quarterly* and the *National Journal* gave glowing descriptions of DPS at the height of its influence.[2] Several of the staff had congressional or executive branch experience, and a high percentage were lawyers. On the other hand, the staff has been criticized as lacking in depth and substantive knowledge, and being spread too thin (see Campbell, 1983, pp. 32, 123). The strongest published criticism comes from Heineman and Hessler: "DPS has consisted of forty to sixty people who specialized *(though they were infrequently expert)* [italics added] in a variety of substantive areas. They attempted to manage great numbers of interagency issues and to maintain close liaison with all manner of constituencies. Too often, DPS has been a complicating factor throughout the government, an institutional rival of OMB in the routine business of government . . . and a powerful magnet for interest group pressures on the White House and thus on the president" (Heineman & Hessler, 1980, p. 208). If the *National Journal* and *Congressional Quarterly* were too positive on the DPS staff, Heineman and Hessler may be too harsh. Some DPS staff were competent, but tremendous pressures on Eizenstat and his staff led to a harried pace that often cut into quality. Weaknesses were magnified as the staff became increasingly overburdened and grew more powerful.

Eizenstat: An Assessment

A sympathetic EOP policy analyst said: "Eizenstat himself is very objective. . . . However, he did look at things primarily in political terms. *Also, it is unclear whether or not he appreciated how little policy analysis he got from his staff.*"

Eizenstat also had management problems within DPS and in DPS's relationships with both other EOP units and the agencies. In the main, DPS staff simply did not have much time to think, and this problem flowed at least in part from Eizenstat's mismanagement. As an EOP policy analyst observed: "Eizenstat felt the president wanted to be involved in a tremendous number of issues and did not block or cut off issues to protect him. This meant that Stu's plate kept getting more and more full. . . . It was extremely difficult to get him to spend much time on an issue."

Eizenstat was the only member of the Carter inner circle who tried to live in the worlds of both politics and policy. On balance he overemphasized politics in the policy/politics equation. He also did not appreciate how little rigorous policy analysis his staff did or its importance in complementing his lawyer generalist orientation. He was not a good manager of staff resources. But in the end, much criticism of Eizenstat is criticism of the Carter presidency in which as staff person Eizenstat tried to carry out faithfully the president's bidding even though he himself did not necessarily agree with what the president wanted.

My final assessment of DPS is that the unit ended up being much less than the sum of its parts. The assessment rests on the assumption that policy analysis should be a central function of the domestic policy unit, a basic assumption for a policy analyst. But is it a fair assumption? A case might be made that the White House domestic policy unit should be made up of broad generalists whose orientation is much more political than policy-dominated. History supports such a claim. Unlike the National Security Council staff, domestic policy units do not have a strong policy analysis tradition. The two most prominent heads before Eizenstat were also generalist lawyers—Joseph Califano and John Ehrlichman. Beyond history, the vacuum at the top in the Carter administration almost forced Eizenstat to overemphasize politics. He and his staff were drawn more and more into political activities, including lobbying on the Hill. Nevertheless, Eizenstat failed to appreciate the necessity for both policy analysts and generalists, and the result was a policy staff incapable of ensuring a flow of sound, timely, relevant expert policy information, analysis, and advice in the domestic area to the president. The link between the president and the institutional analytic structure was damaged.

The Reagan Era, 1981-1988

Ronald Reagan, the first antianalytic president in the modern presidency, moved immediately to downgrade White House policy analysis. The heads of the Office of Policy Development (OPD, the new name for DPS) and the National Security Council staffs, rather than reporting directly to the president as in the past, were placed under Counselor to the President Meese. The quality and size of the OPD and NSC staffs were cut significantly, and staff positions were filled mainly on the criteria of ideological purity and loyalty, not policy capability. OPD in the eight years simply never got off the ground and will not be considered further. Instead, attention shifts to OMB, which did most of the domestic policy analysis in the Reagan White House. OMB Director David Stockman inherited a competent OMB staff and a mandate to develop a budget immediately, before agency political executives were in place. This immediacy meant he operated with no analytic competition from the EOP or the agencies and with no supervision from the top presidential advisers who could not, or did not, follow his budget machinations. Stockman—self-admittedly an ideologue following his own agenda and ready to "rig" the numbers to serve his case—was brilliant, arrogant, and unscrupulous: "Information and analysis in Stockman's hands were weapons to be used fairly or unfairly in the larger battle. Stockman was held in check neither by presidential loyalty, an adherence to analytic standards, challenges from other advocate analysts, nor an underlying commitment to serve the presidency"[3] (Williams, 1990, p. 80).

A Transformed Office of Management and Budget

OMB was transformed in the Reagan years. The most important changes included downgrading career staff, shifting from a primary focus on budget preparation in conjunction with executive branch agencies to a main concern with selling the president's budget in Congress, and taking the lead role in President Reagan's regulatory reform effort. Stockman was the driving force in these institutional changes, dominating the agency to a degree heretofore not seen. His successor, James Miller, continued the Stockman changes, shifting OMB even more toward White House centralization and politicization. By the end of the Reagan era, OMB was more central to White House policy-making, more political than ever before, and had lower credibility.

OMB professional staff were kept out of the major budget decisions. In September 1988 a National Academy of Public Administration panel observed: "Now all OMB staff report to the director or deputy director through one or two of *eleven* appointees (who are supported by 10 to 20 noncareer staff)" (*The Executive Presidency*, 1988, p. 38). Chester Newland argued in terms of the entire EOP: "[T]he Reagan policy apparatus is structured and staffed around strictly partisan and personal presidential loyalty. . . . Institutionalized expertise and professionalism are rarely present at high levels within the EOP" (Newland, 1981, p. 167). OMB professional staff interviewees claimed that the degree of professional staff exclusion was overstated. The weakening of the other White House analytic staffs in the Reagan years meant that OMB staff were used more widely than ever before, including a marked increase in congressional activity by careerists. Here a key distinction needs to be made between budgeting that sets major priorities, such as defense spending, and budgeting that operates on the details after the big budget decisions have been made. An interviewee, who watched OMB from a congressional staff position, observed that during the Reagan years:

> The macro-budgeting decisions were decided ideologically at the top without any regard for analytic input about program effectiveness. However, once the broad framework was set, the agencies, and the [career staff budget] examiners had a lot to say about programmatic details. . . . Whether to cut/add is decided ideologically; how to cut/add is decided by analysis. You might also differentiate between two phases of budgeting—the president's and the actual legislated budget. OMB professionals got used for technical tasks that actually determined the way in which much of the budget bargaining was played out—"scorekeeping," or assessing the budgetary impact of legislation.

Since top OMB political executives cannot possibly cope with the microbudget effort, career staff became heavily involved in "details." That these lower level but still important decisions were influenced by analysis is a positive feature and a reason that a position as an OMB analyst is viewed still as desirable. Obviously, poor decisions at the top, unguided by analysis, can reduce greatly the importance of those at the next level. But important decisions are made in crafting the details, and analysts' professionalism and craft come to fore in this setting.

Whether the OMB staff is used properly and whether it has a significant role in the policy process are two different questions. While OMB career staff working in Congress to help sell the president's budget may not fit the image of the old bureau or be in OMB's long-run institutional interest, OMB may dominate the policy process. The use of OMB career staff in a "new role as a 'packager' and 'seller' of the budget in Congress [has caused] some OMB staff members . . . [to] fear they could jeopardize their traditional reputation as a source of 'neutral competence'" (Johnson, 1984, p. 512). Stockman abandoned the previous practice of delivering the budget to Congress and moving on to other work, arguing that the president's budget had meaning only if Congress passed it. The budget became a full-year effort as OMB career staff joined with staffs such as those of the Congressional Budget Office and the two budget committees to craft budget details. OMB career staff told me that these congressional relationships that so disturb "OMB purists" are similar to those in the past but with congressional professionals rather than agency career staff. But one of my most perceptive interviewees, who has served at OMB and on a congressional staff, pointed out that while the OMB professionals were viewed as competent, the Reagan political appointees gained little trust or respect, so Congress saw the Reagan OMB as two institutions, not one.

One OMB institution was made up of highly professional technicians, supporting the argument that the permanent staff were still performing at a high professional level. But the second, or political, institution was a different story. For example, Director Miller was seen as arrogant but not particularly competent and so loyal to President Reagan that he was ineffective. The *National Journal*'s Lawrence Haas contrasted him with Stockman: "If loyalty has kept Miller in the White House, it has hurt him with Congress. Legislating is a process of compromise. Because Miller has refused to bargain with Congress as Stockman had, and can't match his line-item expertise anyway, lawmakers have wanted less to do with him" (Haas, 1988, p. 2191). The Reagan OMB came to be seen as a political vehicle of the White House, however much its professional staff denied it.

OMB competence in the Reagan era appears to have declined; the case for the decline is not nearly as clear-cut as it is for greater centralization and politicization and lower credibility. First, the level of incoming recruits to OMB continued to rise over time in line with the overall upward trend in substantive and technical analytic competence. Second, greater OMB efficiency has come from a computerized system developed for Stockman in 1982 that allowed comparison of administration and congressional proposals since the two had different accounting/costing systems. Even so, demands on the OMB staff in the Reagan years grew. As it became more central to the White House, the agency's own budget between 1981 and 1989 declined by over 12% in real dollars and staff size fell from 610 to 570 between 1981 and 1988 (Haas, 1988, p. 2191). Although former budget staff have told me that OMB personnel revel in a hair shirt mentality, these cutbacks almost certainly materially reduced competence.

Two other factors likely have diminished the careerists' generalist policy adviser skills. First, in earlier days when the budget season lasted less than a full year, staff had the time to reflect, to visit programs, and, I would argue, to hone their institutional knowledge and generalist policy adviser skills. This loss of "down time" is a critical factor that has made current OMB staff more number crunchers than policy analysts. Being "numbers fixated" is an occupational hazard of budget offices generally; the loss of time for visits and reflection has exacerbated the problem at OMB. Second, to be technically better can be to become more narrow and more uncomfortable with analytic synthesis. Reinforcing this tendency is the fact that careerists today are lower in the organizational structure than in earlier periods. The careerists of the golden days were likely superior to their current counterparts as generalist policy advisers. Even if this is true, it does not necessarily follow that OMB is less capable of serving the generalist policy adviser function than BOB was. To argue that would require me to say that the *combination* of political appointees and careerists at the top in the BOB days had more capacity to generalize than do the political executives in OMB today, supported by careerists who clearly are not as close to the top as in earlier periods.

The Reagan administration antianalytic bent has one important exception: OMB's use of cost-benefit analysis (CBA) in the regulatory reform area. As Frank Fischer has noted: "[C]onservative politicians . . . found cost-benefit analysis to be conveniently compatible with their own biases . . . [and it] emerged as a major *political* methodology of the Reagan administration" (Fischer, 1987, pp. 116, 119). CBA was the perfect analytic weapon to turn against the government regulation that the administration wanted to stamp out, because it gave off the aura of rigor and could be used narrowly to exclude the "soft" variables the administration preferred to ignore. The Reagan administration that generally spurned hard analysis was happy to rest the burden of rigorous proof on those who pushed for greater government regulation of the environment. The approach also fit with the budget mentality of the OMB professionals who sought cutbacks as deficits mounted.

While CBA generally has been packaged in terms of its hardness and neutrality, the technique is but one of the many flawed policy analysis tools available and can be attacked on the same grounds as other policy analysis techniques. CBA did not provide the administration a super weapon to attack and destroy regulation; rather, OMB power forced the use of cost-benefit analysis and was guided more by ideology than scientific principles. CBA, with its narrow focus and its scientific base, did cause turmoil among those who supported government regulation of the environment and the workplace, but the attack on government regulation with analytic techniques was none too successful. The CBA experience offers stronger evidence of the limits of policy analysis than of its technical power.

OMB's move toward regulatory rule making is important in itself and has had major implications for the institutional use of policy analysis. Executive Order 12291, issued in February 1981, just after Reagan became president, and Executive Order 12498, issued in 1985, brought regulatory reform under OMB's Office of Information and Regulatory Affairs (OIRA) that had been established under the Paperwork Reduction Act of 1980. Executive Order 12291 was cast in information and analytic terms. It required that "administrative decisions . . . be based on adequate information," that "regulatory action shall not be undertaken unless the potential benefits to society for the regulation outweigh the potential costs to society," and that agencies must submit formal Regulatory Impact Analyses for major rules, which were defined as those likely to have either a $100 million or more impact on industry each year or major impacts on consumers, industries, and subnational governments. Here was a strong top-down effort to make OIRA the point organization in Reagan regulatory reform.

Implementation became the major stumbling block in an inept performance that was reminiscent of (then) BOB's failure in the mid-1960s in putting the Planning-Programming-Budgeting System (PPBS) into place as a governmentwide policy-making vehicle. Regulatory reform stands as the latest unsuccessful top-down attempt by the budget office to impose the president's will on agencies through a complex new process. Just as with PPBS, the agencies fought back with superior resources. Former OIRA head James Tozzi said: "OMB does not have extreme power. . . . OMB can't send regs to the Federal Register, only the agency can. . . . [An] agency outnumbers OMB by an order of magnitude in resources; they outgun us on data and research money" (*Presidential Management*, 1987, p. 26). The National Academy of Public Administration's Panel on Presidential Management of Rulemaking in Regulatory Agencies noted: "OMB's generalist staff is derogated as lacking the technical expertise necessary for competent judgment in many proposed rulemakings; for the most part, OIRA desk officers are economists, lawyers, and policy analysts with little or no previous experience with government or the programs under its review" (*Presidential Management*, 1987, p. 37). OMB was not selective in its regulation reviews. It spent too much time on minor efforts without concentrating on priority issues, a similar failing under PPBS. Most damning of all is this NAPA panel charge: "Virtually every agency official who has commented on the review process has complained that OMB attention is often focused on 'nit-picking,' on relatively minor provisions of proposed regulations, on choice of wording, and on other differences that do not seem to have much importance. Agency officials widely share the perception that desk officers are expected to be adversaries of agencies, that they are recruited with the promise of being able to push agencies around" (*Presidential Management*, 1987, p. 38).

Lack of technical and organizational mastery was important in OMB's failed implementation effort in regulatory reform. The main problem was that the knowledge demands were great and did not necessarily carry big dollar implications. Major regulatory efforts may have huge cost implications for the firms in a regulated industry, but not for the federal budget. OIRA faced an environment dominated by complex technological, substantive, organizational and procedural issues that did not play to the strong suit—quantitative policy analysis—of the OIRA desk officers. Take as example the 1976 Resource Conservation and Recovery Act (RCRA) that charges the Environmental Protection Agency with the management of hazardous wastes. RCRA regulations ran to 214 pages of the *Federal Register*, and one observer noted: "In the case of standards for disposal, the rules at the time of the Reagan inauguration were still in the interim status stage. Comments from industry and other parties ran into the thousands; the RCRA docket at EPA occupied an entire storage room" (*Surviving*, 1984, p. 2). These rules and regulations, which could be a quagmire for a policy analyst not steeped in them, were central to regulatory reform.

OMB in the Reagan era placed too much emphasis on high-powered, quantitatively based analytic skills. That incoming staff today are "better tooled up" than their predecessors may mean less than meets the eye if staff overvalue analytic tools and undervalue substantive area and organizational mastery. Also, career staff have been pushed farther from the top-level decisions that hone generalist policy adviser skills. The result is that career staff today may be less able to perform top-level synthesis and certainly are less likely to be called on to do so. The bulk of policy synthesis falls to OMB political executives.

Does this shift from OMB careerists to political executives mean a decline in competence? A National Academy of Public Administration panel in a report on the 1988-89 presidential transition argued that "the rapid turnover which characterizes political appointees has . . . contributed to the decline of expertise in [OMB] decisionmaking" (*The Executive Presidency*, 1988, p. 38). Without question, that was the case in the Miller OMB. The extraordinary Stockman period is less certain. But even here, generalist policy adviser depth was less than in the past. The clear implication is that OMB's overall policy adviser skills are more variable than in the past when careerists provided stability. Additionally, the top policy adviser effort benefits less from the institutional memory and wisdom that historically have been a key resource of the budget office. These changes, intensified in the Reagan era, have weakened the institutional presidency. An incoming president may not be able to find the institutional knowledge and generalist policy adviser capabilities that marked the old budget office, before it became politicized in the Nixon administration.

Deterioration in the Executive Branch Institutional Policy Analysis Process

Ronald Reagan in his two terms cut deeply into policy information and analysis staffs and funds and downgraded the role of policy units in the executive branch. His actions struck at the foundation of the executive branch institutional policy analysis process[4]—at the basic statistical information on which policy research and analysis is based. As a 1989 Office of Technology Assessment study observed: "Good public policy demands good information. . . . The cost of a poorly run government program may be many times higher than the cost of improvements to statistical agencies. Unlike other government purchases that can be postponed, statistics cannot be turned on and off—once a gap is created it cannot be easily eliminated" (Office of Technology Assessment, 1989, pp. 1, 6).

Reductions in the capacity to generate sound policy information and analysis during the Reagan years in the nondefense areas are striking. While Defense R&D funding increased 81% between 1980 and 1987 in constant 1980 dollars, all other federal agencies had their

R&D budgets reduced overall by 20% in the same period (GAO, 1988a, pp. 6, 10). The General Accounting Office argued that "the capacity to perform program evaluation [and research are] drying up [in the executive branch], not the least in such areas as . . . health care, education, and the environment, where it is precisely needed most" (GAO, 1988b, p. 8).[5] For example, in the Office of Planning, Budget, and Evaluation—the Department of Education's analytic office—contract awards for evaluation fell from 119 to 25, or nearly 80% (GAO, 1987, p. 30). In the Department of Health and Human Services' Health Care Financing Administration, which funds Medicare and Medicaid, funding for studies within its major research office, the Office of Research and Demonstrations (ORD), fell 43% in constant dollars between 1980 and 1987. The GAO reports that at the same time program costs rose 50% in real terms. Also, congressionally mandated studies in ORD rose from 2% in 1980 to 43% in 1987 (GAO, 1988c, pp. 74-76). The administration did as much analysis and evaluation as it did because Congress mandated the studies in legislation.

The policy staff cuts that marked the EOP were also found in the agencies. Peter May's estimates of full-time equivalent (fte) staff changes in eight agency-level analytic office professional and support staffs show cuts in Commerce (27 to 23), Energy (197 to 60), Health and Human Services (165 to 75), Housing and Urban Development (198 to 140), Interior (35 to 31), Labor (61 to 40), State (41 to 36), and Transportation (32 to 21). The decline was overall almost 43% between 1980 and 1988 (May, 1988, pp. 8, 10). The deep cuts in the HHS analytic office (the Office of the Assistant Secretary for Policy and Evaluation) hit what had been the premier domestic policy analytic office of the Nixon-Carter years. Added to the R&D reductions in HHS cited earlier, the biggest domestic policy funding agency lost much of its capacity to produce sound policy information and analysis to support decision making.

My off-the-record interviews repeatedly indicated an even larger decline in the influence of the agency analytic shops. This decline was seen as particularly severe in the social agencies. Reagan's first Secretary of Education, Terrel Bell, found himself surrounded by highly ideological subcabinet appointees whose appointment was dictated by the White House and who saw rigorous policy analysis as either useless because the needed answers were supplied by the ideology or a threat because the analysis might challenge the underlying ideology

(Bell, 1988). The decline of agency policy analysis was part of an overall White House control strategy. Unlike earlier administrations that sought to balance the cabinet and subcabinet by appointing persons with different views, the Reagan strategy made philosophical consistency and loyalty to Reagan the two most important criteria for selecting the cabinet and roughly 600 key subcabinet appointments at the top of government (Nathan, 1983). As Paul Light observed: "They [the White House] appointed people [to cabinet departments] who would cut their boss's throat to please the president. . . . They [the appointees] are ideologically committed. There is no allegiance to the department, but to the Oval Office or the conservative cause. No administration has penetrated so deeply" (Smith, 1988, pp. 302-303).

The argument of the impact of ideology on policy analysis, using the Reagan administration as an example, should not be read as an implicit argument that policy analysis flowers only in liberal (left-of-center) soil. A far left ideologue is as dangerous to the policy research and analysis enterprise as a far right one. Richard Nixon was pro-analysis and a consummate user of policy information and analysis: "The two [Reagan and Nixon] 'conservative' . . . presidents arrived at diametrically opposite answers on the usefulness of policy analysis, making it clear that policy analysis is an available means to serve any political persuasion. Where it cannot compete is where ideology completely rules out facts that threaten its basic tenets" (Williams, 1990, p. 83).

The most serious damage to the executive branch analytic capacity in the Reagan years appeared to be the decline in the quality of federally generated policy information. How serious the loss of good quality data in the 1980s will be to 1990s analyses that depend on longitudinal comparisons is hard to estimate. It seems clear, however, that the federal underinvestment in basic policy information will continue to diminish the quality of policy analysis, disciplinary and policy research, and federal, state, and local government and private sector policy-making.

A similar argument can be made for government analytic staff competence but with some important differences because of the big increases in the number of policy analysts in the private and nonprofit sectors since the 1960s. This charge has both produced a steady flow of policy analysis and subjected much of that analysis to challenge, often by strong partisans. Multiple advocacy has flowered. Thus, an adequate supply of competent analysts exists to staff federal government policy units, and such units may need less staff in light of the increased flow of nongovernment policy analysis. At the same time, because more and more of the nongovernment policy analyses have a distinct partisan or ideological hue, competence will be at a high premium on federal analytic staffs. The call for "lean and mean" staffs still holds, but I would stress the "mean" (competence) over the "lean" (size) in the current setting. Presidents and agency heads need a high level of analytic competence to vet outside policy analyses for biases and underlying quality, and to determine whether sound analysis is in line with the top policymakers' objectives. Relatedly, the strong supply of outside analysts, some of whom have served in earlier governments, means that analytic competence is the easiest part of the policy analysis base (money, staff, and data) to rebuild.

Concluding Remarks

In the first half of the two-decade period under scrutiny, domestic policy analysis accelerated in the federal agencies after the take-off in the Johnson years, and it made a firm start in the White House. Beyond the executive branch, domestic policy analysis flourished in Congress beginning in the mid-1970s with strong analytic capacity in the independent agencies (Congressional Budget Office, Congressional Research Service, General Accounting Office, and Office of Technology Assessment) and in some committees (e.g., the Senate and House Budget Committees) and in the nongovernmental sector with such prestigious research-oriented organizations as the RAND Corporation, Brookings, and the American Enterprise Institute and with such advocacy groups as the Heritage Foundation. In the second half of the 20-year period, domestic policy analysis and the development of policy information withered in the executive branch but continued strong in Congress and the nongovernmental sector. Let me close with a number of points drawn from this period.

First, the strong lesson drawn from the Johnson period that agency heads are central in whether policy analysis is developed and used in their agencies needs to be modified. A president can set the tone for the entire executive branch with his or her attitude toward policy information and analysis, and key appointments in the EOP and the agencies. An antianalytic presidency can impede executive branch analysis and information development; a proanalysis presidency can foster institutional policy analysis and information development. Of course, in the latter case an agency head still can keep the agency from doing serious analysis, as the PPBS experience made clear.

Second, the executive branch's role is pivotal because it is a primary source of policy information used in the executive branch itself, Congress, subnational governments, nongovernmental research and public policy organizations, the business sector, and by the public. In its *Transition Series* issue in November 1988, GAO argued that Reagan cutbacks had "gravely eroded" data collection capabilities in the executive branch and that the administration, in not developing good information, had failed to carry out the "responsibility of [the U.S.] government to the people of the country" (GAO, 1988b, pp. 1, 7). A number of statisticians and economists have argued that "a combination of budget cuts and deregulation—much of it a legacy of the Reagan era—is eroding important [statistical] yardsticks and undermining policymakers striving to guide the economy" (*The New York Times*, October 30, 1989) and Robert Kuttner has warned researchers that "the official [economic] indexes then become the grist for rigorous-looking academic studies whose ostensible precision is built on statistical sand" (Kuttner, 1988, p. 26). The costs of poor information development reverberate through public and private sector policymaking and into the halls of academe.

Third, analytic weakness in the executive branch decreased the usefulness of sound analysis in Congress and the nongovernmental sector. This point cannot be proved, but it is a fundamental premise of policy analysis that hard scrutiny and challenge (multiple advocacy) enhances decision making. Such challenge does not, and should not, rule out the play of political forces, but sound analysis based on reliable policy information should bound such debate and make the decision process more reasonable.

Fourth, the 20 years has produced an adequate supply of competent policy analysts and institutional devices for fostering more reasonable policy debate.

Fifth, only time will tell if the Reagan antianalytic presidency was an aberration from the trend toward developing sounder policy analysis and information to support federal policy-making, or whether a dramatic sea change has occurred and will continue.

Notes

1. This chapter is drawn from Williams, 1990. The chapter relies heavily on in-depth, off-the-record interviews conducted in 1980-1988 with (then) current or former executive branch political appointees and career civil servants, congressional staff, and print journalists. A number of persons were interviewed several times over the period.

2. The Light (1979) and Bonafede (1979) articles offer extended descriptions of DPS operations, including sketches of individual staff members.

3. For my treatment of Reagan's antianalytic presidency, see Williams, 1990, pp. 64-86. The confession is found in Stockman, 1986, pp. 173, 353. For example, Stockman wrote that he spent April 1981 "rigging the [budget] numbers to the point that even we couldn't understand them" (p. 173).

4. For an in-depth treatment, see Williams, 1990.

5. The OTA study cited is a detailed statement of deficiencies and problems with basic economic statistics.

References

Bell, T. H. (1988). *The thirteenth man: A cabinet memoir.* New York: Free.

Bonafede, D. (1979, June 9). Stuart Eizenstat—Carter's right-hand man. *National Journal,* p. 944-948.

Campbell, C. (1983). *Governments under stress: Political executives and key bureaucrats in Washington, London, and Ottawa.* Toronto: Toronto University Press.

Cronin, T. E. (1976). *The state of the presidency.* Boston: Little, Brown.

The executive presidency: Federal management for the 1990s. (1988, September). A report by an Academy Panel for the 1988-1989 Presidential Transition. Washington, DC: National Academy of Public Administration.

Fischer, F. (1987). Policy expertise and the "new class": A critique of the neoconservative thesis. In F. Fischer & J. Forester (Eds.), *Confronting values in policy analysis,* pp. 94-126. Newbury Park, CA: Sage.

General Accounting Office. (1988a, May). *R & D funding: The Department of Education in perspective* (No. GAO/PEMD-88-18FS). Washington, DC.

General Accounting Office. (1988b, November). Program evaluation issues. *Transition series.* Washington, DC.

General Accounting Office. (1987). *Education information: Changes in funds and priorities have affected production and quality.* (No. GAO/OEND-88-4). Washington, DC.

General Accounting Office. (1988c). *HCFA research: Agency practices and other factors threaten quality of mandated studies* (No. GAO/PEMD-88-9). Washington, DC.

Haas, L. J. (1988, September 3). What OMB hath wrought. *National Journal,* pp. 2187-2191.

Heclo, H. (1976, Winter). OMB and the presidency—The problems of "neutral competence." *The Public Interest,* 89.

Heineman, B. W., Jr., & Hessler, C. A. (1980). *Memorandum for the president.* New York: Random House.

Johnson, B. E. (1984). From analyst to negotiator: The OMB's new role. *Journal of Policy Analysis and Management,* 3(4), pp. 501-515.

Kuttner, R. (1988, May 16). U.S. industry is wasting away—but official figures don't show it. *Business Week*, p. 26.

Light, L. (1979, October 6). White House domestic policy staff plays an important role in formulating legislation. *Congressional Quarterly*, pp. 2199-2204.

May, P. (1988, September 1-4). *Policy analysis: Past, present and future.* Paper presented at the meeting of the American Political Science Association, Washington, DC.

Nathan, R. P. (1983). *The administrative presidency.* New York: John Wiley.

Newland, C. A. (1981). Executive office policy apparatus: Enforcing the Reagan agenda. In L. M. Salamon & M. S. Lund (Eds.), *The Reagan presidency and the governing of America* (pp. 135-168). Washington, DC: Urban Institute Press.

The New York Times. (1989, October 30).

Office of Technology Assessment. (1989). *Statistical needs for a changing U.S. economy: Background paper* (No. OTA-PR-E-58) Washington, DC: Government Printing Office.

Paperwork Reduction Act of 1980.

Presidential management of rulemaking in regulatory agencies. (1987). A report by a Panel of the National Academy of Public Administration. Washington, DC: National Academy of Public Administration.

Resource Conservation and Recovery Act (RCRA) (1976).

Smith, H. (1988). *The power game: How Washington works.* New York: Random House.

Stockman, D. A. (1986). *The triumph of politics.* New York: Harper & Row.

Surviving at the EPA: Gary Dietrich. (1984). Kennedy School of Government Case Program (C16-84-592).

Waldman, R. J. (1976, May/June). The domestic council: Innovation in presidential government. *Public Administration Review, 266.*

Watergate: Its implications for responsible government. (1974, March). Washington, DC: National Academy of Public Administration.

Williams, W. (1986). The Carter domestic policy staff. In S. S. Nagel (Ed.), *Research in public policy analysis and management* (pp. 32-33). Greenwich, CT: JAI.

Williams, W. (1990). *Mismanaging America: The rise of the anti-analytic presidency.* Lawrence: University Press of Kansas.

7

The Office of Policy Analysis in the Department of the Interior

Robert H. Nelson

Introduction

During the 1970s offices were created widely in federal agencies with such titles as Office of Policy Analysis, Office of Program Planning, and Office of Planning and Evaluation (Meltsner, 1976). One of the many new offices of this kind was the Office of Policy Analysis (OPA), created in 1973 in the Interior Department to serve the secretary of the interior (then Rogers Morton). This policy office lasted with only modest changes in organizational structure and responsibility for 15 years (some significant changes recently have been made). I provide here a brief history of the origins of OPA and of the subsequent developments that seem to me of most general interest. OPA's experiences offer a commentary—if in a particular set of circumstances—on some of the broader issues concerning the nature and role of policy analysis. Because I have served in the office since 1975, the chapter does not offer the assessment of a disinterested outsider, but that of a participant-observer. I have neglected also a few subjects such as the impact of individual personalities and capabilities that have been important.

AUTHOR'S NOTE: This chapter is an unchanged version of "The Office of Policy Analysis in the Department of the Interior" by Robert H. Nelson, *Journal of Policy Analysis and Management*, © 1989 by the Association for Public Policy Analysis and Management. Reprinted by permission of John Wiley & Sons, Inc.

Predecessor Policy Offices

The Department of the Interior (DOI) has long housed a diverse collection of agencies, each of which has tended to build strong ties with Congress and with outside constituency groups. Over the years many DOI secretaries found that they possessed only a limited ability to influence the administrative and policy decisions of DOI agencies. A much-quoted remark in the past with respect to Interior has been that it "has none of the attributes of a department except a secretary."

A forceful secretary such as Harold Ickes, however, who also had the strong backing of the president, has been able to give strong direction to DOI. Ickes, who served from 1933 to 1946, began a process of building up the staff resources of the secretary. The rise of a much stronger secretarial administrative and support staff roughly paralleled similar developments in the executive office of the president and in other cabinet departments.

Ickes centralized important functions of the Office of the Solicitor, using it for policy as well as legal purposes, and created a newly professional Division of Budget and Administrative Management. In increasing his staff resources, Ickes tended to move along specialized lines—gradually creating separate staff divisions directly reporting to him for "information" (including public affairs), "territories and island management," "land utilization," and "power." It was not until 1947 that a new secretary, Julius Krug, created the first secretarial policy staff with general responsibilities covering the entire range of DOI concerns. Named the Program Staff, it would have around a dozen professionals typically with social science backgrounds.

Indeed, several would go on to distinguished academic careers, including Harold Barnett, later to be a coauthor of what is now regarded as a classic in the field of natural resources.[1] In 1950, the Program Staff survived a critical test when it was maintained in a large-scale DOI reorganization. An outside study reported at the time that "the idea of a policy staff survived successful trial at the secretarial level. . . . The idea of a Department program had come to be understood and accepted very generally, at least as an ideal, and rudimentary machinery for program making had been preserved (*The Department*, 1951, p. 48).

The arrival of the Eisenhower administration in 1953 posed another critical test. The incoming undersecretary of DOI is reported to have announced an intent to dismiss any staff with a PhD and to have made good partially on the promise. Nevertheless, although renamed the Technical Review Staff, a general policy advisory function was preserved and lasted through the Eisenhower administration. The Technical Review Staff would be a more nuts-and-bolts operation, making less use of formal social science methods.

In 1961, incoming secretary Stewart Udall hired a new director and deputy director and renamed this same staff as the Resources Program Staff, still reporting directly to the secretary. Its director from 1962 to 1966 was Henry Caulfield, who had a close relationship with Udall, assisting him in the writing of his influential book *The Quiet Crisis*.[2] Caulfield played a particularly active role in the field of water policy, helping prepare economic standards for assessing the benefits and costs of proposed dams and other water projects. Legislation as early as 1936 had required explicitly an examination of benefits and costs of water projects, but the economic methods used for such analyses remained primitive until at least the 1950s (Holmes, 1972, 1979). The need for better techniques did much to stimulate the general development of benefit-cost methods within the economics profession. Among the agencies within Interior, only the Bureau of Mines had a tradition of maintaining an economic section staffed with well-qualified professionals.

By 1966 the new governmentwide demands of the Programming, Planning, and Budgeting System (PPBS) had spurred DOI to create a second policy office at the secretarial level. Named the Office of Program Analysis, its relations with DOI agencies became strained, and when PPBS was dismantled, this office was abolished in 1971. Also in 1971, the policy function was placed for the first time under its own assistant secretary (for program policy). Five offices were created to report to the new assistant secretary, having responsibilities for "program development and coordination," "regional planning," "environment and project review," "international activities," and "economic analysis." With the creation of this last office, for the first time an assignment of a formal and explicit economic analysis function existed to serve the secretary of the interior. The leading assignment of the economics office proved to be to assist in the staff work being undertaken for the new oil pipeline from Prudhoe Bay in Alaska.

This organizational arrangement lasted only until 1973, when a comprehensive reorganization of the office of the secretary occurred. The budget function had been under the assistant secretary for administration (which dated to 1950), but it now was brought together with policy advisory functions to form a new assistant secretary for policy development and budget. The merger of budget and policy was partly at the insistence of the new assistant secretary, Larry Lynn, who argued that policy was heavily dependent on budget decisions for implementation.[3] A new Office of Policy Analysis (OPA) was created under Lynn, and by 1974 the economic analysis staff had been blended into OPA.

At this point, OPA contained three staffs for "program" studies, "economic" studies, and "special" studies. This arrangement is still in place as of this writing. The total number of OPA professionals has remained steady over the years at about 20 to 25—fairly small by the standards of Washington policy offices for cabinet agencies. These professionals have held career appointments in the civil service. Unlike some policy offices, OPA has received little money to spend for contract work. Given the size of the staff, OPA at any one time never has focused on more than a limited number of DOI policy issues.

The Nixon-Ford Years

With the emergence of the environmental movement in the 1960s, DOI's responsibilities had become important to a wider set of voters. The national political significance that energy and environmental issues would assume in the 1970s was suggested by the furor that erupted in 1969 when oil spilled from a well drilled on a federal lease off the southern California coast near Santa Barbara. The organizational changes made in DOI in 1973 partly reflected a sense at the White House that stronger management at DOI was needed. John Whitaker, who had been serving under John Erlichman as the lead staff advisor to President Nixon on environmental policy, was dispatched to DOI to become undersecretary (see Whitaker, 1976). He joined with Lynn in leading the effort to bring greater use of policy professionals into the decision-making process at DOI.

Because OPA was new in 1983, DOI political leadership was able to fill the office with staff having the specific qualifications seen as needed. Partly because this promoted the trust and confidence of DOI leadership, and with strong top-level support, OPA achieved the peak of its access to DOI decision making and of its influence in DOI in the first few years. The OPEC oil price shock of 1973-1974 also proved a decisive event for OPA because federally owned onshore and especially offshore lands contain a major part of the energy resources of the United States. More rapid exploration and development became a high priority, yet the DOI agency principally responsible, the Bureau of Land Management (BLM), had a long history devoted almost entirely to public land sales, grazing, and other surface uses and was ill equipped to handle the major leasing responsibilities suddenly being thrust on it. Moreover, BLM had to rely on a separate Interior agency (the U.S. Geological Survey) under a different assistant secretary for energy resource estimates, tract evaluations, and other key assistance. Coordination was frequently poor between these two agencies, and on occasion outright conflict existed.

The secretary of the interior and his close aids therefore decided to elevate to their level the direct responsibility for policy decisions with respect to energy leasing and for much of the implementation as well. OPA began providing key staff for DOI policy development for federal energy resources, the most important area of involvement in DOI policy-making throughout OPA's history. The head of the economics staff in 1974 was Darius Gaskins, who also later served in DOI as Director of the Office of Outer Continental Shelf Program Coordination (OOCSPC), another Interior policy shop at the secretarial level with which OPA worked closely.

A series of important issues had to be resolved before the expanded OCS leasing program could get under way, including the proper rate of leasing, the method of selecting the most promising OCS acreage to be offered, the type of bidding (whether bids would be submitted as lump sum payments, royalty shares, or profit shares), the level of any royalty rates fixed in advance, and the maximum time allowed lessees to begin development without forfeiting the lease (the "diligence requirement"). By longstanding policy, and in some cases as required by law, the government seeks to ensure that "fair market value" is received for its leased resources. If bidding competition were strong, however, why second guess the results of the competitive process? Illustrating the OPA tendency in many areas to try to make use of market forces and information, OPA and OOCSPC staff proposed a "bid averaging" rule, which DOI adopted and is still being employed today. DOI's internal estimate of a tract's value is averaged with all individual bids received. The rule then is that if the high bid exceeds this average, the lease is issued—otherwise, the high bid normally will be rejected.

The early involvement of OPA in OCS policy would prove to be typical in a number of ways of future circumstances in which OPA would be called on. It involved a high profile issue that had been elevated to the secretarial level. The secretary wanted his own staff assistance, partly because he lacked confidence in the line agencies involved. The secretary also preferred to have a second opinion for an important policy matter in which he had a large personal stake. OPA has been most likely to be brought into the picture when these circumstances were combined with a third factor—the issue was amenable to economic analysis.

Yet, the circumstances most likely to bring about OPA involvement may be temporary. Changes in the person of the secretary may cause abrupt changes in the areas of greatest secretarial interest. Some secretaries are much more interested in receiving economic inputs into their decision making. A particular secretary may be comfortable with staff work only from his or her own personal aides, while other secretaries are comfortable in working with career professionals. Other important circumstances may change, such as the shift in the 1980s in international energy markets that would cause a decline in the overall level of DOI interest in energy policy issues. OPA has had to be flexible and prepared to make significant reorderings in the allocation of staff efforts. Over the years, OPA staff have spent considerable time reviewing the internal functions of the office within DOI and how the OPA role might respond to changing circumstances.

During the Nixon-Ford years OPA also played a major role in the design of the program for leasing federally owned coal (about one third of U.S. coal reserves).[4] The BLM was responsible initially for designing the new coal program and sought to base leasing plans on a set of calculations to estimate future coal production and the amounts of federal coal that would have to be produced to satisfy these production plans. This design set off a major debate within DOI as OPA staff, among others, argued that less reliance should be placed on central planning calculations and greater reliance on use of the market mechanism. OPA advocated that DOI simply should lease any federal coal for which the high bidder had offered the full fair market value. OPA further argued that the requirement for fair market value would prevent a wholesale transfer of federal coal reserves into private hands. Moreover, if coal under lease exceeded demands, then it would be returned to the government after 10 years for failure to meet the diligent development requirement.

BLM might have responded—although it did not—that OPA was ignoring or minimizing the distortions that might result from premature development caused by the diligence requirement itself, as well as major practical difficulties in calculating fair market value with any precision (Nelson, 1983). But whatever the exact merits of the approach advocated by OPA, this debate proved pivotal in a transfer of basic responsibility for coal policy from BLM to the secretary and his close aides. OPA ended up providing the staff support for the development of the department's coal leasing program, much as it was doing for OCS leasing at the time.

In areas other than energy leasing, the OPA role was much less prominent. Indeed, the first assistant secretary for policy, development, and budget, Larry Lynn, left within a year of arriving, partly out of frustration with the resistance he encountered. Lynn devoted considerable personal attention to issues in the fields of Western water development and policy toward American Indians, yet found that in these areas the national and economic perspective of OPA was given short shrift. The office had little impact on such important policy issues as the surface use of public lands, the management of national parks, fish and wildlife management, and geological and mining research. Economic analysis in some of these areas simply was unable to yield any clear policy conclusions. In other areas the conclusions were clear enough but were politically unacceptable. The experiences of the Nixon-Ford years showed that in the proper circumstances professional policy analysts could play a key role in DOI decision making but that these circumstances might be limited.

The Carter Years

Changes in administration can be trying times for a policy office, raising questions of the real loyalties of office staff and personal commitments to the policies of the previous administration. The arrival of the Carter administration thus confronted OPA with some new and difficult questions. Energy leasing was a special concern for new Carter appointees. Indeed, a number of them had entered national politics as staffers to environmental groups fighting DOI leasing policies. More generally, these appointees typically favored heavy reliance on formal government planning and distrusted the influence of market forces, viewpoints at odds with those of OPA staff. Some segments of the DOI bureaucracy had resented also the close ties of OPA to top DOI leadership during the Nixon-Ford years and recommended to incoming Carter appointees that the role of secretarial staff be curtailed sharply, leaving policy responsibility to the line agencies. In principle, this approach was also congenial to the management preferences and style of the incoming secretary of the interior, Cecil Andrus.

The new Carter team quickly found, however, that a goal of line authority and greater policy decentralization was not always realistic. The most obvious conflict emerged in water policy. The Carter administration announced in the first few months the "hit list" of Western water projects—some of them already well under construction— that it planned to cancel. When the West erupted in protest, not only Secretary Andrus, but President Carter himself became personally involved. Because the administration could hardly look to the Bureau of Reclamation, the agency whose traditional policies were being attacked, OPA and other secretarial-level staff were pressed quickly into service. Although Carter appointees opposed dams and other projects mostly for environmental reasons, they recognized that economic analysis could be put to the cause.

The hit list episode was only the first instance of what proved to be a long-term and significant OPA involvement in Western water policy—if perhaps never reaching the prominence of the OPA role in energy leasing. OPA staff bore much of the technical review responsibility for the final version of a revised *Principles and Standards* that set the ground rules for conducting benefit-cost and other analyses of water projects (and a few years later would represent DOI on an interdepartmental working group that further rewrote these ground rules in what then became the *Principles and Guidelines*). OPA encouraged and then assisted in performing studies that elaborated and clarified the extent of federal subsidies for Western water projects— subsidies not only in covering capital expenditures but also often for operating and maintenance costs. OPA efforts of this kind helped lay the groundwork for the later adoption in the 1980s of DOI policies seeking to obtain a greater share of the costs of water projects from Western states and water interests. OPA also prepared an analysis showing that, even though 90% of the Tellico Dam in Tennessee was completed, the benefits from completion were still smaller than the remaining additional costs (Davis, 1988).[5] After hearing this analysis, a cabinet committee voted to deny an exception to the Endangered Species Act and to leave Tellico uncompleted (although Congress later reversed this decision).

OCS leasing proved to be another area in which Secretary Andrus, ignoring his general principles of decentralization and line authority, instead found a need to concentrate policy responsibility in himself and his immediate staff. A former director of OPA, Heather Ross, became a deputy assistant secretary for policy, budget, and administration (which in 1977 replaced the assistant secretary for program development and budget) and also, in effect, the department's principal coordinator for OCS leasing. OPA staff thus became heavily involved in the debates and negotiations that led up to passage of the Outer Continental Shelf Lands Act of 1978, the most important legislation concerning OCS leasing since the 1950s. OPA staffers also helped oversee the preparation of the OCS option papers for each lease sale, negotiate with the Department of Energy on issues of joint interest because of the division of OCS leasing responsibilities, oversee bidding system design and the adequacy of bid review procedures, and generally participated closely in the overall development of policy for the OCS program. Indeed, the OPA staff may have reached its maximum influence on OCS policy in the later Carter years.

When the Carter administration decided to redo the entire coal program, key issues raised included the role of industry nominations in selecting coal leasing sites, the role of coal production projections versus market mechanisms in deciding the levels of leasing, planning procedures for declaring some areas off limits entirely to coal leasing, the determination of appropriate rates of coal recovery from individual mines, proper methods of calculating fair market value, and techniques for stimulating greater bidding competition. OPA fought to allow the coal industry to submit nominations for specific tracts to be leased (some Carter appointees viewed such nominations as inherently biasing the planning process in favor of industry), offering more coal tracts for lease, and leaving companies to decide the specific level of coal recovery for coal mines on federal leases.

The tolerance of Carter appointees for advocacy of what was in many cases an opposing point of view reflected several factors. A few Carter appointees were sympathetic to or agreed with the stronger economic and market orientation typically favored by OPA. Other Carter appointees believed such views should have adequate representation, even when they personally disagreed. Although provoking less public uproar than the water project hit list, the initial Carter efforts in energy leasing quickly stirred widespread criticism and accusations of political and economic naivete. The Andrus team responded in part by paying greater heed to its own professional policy analysts (who sometimes gave a forewarning of future outside concerns) and argued that they had installed a "balanced" DOI decision process in which all viewpoints found advocates, replacing a previously biased process in which only views favoring growth and development had been heard. The OPA viewpoint thus acquired an outside political value in helping make more credible this claim of balanced internal decision making.

The OPA activities in developing the coal program involved roles not only of advocate, but also of neutral analyst laying out all the policy options. Indeed, OPA staff prepared several of the key DOI option papers in the design of the coal program, including those that produced decisions on whether to use industry nominations and finally decisions on whether to resume leasing and at what levels after a long moratorium. This dual role—both advocate and disinterested policy broker—creates a tension found in many Washington policy offices, one that can lead easily to accusations that the advocate role is intruding on the role of neutral broker. As in the coal program, OPA frequently has provided staff assistance to the offices of line assistant secretaries and in many cases to individual DOI agencies. When OPA later recommends policies to the secretary of the interior that conflict with the preferences of such an assistant secretary or agency, it is not surprising that ill will has from time to time resulted.

During the Carter years, OPA staff also conducted studies addressing such matters as the economic value of wilderness and national park experiences, the value of hunting and other wildlife-related uses on public lands, the fees charged ranchers for livestock grazing on public land, and the fees charged visitors to the national parks and other recreational lands. An OPA study of BLM timber harvest policies on lands in western Oregon contributed to a policy decision by BLM to allow limited exceptions to its previous absolute prohibition on departures from an "even flow" rate of timber harvest (Nelson & Pugliaresi, 1977).[6] The most influential OPA argument was to develop estimates of the physical volumes of timber that were literally being wasted as a result of the even flow policy. In many cases policy analysts make their greatest contribution, not with highly sophisticated economic analyses, but with simple arguments that challenge practices and ideas that have simply become part of agency tradition, culture, and ideology—even in the face of common sense.

OPA had little involvement in the work leading up to the passage in late 1980 of legislation to transfer about 100 million acres of Alaska lands from their traditional BLM management to the Park Service,

Fish and Wildlife Service, and Forest Service. Along with OCS leasing and federal coal leasing, the future management of Alaska lands ranked among the three most important DOI policy issues of the Carter years. The small OPA involvement reflected several factors: the limited earlier OPA experience in this area during the Nixon-Ford years; the lack of OPA staff with a background that would cause them to seek out this policy issue; the generally greater difficulty of applying economic analysis to surface land management issues; and a skeptical attitude within the Andrus team towards applying OPA's economic efficiency perspective to what was seen internally as a DOI environmental protection imperative.

The Watt Years

In the change from the Carter to the Reagan administration, the normal uncertainties were magnified by the announced desire of the new secretary of the interior, James Watt, to shake up the department and to bring about "radical change" in Interior policies. One obvious step might be to eliminate as much of the holdover staff from the Carter administration as possible, including OPA. Moreover, some Reagan supporters were actively hostile to OPA. In 1981 the Heritage Foundation report, *Mandate for Leadership,* directly attacked OPA, warning (surprisingly in light of OPA's actual views) that "the ivory tower modeling mentality and the voodoo economics exercised by the AS/PBA's Office of Policy Analysis has demonstrated with some facility the Carter Administration's bias against timely resource development" (Heatherly, 1981, p. 396).

The Watt team was also skeptical of the very enterprise of policy analysis. Policy analysis was on occasion derided as "policy paralysis." It was seen as a means of better government planning when the objective should be to abandon many government functions. Policy analysts had their own interests in preserving programs to which they could apply their analytical tools. Policy analysis was perhaps not the value-neutral activity that it claimed to be, but was closely associated with a progressive and liberal tradition of faith in the socially beneficial powers of rational analysis and scientific methods. Watt himself tended to think in sweeping categories and to generalize quickly, habits of thought not especially congenial to the methods of policy analysis. The Watt team in fact eliminated two policy offices that had been created in the 1970s and were located in the Office of the Assistant Secretary for Energy and Minerals and in the BLM.

OPA's survival seems to have reflected several factors. First, some former DOI officials from the Nixon-Ford years recalled its past assistance to them and personally recommended to Watt that it could perform similar functions for him. Second, Watt recognized the need for staff resources that could assist him in keeping track of activities in the department and in carrying out the policy directions he sought for DOI. Watt had served in high-level DOI positions from 1969 to 1975 and knew much better than most incoming secretaries the obstacles he would face. Another helpful factor for OPA was a reputation the office had acquired of having well informed and capable staff— potentially a significant asset to any secretary who knew how to use it. Finally, Watt may have recognized that many of the specific policy changes he sought to make were at least compatible with the orientation that over the years had characterized OPA staff.

For the first two years of the Reagan administration, the OCS program kept its anomalous organizational status, as authority for overall policy coordination resided outside normal department lines, and instead in the assistant secretary for policy, budget, and administration.[7] But in 1982 Watt shifted the OCS program, eventually placing it in the newly created Minerals Management Service (MMS). As a result, after 8 years of close involvement, the OCS role of OPA was diminished sharply, limited to cases in which OPA expertise and institutional knowledge were tapped by lower level agency staffers with whom OPA staff had long worked. After a year or two, some OPA staff members found it desirable to move to the MMS, where they performed OCS functions closely related to their previous OPA service.

The transfer of basic policy responsibility to a line assistant secretary had already occurred in the case of coal leasing during the Carter years. In contrast to OCS leasing, the input of OPA into coal leasing started small and then grew during the course of the Watt years. By 1982, the Reagan administration had run into strong opposition to its plans to lease large amounts of coal, and Watt was facing congressionally mandated investigations and sharp criticism for the conduct of the Powder River coal lease sale in Wyoming and Montana. OPA possessed technical and institutional knowledge that was recognized as valuable to the Watt team in defending against criticisms. Among other assets, OPA itself had long made a case for more rapid coal leasing, but in an economic and policy language more acceptable to influential and politically powerful Washington audiences (Bieniewicz & Nelson, 1983).[8]

It was not unusual that a secretary or a line agency would come to OPA to obtain greater legitimacy for a DOI policy by presenting this policy in a technical and analytical language that commanded greater social acceptance. Such OPA efforts might then be mixed with a genuine OPA search for economic answers and improved policies. Indeed, OPA and the agency might have different and to some degree conflicting motives. OPA might agree to provide a symbolic and legitimizing function useful to the agency in return for some real input into the substance of agency policy decisions. If the agency need in this regard persists long enough, however, then the agency is likely to respond by developing its own policy office, which it can put under tighter reins.

The Watt years also resulted in a significant involvement for OPA in two new policy areas—onshore oil and gas leasing and tenure for public lands. Instead of competitive bidding, most onshore oil and gas leases were issued through a special lottery in which each player was allowed to purchase only one lottery ticket per lease. When outside critics demanded a leasing system based solely on competitive biding, and other controversies arose, onshore leasing issues were also elevated to the secretarial level. OPA provided analyses of the revenue and other economic impacts of different prices for lottery entries or of switching to an "all-competitive" system.

In a departure from its usual posture of favoring a competitive approach, OPA argued in this instance that many marginal oil and gas tracts were not worth enough to justify the sizable costs of operating an all-competitive system (costs such as calculating fair market value) and that a simple lottery would both ensure quick access to such low value tracts for exploration and probably also yield more revenue. OPA staff also played a key role in developing a DOI legislative proposal for a new "two-tier" onshore leasing system (Halspel, 1985).[9] All oil and gas tracts would be offered first competitively, but with a uniform required minimum bid set high enough that only the more valuable tracts could meet it, leaving other tracts to be offered through a lottery in a second tier. In 1987, Congress enacted the Federal Onshore Oil and Gas Leasing Reform Act, containing the most significant changes in the onshore oil and gas leasing system since the

Mineral Leasing Act of 1920, following in some key areas concepts that had been advocated by OPA staff since the early 1980s.

As a result of the "Sagebrush Rebellion" and "privatization" controversies, OPA was drawn into still another new area, the future ownership and management of the public lands (Nelson, 1982, 1984a). OPA staff studies had shown that most public lands—even those ostensibly having a commercial purpose—cost the government considerably more to manage than they returned in revenues. In the extreme, by some estimates the management of livestock grazing cost the government from $100 million to $200 million annually (depending on rules for overhead and other cost allocation), while bringing in grazing fee revenues in many years of less than $20 million. Even allowing for the high subsidy contained in the fee, management costs substantially exceeded the market value of the grazing—worth no more than $50 million to $70 million. Such calculations entered into the rationale for ill-fated Reagan administration proposals in 1982 to sell off several million acres of public land. Much of this land consisted of scattered small parcels and was located in such urbanized areas as Palm Springs; it had an estimated total value of several billion dollars (Nelson, 1984b, 1984c).

As in previous administrations, OPA during the Watt years continued to have a limited role in setting the directions for Indian, national park, fish and wildlife, science research, and other important DOI responsibilities. Despite their original decision to retain OPA, the Watt team never seemed to have a clear idea of the role OPA was expected to play in DOI decision making. Watt's natural inclination was to rely on his own judgments and intuitions in important policy matters. But he did look to OPA for specific proposals for basic policy changes that would further his overall objectives. Rather than a skilled technical analysis, Watt's real hope was that OPA could provide him with promising flashes of insight or other valuable thoughts. His ideal product from OPA would be a "one pager" laying out the basic concept for some fundamental change in a DOI policy or agency. OPA sought to comply, in one instance going through a formally structured exercise to produce a full set of such brief concept papers. One paper, for example, proposed the transfer of the California Desert Conservation Area, a massive block of land containing 12 million BLM-administered acres (more than 10% of the land in California), from the BLM to the state of California. A few efforts were made to implement some of these proposals, if in toned-down form, but most proved to be politically or administratively infeasible. Watt appeared somewhat frustrated by OPA's inability to generate new policy proposals with a more realistic potential for achieving the fundamental changes that he hoped to make.

More so than in the Carter administration—and in contrast to the standard views of the proper role of professional policy analysis—the policy advice that OPA had to offer during the Watt years was often as much political as technical. OPA sometimes sought to persuade Watt to soften and otherwise modify proposed DOI policy changes in order to make them politically more acceptable and to explain constructive policy proposals in analytical terms more likely to enlist congressional and public support. Watt was sometimes receptive but, not surprisingly, usually preferred to handle the politics and the explanations his own way. As public criticism of Watt swelled, OPA staff from time to time were chagrined to find that policies they had advocated internally and believed to be sensible were being tarred simply by the way the media and his critics were reacting to the Watt embrace.

Since Watt

Few major developments have occurred for OPA in the years since Watt's replacement in the fall of 1983 by William Clark, the long-time associate of President Reagan and former director of the National Security Council (and who was succeeded as secretary by Donald Hodel about 1 year later). A main goal for them was to defuse the antagonisms that Watt had created towards DOI and to avoid controversy. The post-Watt years did see the coming to fruition of some long-term efforts by OPA in the area of water policy (see Wahl, 1986; Wahl & Osterhoudt, 1985).[10] When first raised, proposals to buy and sell water had been given scant attention. Many Westerners had long regarded the outright sale of water as virtually offensive to moral principles. Yet, these attitudes were changing rapidly by the mid-1980s, as environmental concerns, demands for water conservation, and new political constituencies were leading Western political leadership to examine actively the potential for greater water marketing. OPA staffers contributed to a network of economists—most of them outside DOI—seeking to demonstrate the social benefits and to give greater intellectual legitimacy to these trends.

Internally, OPA staff often found it tactically more effective to avoid the rhetoric of markets (water "sales" became water "transfers") or the language of economic efficiency. Studies were undertaken of the limited past experiences in water markets and of such engineering and legal concerns as the quantities of water involved, return flow measurements, and legal provision necessary for water sales. Major changes in policy frequently occur gradually and incrementally through the evolution of operating procedures and in other details, rather than in wholesale jumps. Even when the goal is a major policy innovation, OPA's pursuit of this goal often has had to reflect a long-term commitment and has required the influencing of many small decisions in small ways.

Issues relating to the possible sale of oil and gas leases in the Arctic National Wildlife Refuge began to occupy a significant amount of staff time in the mid-1980s. OPA supported and oversaw a major study of the impact of federal policies and subsidies on the loss of U.S. wetlands, seeking to show that reductions in subsidies that offered significant budgetary savings could also have beneficial consequences for wetlands preservation (*The Impact*, 1988; Goldstein, 1988).[11] OPA contributed significantly to a major study to provide methods for calculating the dollar value of environmental damages that might be judged in court to have been caused by waste dumps and other toxic substances on public lands—and thus to require some compensation.

Finally, despite a longstanding office skepticism concerning involvement in the field of Indian affairs, OPA staff conducted two major studies in this field. The first was the report of a task force chaired by an OPA staffer recommending the creation of enterprise zones and other measures to promote economic development of Indian reservations (*Report*, 1986). The second was a report examining the problems of Indian education in schools serving about 38,000 Indian children all over the United States that are operated or funded by the Bureau of Indian Affairs (BIA) (BIA, 1988). This greater OPA attention to Indian affairs reflected several factors: a recognition that BIA had been neglected in the past, even though it had the largest budget of any agency in DOI (around $1 billion); a declining demand for OPA staff services in the field of energy policy-making, as the "energy crisis" waned and DOI line agencies developed stronger analytical capabilities of their own; the vacuum created by a major shortage of analytical and policy study resources within the BIA itself; and the sense that the continuing severe economic and social deprivation on Indian reservations demanded some form of response, whatever the policy complexities and obstacles might be.

Concluding Reflections

Reflecting on 15 years of OPA history, it seems to me that OPA has made its greatest contributions to the Interior Department in the following ways. First and foremost, OPA has been an advocate for what it saw as the national interest in a political process in which many other participants were advocates of narrower interests, such as particular industries or particular sections of the country. OPA further tended to define the national interest in economic terms, seeking to maximize national benefits minus national costs in administrative actions and seeking to rely heavily on the national allocative efficiency promoted by use of a market system. OPA's economic orientation has been reflected in the fact that the first five directors of OPA all had Phd degrees in economics.

To say that OPA frequently adopted an economic perspective is far from saying, however, that it ignored other social values and concerns. Indeed, if that had been the case, OPA would have fallen outside acceptable bounds to DOI leadership. Instead, OPA staff had to show a keen sensitivity to the full range of political and social considerations. In its advocacy role, OPA typically fought for policies that moved the system in the direction of greater national economic efficiency, yet had sufficient attractiveness in other respects that they were politically feasible. In proposing policy measures, the selection of the appropriate blend of economic and other features has been an essential talent for an effective OPA staffer (Leman & Nelson, 1981). It is also an exercise in judgment that is difficult to teach.

The OPA advocacy efforts clash somewhat with the formal description of the office role and with the characterization often given to outside parties. Officially, OPA conducts technical analyses, raises options but takes no positions, and analyzes the consequences of alternative policies. Such a neutral expert role does in fact characterize a number of activities undertaken by OPA, but it is only a limited part of the picture. Indeed, DOI political leaders have sought a more aggressive and entrepreneurial OPA involvement in policy-making. Otherwise, OPA might not have made enough difference to justify the continued existence of the office.

OPA's actual role also clashed with the idea that policy analysts should not advance an ideology of their own. In practice, OPA has been an advocate not so much of specific solutions as of a broader way of thinking and an overall outlook on the world (Nelson, 1987). This outlook, derived in significant part from economics, is often at odds with other ways of thinking that are well represented in the DOI policy-making process. OPA economic analysts, for example, have found themselves often at odds with environmentalists on what came down to basic questions of value. Although there need not be a conflict, in practice many economists see in nature an instrument for achieving human purposes, while many environmentalists see in nature an end in itself that requires protection from human violation. Many DOI policy debates reflect deep disagreements with respect to these two very different outlooks.

The sizable gap between the OPA role in practice and the formal job description for the office raises the question of the real source of legitimacy for OPA's actual role. Officially, OPA is justified as a representative in government for scientific thought and neutral technical expertise, but in fact great skepticism exists within DOI towards any such claims. In practice, OPA is seen much as this article has described, as a representative of a certain set of values and a general outlook associated with the pursuit of national economic efficiency—a viewpoint shared in some degree across the spectrum of American political thought. Moreover, American government and politics are regarded widely by participants as an adversarial process in which diverse interests and viewpoints are legitimately represented. OPA thus in practice derives its basic legitimacy within DOI, not from a claim to dispense scientific truths, but from an acceptance that the OPA view of the world deserves a vigorous and forceful advocate within DOI.

This source of legitimacy raises the further question of whether the type of staff within OPA—largely social science professionals holding career appointments—are the best people to perform the actual OPA role. For example, would it be better to staff OPA with politically skilled advocates who have some knowledge of economics, as opposed to professional economists and policy analysts, some of whom may be out of place in the rough and tumble of political controversy and debate? Unlike OPA, some policy offices, such as those at the State Department and the White House, are staffed heavily with political appointees who turn over with each change in administration.

The case for existing OPA staffing practices might be made as follows. The rapid turnover characteristic of political appointees places them at a major disadvantage in terms of institutional knowledge. They would not have time to build up a network of personal connections and contact within DOI agencies. At present, the typical OPA staffer has a tenure of 5 to 10 years, and several have stayed more than 10. Another important factor is that political appointees, partly because they have a shorter tenure and must be concerned with future employment, are likely to be associated more closely with outside groups, regions, and interests. It thus may be more difficult for a political appointee to sustain a credible claim within DOI to speak for a national interest that is above regional and other parochial concerns.

This issue also raises the important subject of the role and character of professionalism in government. It may be that members of such professions as economics and policy analysis are needed in government as much for their sense of loyalty and commitment to the ideals and values of the profession as they are for their knowledge of the specific subject matter of the profession. In the experience of OPA, the mathematical, econometric, and other more sophisticated techniques of the social sciences are frequently out of place and inapplicable in the world of government policy-making. A more important factor when OPA hires professionally trained economists and policy analysts may be that their training typically has formed a set of professional allegiances and a style of thinking. Acquiring this way of thinking seems to require long practice in order to ensure that it becomes an ingrained habit. It is possible for many people to obtain an intellectual understanding of the key concepts of policy analysis in a few short courses; it nevertheless may take years to become a committed economist or policy analyst in the full professional sense.

To be sure, many decision makers in government have never understood the content of basic economic ideas, such as the workings of markets. Their tendency often is to decide questions on distributional, moral, and ethical criteria of various sorts—if not on the basis of the impact on some parochial interest. The one most important message of OPA over the years has been to try to explain the workings of the market mechanism, a message that seems to require constant repetition. At the same time it has been acknowledged that, even when fully understood, some people will have their own reasons for rejecting the reliance on markets, reasons that cannot be refuted or denied as a matter of logical consistency.

OPA also contributed over the years by doing many useful and practical things. It provided an institutional memory that was especially valuable on changes of administration and for newcomers generally. The office has organized and managed the internal DOI budget process, reviewed correspondence and legislative proposals, overseen reviews of regulations, helped write environmental impact statements, and undertaken a number of other practical tasks. This chapter has said little about these tasks, but they have been an important part of office life and in sustaining OPA, especially in difficult times. OPA also has served informally as a source of political advice and as the eyes and ears for top political leadership with respect to important new policy developments—external as well as internal to DOI.

Nevertheless, I have focused in this chapter on the larger policy initiatives and on the importance of economic and market advocacy from a national perspective, because I believe (some OPA staffers may disagree) that these features have been the heart and soul of OPA. They motivated OPA staff and gave the office a sense of direction that served it well under four different presidents and diverse secretaries. OPA's outlook has been further compatible with the deregulation movement, tax rate reduction, and other broad shifts in public opinion toward a greater attention to economic ideas that have occurred on a bipartisan basis during the years OPA has existed. What would happen if public opinion were to shift sharply in a different direction— whether OPA would change its focus, adapt in some other way, or perhaps even disappear—is a concern that has not yet had to be confronted.

Notes

1. Barnett & Morse, 1963.

2. Udall, 1963.

3. For an explanation of the rationale for DOI arrangements, see Lynn & Seidl, 1977.

4. The history of DOI coal policy-making from 1971 to 1981 is described in Nelson, 1983.

5. See Davis, 1988. Davis (1975-1985 in OPA, the last 10 as head of the economics staff) was the person most responsible for the Tellico analysis.

6. Nelson & Pugliaresi, 1977, subsequently appeared with some modification under the same title in Nelson & Pugliaresi, 1985.

7. For a review of OCS debates and the role of policy analysis, see Heintz, 1988. Heintz writes with the benefit of many years (1974 to the present) of close involvement as a key OPA staffer on OCS policy issues.

8. Bieniewicz has been an OPA analyst of both OCS and coal leasing issues from 1975 to the present.

9. Haspel, who was an OPA analyst from 1978 to 1985 and is now with the Minerals Management Service, did most of the OPA staff work on the onshore oil and gas leasing system.

10. Wahl has been an OPA staff economist focusing on water issues from 1979 to the present. Osterhoudt also has worked in OPA since 1984, including on water issues.

11. Goldstein has been an OPA economist covering endangered species, wildlife, and environmental issues from 1979 to the present.

References

Barnett, H. J., & Morse, C. (1963). *Scarcity and growth: The economics of natural resource availability*. Baltimore: Johns Hopkins University Press for Resources for the Future.

Bieniewicz, D. J., & Nelson, R. H. (1983, July). Planning a market for federal coal leasing. *Natural Resources Journal,23,* 593-604.

Bureau of Indian Affairs. (1988, March). *Report on BIA education: Excellence in Indian education through the effective school process (Final review draft)*. Washington, DC.

Davis, R. K. (1988). Lessons in politics and economics from the snail darter. In V. K. Smith (Ed.), *Environmental resources and applied welfare economics: Essays in honor of John V. Krutilla*, pp. 211-236. Washington, DC: Resources for the Future.

The Department of the Interior: Evolution of program and administration. (1951, October 5). A research project of the Woodrow Wilson School of Public and International Affairs, Princeton University, directed by George Graham. (Available at DOI library).

Endangered Species Act (1973).

Federal Onshore Oil and Gas Leasing Reform Act (1987).

Goldstein, J. H. (1988, March). *The impact of federal programs and subsidies on wetlands*. Paper presented to the 53rd North American Wildlife and Natural Resources Conference, Louisville, KY.

Haspel, A. E. (1985, July/August). Drilling for dollars: The federal oil-lease lottery program. *Regulation*, pp. 25-31.

Heatherly, C. L. (Ed.). (1981). *Mandate for leadership: Policy management in a conservative administration*. Washington, DC: The Heritage Foundation.

Heintz, H. T. (1988). Advocacy coalitions and the OCS leasing debate: A case study in policy evolution. *Policy Sciences, 21,* 213-238.

Holmes, B. H. (1972, July). *A history of federal water resources programs, 1800-1960*. Washington, DC: U.S. Department of Agriculture, Economic Research Service.

Holmes, B. H. (1979, September). *History of federal water resources programs and policies, 1961-1970*. Washington, DC: U.S. Government Printing office.

The impact of federal programs on wetlands: Vol. I—The lower Mississippi alluvial plain and the prairie pothole region. (1988, October). A report to Congress by the Secretary of the Interior.

Leman, C. K., & Nelson, R. H. (1981, Fall). Ten commandments for policy economists. *Journal of Policy Analysis and Management, 1,* 97-117.

Lynn, L. E., Jr., & Seidl, J. H. (1977, January/February). "Bottom-line" management for public agencies. *Harvard Business Review, 55,* 144-153.

Meltsner, A. J. (1976). *Policy analysts in the bureaucracy.* Berkeley: University of California Press.

Mineral Leasing Act of 1920.

Nelson, R. H. (1982). The public lands. In P. R. Portney (Ed.), *Current issues in natural resource policy,* pp. 14-73. Washington, DC: Resources for the Future.

Nelson, R. H. (1983a). *The making of federal coal policy.* Durham, NC: Duke University Press.

Nelson, R. H. (1983b, January/February). Undue diligence—The mine-it-or-lose-it rule for federal coal. *Regulation,* pp. 34-38.

Nelson, R. H. (1984a). Ideology and public land policy: The current crisis. In S. Brubaker (Ed.), *Rethinking the federal lands,* pp. 275-298 Washington, DC: Resources for the Future.

Nelson, R. H. (1984b, May/June). Why the sagebrush revolt burned out. *Regulation,* pp. 27-35.

Nelson, R. H. (1984c, July/August). The subsidized sagebrush: Why the privatization movement failed. *Regulation,* pp. 20-26, 39-43.

Nelson, R. H. (1987, March). The economics profession and the making of public policy. *Journal of Economic Literature, 25,* 49-91.

Nelson, R. H., & Pugliaresi, L. (1977, March). *Timber harvest policy issues on the O&C lands.* Washington, DC: Department of the Interior, Office of Policy Analysis.

Nelson, R. H., & Pugliaresi, L. (1985). Timber harvest policy issues on the O&C lands. In R. T. Deacon & M. B. Johnson (Eds.), *Forestlands: Public and private,* pp. 149-168. San Francisco: Pacific Institute for Public Policy Research.

Outer Continental Shelf Lands Act of 1978.

Report of the Task Force on Indian Economic Development. (1986, July). Washington, DC: U.S. Department of the Interior.

Udall, S. L. (1963). *The quiet crisis.* New York: Holt, Rinehart & Winston.

Wahl, R. W. (1986, October). *The role of economics in the making of federal water policy.* Paper presented at the Annual Research Conference of the Association for Public Policy Analysis and Management, Austin, TX.

Wahl, R. W., & Osterhoudt, F. H. (1985). Voluntary transfers of water in the West. *National water summary—1985,* pp. 113-124. Washington, DC: U.S. Geological Survey.

Whitaker, J. C. (1976). *Striking a balance: Environmental and natural resources policy in the Nixon-Ford years.* Washington, DC: American Enterprise Institute.

8

Policy Analysis in the Office of the Assistant Secretary for Planning and Evaluation in HEW/HHS: Institutionalization and the Second Generation

Beryl A. Radin

The oldest of the departmental level federal domestic agency policy analysis units—the Office of the Assistant Secretary for Planning and Evaluation (ASPE) in the Department of Health and Human Services (HHS), formerly the Department of Health, Education, and Welfare (HEW)—celebrated its "official" 20th birthday in 1988.[1] As others have recently noted (Lynn, 1989; Nelson, 1989; Pugliaresi & Berliner, 1989), most of the offices that we have claimed as policy "shops" have ancestry that harks back to the 1961 creation of the Office of Systems Analysis in the Department of Defense. Indeed, ASPE's connection to the McNamara "whiz kids" was particularly direct since several of its first staff came directly from staff positions in Defense. ASPE provided experiences that were pivotal to the development of an inchoate field.[2]

This chapter is based on data collected in 1988 on 70 professional staff members who were in the HEW/HHS policy analysis office within the Office of the Secretary some time between 1965 and the present.[3] The study examined the background of these individuals, their views on skills needed to be an effective policy analyst, their role

AUTHOR'S NOTE: I am appreciative of the comments made on an earlier draft of this paper by Christopher Bellavita, Sally Cobberly, Harry Hatry, Peter May, Duncan MacRae, Arnold Meltsner, Carroll Seron, Carol Weiss, Joseph Wholey, and William Zumeta.

definition, and their assessment of an optimal location for the policy analysis function. In addition, the study elicited information on the process of "doing" policy analysis by asking them to recount two examples of work—one that they view as their most successful assignment, and one that they view as least successful.

Although the study was designed as an "update" to Arnold Meltsner's 1986 work on the role of policy analysts,[4] it can be seen also as an exploration of the institutionalization of the policy analysis function through historical analysis of the office. It examined several questions. First, what are the elements of the policy analysis experience that allow practicing policy analysts to view their work as "successful" or "not successful"?[5] Second, does the typology of policy analysts developed by Meltsner continue to describe types of clients, skills, and perceived roles of analysts? Third, did the policy analysis function change over time in response to shifts in the office size, staff recruitment patterns, development of competing sources of analysis, and shifting expectations within the external environment? Finally, do these changes indicate that we should reexamine our assumptions about the structure and organization of policy analysis units?

ASPE: A Historical Look

Policy analysts' activities came to HEW in 1965 in the guise of an Office of Program Coordination. A staff of eight reported to an assistant secretary who, in turn, reported to the undersecretary of the department. The functions of this small staff were driven originally by the Program, Planning, and Budgeting System process (PPBS); individuals within the unit had specific areas of program responsibility and collected and analyzed data to inform the multiyear PPBS planning process. The first director of the office, William Gorham, was followed in 1968 by Alice Rivlin, who headed an office of 30 staff.

The office was elevated in stature and rank at the beginning of the Nixon administration during the tenure of Assistant Secretary Lewis Butler. While neither the size nor the functions of the office changed appreciably, the status changes gave the staff formal credibility within the department. Despite its sense of permanency, however, the office was (and continues to be) dependent on the highly individualized expectations of the secretary; some Assistant Secretaries of Planning and Evaluation had the "ear" of the secretary while others were not linked to the top policy-making process. The early ASPE continued to play out a residue of the PPBS system, conducted some evaluation studies, and scrutinized issues that were of interest to the assistant secretary.

The first significant staff growth within ASPE came in the early 1970s due to two factors: the interest of the HEW secretary in policy analysis activities, and the transfer of staff from the research office of the Office of Economic Opportunity (OEO). The OEO infusion into HEW not only brought an increase in staff but also introduced ongoing welfare reform experiments and computer capacity to ASPE. The Negative Income Tax and Health Insurance experiments were the centerpiece activities of the office. The OEO contingent was absorbed into a unit that mirrored the major parts of HEW. Staff were assigned policy development and analysis responsibilities in the program areas of education, health, income security, and social services. Other staff focused on process issues (planning and budgeting[6] activities) or on evaluation. This organizational form was begun by Laurence Lynn and continued, slightly modified, by William Morrill. When Morrill left the department in 1976, the unit had a staff of more than 200, with activities that responded to ongoing processes within the department, as well as the policy interests of the assistant secretary and the secretary.

Another increase in ASPE staff came during the tenure of Henry Aaron, the assistant secretary through the first part of the Carter administration. Extensive use was made of temporary appointment authority—individuals were brought into the government for fixed terms or on leave from academic or research institutions. It was during this period that ASPE reached its largest size—more than 300 individuals, many of whom were involved in work on administration initiatives in welfare reform and health. The staff was viewed by Secretary Joseph Califano as his "think tank," and he tended to use other units within the department for strategic and political advice (especially the Executive Secretariat).

By the Carter years, policy analysis staffs had multiplied throughout the department; they were attached not only to the Office of the Secretary (ASPE) and the program assistant secretaries, but also to program offices and units farther down the bureaucratic chain. Analytic turf battles were common. Evaluation activities were bifurcated between ASPE's evaluation unit and evaluation units in the substantive programs. Attempts were made to sort out the different approaches to evaluation, but the boundary lines between them were increasingly fuzzy. In addition, the Office of the Inspector General was becoming involved in a short-term evaluation form called service delivery assessments to provide service-level information to the secretary, bypassing the "normal" bureaucratic decision chains.

In many ways, ASPE exhibited the characteristics of a line agency with predictable positions on policy that transcended the policy directives of the secretary or the White House. This appearance can be attributed to its large size, its struggle with other staff units for "turf" within the department, and ascendancy of the authority of the Office of the Secretary during the Califano regime. At the same time, the proliferation of policy analysis activities gave the ASPE staff some colleagues spread around the department who shared a common language and training.

By the end of the Carter administration, ASPE staff was beginning to shrink, largely because of the termination of fixed-term appointments and the exodus of a few staff members who had worked on education issues to the newly formed Department of Education. This decrease was intensified by policy initiatives of the Reagan administration in many of the program areas under the jurisdiction of the department (now called Health and Human Services)—block grants, total elimination of programs, and reliance on ideological arguments rather than analysis. In addition, the private sector Grace Commission, appointed to reduce government waste, advised the scaling down of many functions within the Office of the Secretary, and the administration called on federal departments to increase their contracting-out of government functions.

In 1990, ASPE had approximately 100 staff members. While continuing to perform the same broad array of functions through the same organizational structure, the office tried to systematize policy support for departmentwide functions (e.g., legislative formulation, research, evaluation, and data planning). In contrast to the Carter years, ASPE plays a minor role in devising major policy initiatives (see May, 1988). Most program evaluation is undertaken by the inspector general's office or by the operating program components.

The Study Participants: A Staff Glimpse of History

As Arnold Meltsner noted, "policy analysts are a highly variegated species"[7] (Meltsner, 1986; p. 14). While they are all individuals who give information and advice, policy analysts differ in terms of educational background, policy areas of interest, incentives, and views about policy analysis and its impact on policy-making. His assessment of variety seems to be an accurate depiction of the ASPE group. Of the 70 individuals who participated in the ASPE study, a majority are now in their 40s, are largely white, and two thirds are men. Of these, 4 individuals were in ASPE at the time the questionnaire was administered; 4 had been in ASPE twice during their career. Data about their tenure at ASPE include: less than a year, 8; 1 to 2 years, 20; 2 to 4 years, 25; 4 to 8 years, 12; over 8 years, 5.

Ph.D. degrees were held by 34; master's degrees by 19; and bachelor's degrees by 5. Others held specialized degrees (such as LLDs, MDs, or EdDs). Also, 21 were trained as economists; 12 had public policy or public administration degrees; 8 were political scientists; 6 held social work or social welfare degrees; 5 had degrees in health; 4 had degrees in management or business; and the rest studied sociology, psychology, physics, math, law, philosophy, and other fields. Recruitment seems to have varied over the years: Economists were always hired; political scientists were hired in the 1970s, and none were hired after 1978; public policy/public administration degree holders were hired in the mid- to late-1970s, although a few were hired in the 1980s.

Distribution in ASPE subunits generally reflects the size of the units. For example, 21 respondents were in the income security program, working on welfare and Social Security; 14 in health; 7 in social services; 4 each in evaluation and program systems; and 2 in education. Respondents include 7 former assistant secretaries; 10 at the supergrades (senior executive service or deputy assistant secretary level), 5 at GS-15, 14 at GS-13/-14, 12 at GS 11/12. Others were either at a lower level or lacked a federal government grade classification. Experience before coming to ASPE included government jobs, 24, 11 of whom had worked elsewhere in the department; think tanks or consulting firms, 14; university faculty, 10; university researchers or staff, 6; and students, 4. The rest ranged from interest group employment to high school teaching.

Stories From the Trenches: Successes and Failures

The questionnaire asked respondents to pick two policy issues that they had worked on at ASPE, one that they viewed as the most successful assignment and the other the least successful. Of the respondents, 51 told a story about a "success" and 32 told about a "failure."[8]

Substantive Focus

Both the "success" and "failure" examples covered a wide range of issues. Several issues were perceived by some to be "successes," while others cited them as failures. For example, 6 individuals used welfare reform as their successful example, and 2 cited it as a failure. Child support policy and bilingual education also appeared in both categories. A few issues were clear failures: Five people used national health insurance as their negative example. Three cited projects on the National Health Services Corps as positive experiences.

The negatives included five examples of departmentwide initiatives (e.g., the PPBS system, the secretary's Policy Statement, and evaluation for the department), while the positive tales included two such issues (block grants and the 1% evaluation set-aside). Health issues were more likely to appear on the "failure" side of the ledger than were income support issues. Social services issues were divided equally between the two categories. Technical issues of measurement, modeling, and estimation were more likely to appear on the positive than the negative listing.

Definitions of Project Success or Failure

Respondents were asked why they thought that each example was or was not a success. Responses fell into five categories: political reasons, the substance of the policy issue, attributes of the work situation, bureaucratic factors, and outcomes of the work. Successful examples were divided equally among the first three categories. Political reasons included "the right time," serious congressional interest, agreement in the administration, political support or pressure, and presidential support. Reasons linked to the substance of the issue had to do with information available, a clear charge, a problem that had to be solved, ability to define evaluation criteria, and an issue that was well thought out. Elements of the work situation were a dedicated staff, talented or motivated people, freedom to proceed, resources available, a good environment for work, and ability to work with peers. Less frequently noted, bureaucratic factors included commitment of agencies, good working relationships and support by operating program staff, and willingness of agencies to work together.

By contrast, the reasons given for negative examples were overwhelmingly political: lack of support in the administration or the department, not enough political will, lack of interest, politics were "too rough," "the window of opportunity closed," congressional resistance, or collision with political ideologies. Very few substantive or bureaucratic reasons were given for "failure," and even fewer reasons involved the personal work situation.

The Assignments

In the "success" category, the source of most of the assignments was individuals or processes inside the department: the assistant secretary, departmental processes (such as planning, budgeting, or regulation development), ASPE itself, or other department programs or offices. Other issues originated from the White House or the secretary. A few examples originated with the analysts themselves, were just "out there," came through "natural progression" of issues, or developed in reaction to Congress, the Supreme Court, or other external actors.

In contrast, most examples in the "failure" category came from the political agenda within the executive branch—from the White House or the secretary. A few examples emanated from inside the department (the assistant secretary, normal processes, or other agencies). None of the negative examples originated inside ASPE, but several came from individual analysts. A few examples (about the same number as the successes) came in response to congressional or Supreme Court action.

In a majority of the "success" examples, respondents could identify a specific client for the analysis—the secretary, assistant secretary, undersecretary, or others in the department. A sizable number of respondents identified multiple clients—collective bodies or a chain of decision makers ranging from the assistant secretary level up to the White House and Congress. A few individuals thought that their client was the public, the aging network, Hispanic children, or the poor and minorities. Five individuals were not aware of a client for their work.

The negative examples showed a loftier set of expectations regarding clients. More respondents thought that their client was the president than anyone else. Some cited the secretary or the secretary's chief of staff and the assistant secretary. Several identified collective bodies or a chain of decision makers. A few named external clients—the U.S. taxpayer or the research community. Four were not aware of a client for their work.

Respondents were asked whether they had prior knowledge of the issue before working on the assignment. In the "success" examples, analysts overwhelmingly had prior knowledge (either extensive background or at least some familiarity with the topic). About half the respondents on the "failure" cases had knowledge of the issue.

Both "success" and "failure" responses indicated a wide range of analytic techniques. Many of the successful examples included computer simulation, statistical analysis, microeconomics, modeling, regression analysis, and econometrics. Techniques mentioned less frequently were demography, legal analysis, political analysis, evaluation techniques, and survey research methods. Other respondents noted that their analytic approach included "clear thinking," synthesis, and trial-and-error techniques. The pattern in the negative examples was similar, but even more reliance appeared to be on the quantitative cluster of techniques and less on qualitative approaches.

The examples of successful projects indicated that analysts at all grade levels and throughout ASPE's history have had extensive relationships with others during their projects. Almost all respondents interacted with others inside ASPE, and almost as many indicated relationships with individuals in the department, largely in the program units but also in other parts of the Office of the Secretary (e.g., the budget office, general counsel's office, office of legislation). Similarly, most respondents worked with other federal agencies during the course of the project, including OMB, the White House, GAO, and congressional offices, as well as other program departments (such as the Department of Labor or the Department of Agriculture). About half of the respondents had contacts with others outside the government during the project; these included researchers in academic settings and think tanks, interest groups, and state and local officials.

The negative examples showed a very different pattern. Although most of the respondents indicated that they had relationships with colleagues inside ASPE during their work, significantly fewer of them had other types of interactions. Fewer than half worked with individuals in other parts of the department, about a third had interactions outside of the government, and very few developed relationships with individuals in other agencies.

The Final Product

Respondents were asked whether their final product included elements of "classic" policy analysis: alternatives, recommendation, strategy for adoption, implementation issues, and cost estimates. Most of the successful examples included all of the elements. Final products were more likely to include recommendations than any other element. In rank order, responses were recommendations, alternatives, cost estimates, adoption strategy, and implementation. Fewer of the negative examples contained all of the elements. Indeed, a number involved work that was never completed. The product was more likely to contain alternatives than anything else. Responses in rank order were alternatives, cost estimates, implementation, adoption strategy, and recommendations.

In the successful examples, memoranda were the most frequent product of the analytic work. Other products were proposed legislation, briefings, reports, meetings, and policy papers. A few people mentioned regulations, a budget package, or articles. Negative examples were most likely to result in oral briefings, followed by reports, papers, and memoranda, plus a scatter of regulations, new process, legislative proposals, or options papers.

Skills, Roles, and Clients

ASPE analysts employed a wide variety of skills, defined their "clients" in multiple ways, and played a wider variety of roles than the four types of analyst that Meltsner (1976, 1986) described (i.e., entrepreneur, politician, technician, pretender). Their responses to questions on skills and roles do not appear to indicate different perceptions based on the period in which they were in ASPE. Responses about types of clients, however, do suggest a change over time in the way that clients for analysis are identified. This shift reflects the changes that occurred within the department as a whole, as well as modifications within the larger political environment.

Respondents were given an inclusive list of 21 skills that have been viewed as important for policy analysis training. They were asked to indicate whether these skills were *essential, important,* or *not very important.*

Specific program knowledge emerged as the most essential skill; 39 of the 70 respondents ranked this item as one that should be a part of

ASPE, Department of Health and Human Services

policy analysis training. This ranking was surprising, given the tendency to think of policy analysts as individuals with analytic abilities and techniques that are transferable from one policy setting to another. The ASPE group, by contrast, seemed to be emphasizing their skills as policy experts, rather than policy *analysis* experts. Economists ranked specific program knowledge highest, then statistics, microeconomics, and cost-benefit analysis. Political scientists ranked research design as the most essential skill, followed by implementation analysis, statistics, survey research methods, and political analysis. Those trained in public policy or public administration ranked specific program knowledge highest, followed by statistics, evaluation techniques, implementation analysis, cost-benefit analysis, organizational analysis, and microeconomics.

Respondents were given a list of 17 descriptions of policy analysts and were asked to indicate which of those terms describe the role that they played in ASPE. They were asked also to indicate which *one* of the terms best described their own role. Their answers were:

Roles	Among roles	Major role
Advice giver	54	9
Researcher	49	7
Evaluator	44	4
Expert	43	11
Coordinator	41	7
Technician	36	7
Broker	32	4
Negotiator	32	0
Institutional Memory	28	0
Conflict Manager	20	0
Entrepreneur	19	2
Conscience	18	2
Traffic Cop	15	0
Politician	15	0
Implementer	12	1
Lobbyist	12	0
Fall Guy	8	0
Other		6
No Response		10

Economists tend to emphasize their roles as technician, researcher, and expert. Political scientists tend to emphasize roles as advice givers and experts. Public administrators emphasized their role as coordinator. Most of the respondents, however, reported that they played multiple roles. Practicing policy analysts do not see their roles simply

as producers of reports. Indeed, the almost universal acceptance of
advice giver as a role played in ASPE suggests a reaching for a more
encompassing term to describe their work in the agency. In this
instance, as in the "success" stories, the respondents seemed to indicate the importance of blending the traditional analytic posture with
an interactive role.

Types of Clients

Much of the literature in the policy analysis field draws its view of
the client from Machiavelli; that is, the policy adviser provides advice
to the ruler (see Meltsner, 1990). The origins of the policy analysis field
were linked clearly to efforts by top officials in an agency to gain
control over those within it (see Dror, 1967; Stout, 1980; U.S. Department of Justice, 1979). A basic assumption has been that analysts are
providing advice to a specific decision maker or group of decision
makers identifiable by name and title. This study suggests that over
the years other client types have emerged. Clients fell into four
categories:

Decision Maker as Client

Clients, in this category, are individuals who are a part of the
decision-making process. While they may not have clear authority to
make a decision, they are a part of the decision chain. Given the
fragmented and complex decision process in many federal agencies,
this category may include many different actors, from top political
officials to midlevel career individuals involved in deciding elements
of implementation. Analysts may or may not have direct contact with
their clients, but they believe that specific individuals will be recipients of policy advice. An analyst who operates with an individual
decision maker as a client may assume a number of different roles:
technician, politician, broker, expert, or evaluator.

Institutional Processes as Client

Here the client is the processes that are a part of standard operating
decision procedures, such as planning, budgeting, regulation drafting, or legislative drafting. These processes are predictable and
defined by law, internal decision rules, or externally imposed calen-

dars. Most federal agencies create venues to develop decisions around these processes, frequently designed as ad hoc task forces composed of individuals representing various parts of the agency. Although an official of the agency may actually sign off on the decision, much of the authority of the process is delegated effectively to the task force. Policy analysts may play two different roles in these bodies—either staff to the task force or as members of the group. Individuals who see their client as institutional processes may assume the roles of technician, negotiator, traffic cop, expert, or evaluator.

Organizational Maintenance as Client

Unlike the first two cases, here the analyst does not produce advice for either an individual or a collective decision group. Instead, the client is the organization itself; the analyst's imperative is response to issues that are seen to threaten the agency. Thus, survival of the agency and maintenance of its programs become the implicit client for the analytic work. Policy analysts of this type are likely to have been in the agency for some years and, in many ways, identify with its mission and goals. In this sense, they are like other career public servants. This type of response may be the way that individuals who disagree with current policy direction justify their continuation in the agency. Analysts may work on issues to keep them from being decided by top officials; that is, the goal of the analysis may be decision *avoidance* rather than decision *making* as a way of protecting the status quo in the organization. Individuals whose imperative is organizational maintenance may operate in roles as researchers, conflict managers, coordinators, institutional memory, or evaluators.

Self as Client

Some policy analysts always have operated in response to their own personal agendas. In some cases, they seek a situation like an academic research enterprise. In other cases, the fluidity of a situation gave analysts a sense of moving as policy actors, responding to their view of what is appropriate. During the past decade, a nonclient situation has been a way that policy analysts who are not comfortable with the policy direction of the agency maintain their sense of professional autonomy. Policy analysts who see themselves as the client may assume the role of researcher, entrepreneur, or conscience.

Institutionalization and Transformation

During the 20 years of its life, ASPE has undergone a significant shift in its mode of operation and its role within the department. Some of these changes are attributable to changes within the office itself. Sudden growth changed the office from a small, almost intimate work group to a compartmentalized and specialized bureaucracy. Recruitment patterns over the years broadened the methodological approach; an early reliance on economics was complemented by other approaches. As the years passed, some individuals became career ASPE officials and created norms that socialized shorter term employees. Longevity and specialization combined to create organizational units made up of staff members with strong commitments to specific policy areas (often to particular approaches to those policies) and to the agency itself.

At the same time, changes also were taking place within the department and the external environment that modified ASPE functions. As policy analysis units proliferated throughout the department, ASPE analysts could no longer view themselves as holding a monopoly on the production of policy advice. Increasingly, policy development took on the quality of debate or bargaining with policy analysts from other parts of the department. ASPE staffers found that these debates did not entirely rely on methods associated with formal social science or economic reasoning. Relationships with other analysts became even more important by the late 1970s, when limited resources meant that debate focused more on the modification of existing programs than on the creation of new policies. ASPE analysts were likely to be working on issues for which they already had a track record, either in terms of substantive policy approaches or relationships with others within the department.

These developments took place amid the uncertainties always found in a policy analysis office attached to the Office of the Secretary: the vagaries of the secretary himself or herself. Some secretaries of HEW/HHS involved the ASPE unit directly in the crafting of policies. Others wanted the office to operate as a "think tank," producing information that might (or might not) be used in the decision-making process. Still others saw the role of ASPE as the rationalizer and justifier of specific policy changes that had been determined already.

This study has indicated that ASPE experienced a transformation as these forces played out. ASPE staffers thought differently about policy-making within the department than they had in its early years. Policy-making was not simply what top officials explicitly decided to do, but also involved the machinery of the organization itself—its decision processes, its standard operating procedures, and the survival of its programs. Analysts became more entrenched in the bureaucracy, moving to assignments at which their specialization could be linked to some level of predictability in the turbulent political, social, and economic environment. They sought to protect themselves from external overt political pressure or agendas, often moving away from high-profile assignments to less visible activities. Some of these projects were technical in nature, but more often they involved the satisfaction of working on interesting topics with good colleagues in ASPE and with others interested in the work.

Conclusions

Six general themes emerged from this inquiry that indicate patterns of institutionalizing the policy analysis function as it moved into its second generation.

First, *the changes in the office over the years are directly related to changes that occurred in the external environment of the department.* Changes occurred in the availability of funds for new or enlarged programs; shifts occurred in the political orientation of the department (both partisan political changes, as well as ideological changes in the Reagan years); changes occurred in the policy communities and advocacy coalitions surrounding the programs; and sophistication grew in the academic community about the importance of implementation issues as a part of the policy process.

Second, *changes in the office are related to the process of bureaucratization.* As time went on, staffers appeared to become increasingly socialized to the policy cultures and political structures with which they were dealing. Those staffers who stayed in the office for significant periods of their careers became attached to and identified with specific program areas and took on the characteristics of specialists, sometimes serving as the institutional memory within the department (Rein & White, 1977). At times they became players with a parochial interest (Lynn, 1989) and advocates for specific policy alternatives. While working relationships with the operating programs in the department varied, the adversarial tension between policy analysts and program officials was replaced by an evaluative or developmental working style. As policy analysis activities proliferated in the program offices, the centralized policy analysis officials in ASPE became highly interactive in their dealings with analysts and officials in other parts of the department. In addition, ASPE staff found they shared an interest in activities performed by other offices within the Office of the Secretary (such as the inspector general, Office of Management and Budget). In many ways, staffers behaved more like career bureaucrats than the in-and-out analysts envisioned in the early period of the profession's development (Dror, 1967).

Third, *clients for analysis extended beyond the top officials in the department and its agencies.* As the office matured, staff redefined the concept of "client." In part this was understandable as analysts developed predictable relationships with programs and program officials over time. But the change also reflected a response to the environmental changes affecting the programs of the department. Not only were clients the individuals (or groups) who occupied top-level positions within the organization, but they were also the institutional processes within the agency. The institutional processes included the standard operating decision procedures in federal agencies (such as planning, budgeting, regulation drafting, and legislative drafting) that are predictable and defined by law, internal decision rules, and externally imposed calendars (Nelson, 1989). Organizational maintenance as the "client" for analysis seems to have developed as the analyst's imperative became the survival of the agency and maintenance of its programs.

Fourth, *the operational goals of the policy analysis function were modified over the years.* While some analysts continue to define their success in terms of the impact of their analytic work on specific societal problems, other clearly developed suboptimal goals for their work. Analysts valued their ability to influence decision makers and to sustain that influence over time. Goals became more modest in scope and, at the same time, reflected an awareness of the multiplicity of subgoals contained in programs. Analysts often recognized the complexities involved in the implementation of their recommendations and moved to rethink the way they structured problems and thought about policy design (Dunn, 1981; Ingraham, 1987). Some analysts defined success in response to political realities, while others focused on the elements of the work situation in which they operated or on bureaucratic support for their efforts. Overall, few analysts held the optimistic goal of achieving an applied social science that was both scientifically rigorous and practical.

Fifth, *a patterned relationship exists between skill areas, type of client served, and the role definition adopted by an analyst.* The skills identified by analysts as essential or important to their work cluster around several poles and relate to different perceptions of their roles as policy analysts. Skills may be classified as technical, political, organizational, issue-specific, and evaluation skills. Seasoned analysts tended to emphasize interactive and "persuasive" (Majone, 1989) techniques (particularly political and organizational skills) and to perceive their roles as coordinators and brokers of multiple interests rather than controlling seekers of "truth." While some analysts continued to use normative decision models, others moved toward contingency models, social processes, and a focus on symbolic action.

Sixth, *the centralized policy analysis office contains a diverse array of staff capabilities and interests that allow it to respond to changing department demands and functions.* Despite the dramatic changes that have taken place within the department and its program areas, ASPE staff continue to play a role in decision making. ASPE looks different today from its early period (May, 1988); its products are much less visible to the external world, and it is no longer associated with large-scale policy initiatives (such as national health insurance or welfare reform). While this approach makes ASPE less attractive to some, it is testimony of the ability of a policy analysis institution to survive in the face of major changes in the nation's economic and political environment.

Notes

1. The Office of Research, Plans, Programs, and Evaluation in the Office of Economic Opportunity was the first policy analysis office in a domestic policy agency. OEO did not have the status of cabinet department. The forerunner to ASPE in HEW was created in 1965.

2. Alice Rivlin (1971) and Joseph Wholey (1970) drew directly on their HEW experiences. Others, such as William Gorham, the president of the Urban Institute, brought experiences drawn from the HEW setting to other institutions.

3. While the study respondents do not constitute a random sample of ASPE staffers, they do appear to be representative of the broad characteristics of staff through the years. The questionnaire was sent to individuals who were identified by the planning committee for the 20th anniversary celebration. The total number of individuals who were a part of the ASPE staff over the years is unknown. The questionnaire itself is a combination of open- and closed-ended questions.

4. Meltsner's interviews, however, were done in 1970-1971, the earliest days of the policy offices. Martha Feldman's book (1989) is based on a study of analysts in the Department of Energy; she focuses mainly on the information production function of

the analytic staff. Carol Weiss's study (1989) looked at congressional staffers as users of analysis through a series of systematic interviews. Other extremely helpful essays have drawn on personal experience and used participant observation as the methodology for presenting information on the offices.

5. Pugliaresi and Berliner (1989) note that analysts in the Department of State valued their ability to influence decision makers and to sustain that influence over time.

6. By this point, the PPBS process was eliminated.

7. Meltsner himself worked in ASPE for a short period of time.

8. The disparity between the response rate to the two sections suggests that the individuals who were willing to respond to the questionnaire were, over all, positive about their experience in ASPE.

References

Dror, Y. (1967, September). Policy analysts: A new professional role in government service. *Public Administration Review*, 197-203.

Dunn, W. N. (1981). *An introduction to public policy analysis*. Englewood Cliffs, NJ: Prentice-Hall.

Feldman, M. S. (1989). *Order without design*. Stanford, CA: Stanford University Press.

Ingraham, P. W. (1987, June). Toward more systematic consideration of policy design. *Policy Studies Journal, 15*(4), 611-628.

Lynn, L. E., Jr. (1989). Policy analysis in the bureaucracy: How new? How effective? *Journal of Policy Analysis and Management, 8*(3), 373-377.

Majone, G. (1989). *Evidence, argument, and persuasion in the policy process*. New Haven, CT: Yale University Press.

May, P. J. (1988). *Policy analysis: Past, present, and future*. Paper presented to the 1988 annual meeting of the American Political Science Association, Washington, DC, and the Minnowbrook II Conference, Minnowbrook Conference Center, New York.

Meltsner, A. J. (1986). *Policy analysts in the bureaucracy* (2nd ed.). Berkeley: University of California Press. (First edition 1976.)

Meltsner, A. J. (1990). *Rules for rulers: The politics of advice*. Philadelphia, PA: Temple University Press.

Nelson, R. H. (1989). The Office of Policy Analysis in the Department of the Interior. *Journal of Policy Analysis and Management, 8*(3), 395-410.

Pugliaresi, L., & Berliner, D. T. (1989). Policy analysis at the Department of State: The policy planning staff. *Journal of Policy Analysis and Management, 8*(3), 379-394.

Rein, M., & White, S. H. (1977, Winter). Policy research: Belief and doubt. *Policy Analysis, 3*(1), 239-271.

Rivlin, A. (1971). *Systematic thinking for social action*. Washington, DC: Brookings Institution.

Stout, R., Jr. (1980). *Management or control?* Bloomington: Indiana University Press.

U.S. Department of Justice, Office of Management and Finance. (1979, Summer). *Policy formulation and implementation at the federal level: A comparative analysis of structure, functions and staffing in ten cabinet departments*. Washington, DC: Author.

Weiss, C. H. (1989). Congressional committees as users of analysis. *Journal of Policy Analysis and Management, 8*(3), 411-431.

Wholey, J., Scanlon, J. W., Duffy, H. G., Fukumoto, J. S., & Vogt, L. M. (1970). *Federal evaluation policy*. Washington, DC: Urban Institute.

9

Policy Analysis in the Office of Inspector General, U.S. Department of Health and Human Services

Penny R. Thompson

Mark R. Yessian

When we tell people that we work at the Office of Inspector General (OIG) at the U.S. Department of Health and Human Services (HHS), often the first question we're asked is, "Are you an auditor or an investigator?" The general public, as well as many public administrators, policy analysts, and evaluators, conceive of OIGs as offices solely concerned with conducting financial audits of federal grantees and contractors and investigating recipients, providers, and managers of public programs. Indeed, the investigators and auditors within federal OIGs have been immensely successful in fulfilling this part of the OIG mission. Yet the HHS OIG also emerged in the late 1970s and 1980s as an important player in the larger policy and program assessment process within the department, both by establishing a distinct office dedicated to policy analysis and evaluation and by identifying and emphasizing policy implications that arise as a result of investigations and audits. In other words, the HHS OIG, led by Richard P. Kusserow since 1981, uses policy analysis and program evaluation as tools of oversight.

AUTHORS' NOTE: Penny R. Thompson is a program analyst in the Office of Inspector General, Office of Evaluation and Inspections, Washington, DC. Mark Yessian is the Regional Inspector General for Evaluation and Inspections, Office of Inspector General, Boston, Massachusetts. The views expressed in this article are those of the authors and not necessarily those of the Department of Health and Human Services or of the Office of the Inspector General.

Background

HHS is the largest of all cabinet agencies. Its total budget for the fiscal year 1990 is expected to top $436 billion. Under its umbrella are the following:

- the Social Security Administration
- the Health Care Financing Administration (which oversees the Medicare and Medicaid programs)
- the Public Health Service (including the Alcohol, Drug Abuse, and Mental Health Administration, the National Institutes of Health, the Centers for Disease Control, the Food and Drug Administration, and the Health Resources and Services Administration)
- the Family Support Administration (including the Office of Family Assistance, the Office of Child Support Enforcement, the Office of Refugee Resettlement, and the Office of Community Services)
- the Office of Human Development Services (including the Administration on Aging, the Administration for Native Americans, the Administration on Developmental Disabilities, and the Administration for Children, Youth, and Families)

HHS programs affect the lives of virtually every American citizen. Providing the elderly and poor with health insurance through Medicare and Medicaid, providing financial support for poor families with children through Aid to Families with Dependent Children, administering the Social Security trust fund, funding medical research, and ensuring that foods, drugs, and devices are safe for use by American consumers are but a few of the myriad of responsibilities assigned to the department.

In 1976, to protect the integrity of these programs, Congress passed and the president signed into law Public Law 94-505, which created the HHS Office of Inspector General (then the Department of Health, Education, and Welfare [HEW]). Public Law 94-505 required that the HEW inspector general be appointed by the president and confirmed by the Senate. Since 1976, OIGs have been established in over 60 other federal agencies. About a third of the IGs, like the HHS IG, are selected through presidential appointment.

By law, the HHS IG is responsible for oversight of the wide range of HHS programs and functions. The Inspector General Act of 1978, as amended,[1] states that the IG shall "provide leadership and coordination and recommend policies for activities designed (A) to promote economy, efficiency, and effectiveness in the administration of, and (B) to prevent and detect fraud and abuse in, such programs and operations . . ." (5 U. S. C. App 3 § 2(2).). Congress wished to create offices that were both "objective" and "independent" and that would have the authority to question, challenge, and debate departmental managers on a wide range of programmatic and managerial issues, with Congress listening in. To ensure this objectivity and independence, the law required that:

- Inspectors General are to be appointed "without regard to political affiliation, solely on the basis of integrity and demonstrated ability in accounting, auditing, financial analysis, law, management analysis, public administration, or investigations" (Inspector General Act of 1978, p. 2).
- The IG is to "[keep] the head of the agency and Congress fully and currently informed concerning fraud and other serious problems in the operation of programs" (Inspector General Act of 1978, p. 2). The law requires the IGs to report semiannually to the secretary and to Congress summarizing activities of the office during the previous 6 months. Also, the IG must report immediately to the secretary and Congress on particularly serious or flagrant problems, abuses, or deficiencies related to program administration or operations.
- The agency may not "quash" reports through its clearance process; IG findings and reports are to be issued on the IG's authority, without necessary clearance or concurrence from the head of the agency.
- The IG has access to all "records, reports, documents or materials available to the agency relating to programs over which the [IG] has responsibility" (Inspector General Act of 1978, p. 3) and may subpoena documents if necessary.

A number of factors influenced the desire to establish such offices with such substantial authority and power. William C. Moran, Regional Inspector General for Evaluation and Inspections, has suggested that such factors included congressional distrust of the executive branch in the aftermath of Watergate and the rapid increase in the federal budget experienced in the 1970s (Moran, 1990). General suspicion toward the federal bureaucracy and a belief that the federal government was inefficient, views held by both the Carter and Reagan administrations, surely contributed as well to the creation and growth of the OIGs (Moore & Gates, 1986).

Organizational Structure

The HHS OIG is composed of three primary offices: the Office of Investigations, the Office of Audit Services, and the Office of Evaluation and Inspections. Because each of these offices is structured somewhat differently, contains very different kinds of staffs, and reflects different cultural traditions, we will discuss each of them briefly in turn.

Office of Audit Services

The Office of Audit Services (OAS) conducts and oversees audit work for HHS. Audits include examinations of records and accounts to check their accuracy and program conformance to laws and regulations, and performance reviews to assess the success of HHS programs and/or its grantees and contractors in fulfilling their responsibilities. Currently, the HHS OIG has over 700 auditors, located throughout the country in 8 regional offices and 29 field offices. HHS OIG auditors are trained in auditing and accounting and conduct their work in accordance with government auditing standards (the "Yellow Book"), issued by the comptroller general of the United States.

Office of Investigations

The Office of Investigations (OI) conducts criminal, civil, or administrative investigations of allegations of wrongdoing in HHS programs or by HHS employees, recipients, providers, or contractors. Currently, the HHS OIG has over 300 investigators located throughout the country in 8 regional offices and 41 suboffices. HHS OIG investigators receive special training in law enforcement when they are first hired and throughout their employment, and many were employed as law enforcement officers prior to their employment with the OIG.

Office of Evaluation and Inspections

The Office of Evaluation and Inspections (OEI) conducts short-turnaround policy analysis and program evaluations, referred to as program inspections, on a wide variety of issues of importance to the department, Congress, and the public. The smallest office in the HHS OIG, OEI has approximately 140 staff located in the Washington-Baltimore area and eight regional offices. OEI staff represent a wide variety of backgrounds and disciplines: statisticians, social scientists, journalists, health professionals, and policy analysts.

A fourth office within the OIG, the Office of Management and Policy, is responsible for coordinating OIG analysis and information and bringing that knowledge to bear on the review of current and proposed legislation and regulation. By law, the IG must review existing legislation and proposed regulations and make recommendations "and offer guidance concerning their likely impact on fraud and abuse control as well as economy and efficiency" (Inspector General Act of 1978, p. 8). This office reviews annually hundreds of regulations and laws. The OIG comments on these regulations and laws based primarily on its expertise in promoting efficiency and effectiveness and preventing fraud, waste, and abuse, and on the specific findings of the audits, investigations, or evaluations performed by the office.

The OIG and Policy Analysis

The HHS OIG's involvement in policy analysis and evaluation has grown considerably in the last decade. In those years, the staff dedicated to policy analysis and evaluation within the Office of Evaluation and Inspections has grown geometrically. Even the investigators and auditors in the OIG have become involved in work that falls under the umbrella of analysis and evaluation.

In 1977 the OIG employed about 50 analysts who conducted Service Delivery Assessments, or SDAs. SDAs were field-intensive studies usually reporting the opinions and perspectives of frontline managers and caseworkers, program recipients, and other "grassroots" individuals on the success of HHS programs and initiatives. SDAs were the brainchild of Joseph Califano, Jr., then secretary of the department, who wanted "continuing, rapid access to information about how HEW programs function from many perspectives at the local level" (Mitchell & Hendricks, 1984-1985, p. 39).

During the 1980s, under the direction of Richard Kusserow, SDAs gave way to more rigorous evaluations termed "program inspections," conducted by staff more than double the size of the SDA contingent. Program inspections retained some of the characteristics of SDAs, notably the idea of rapid response, but concentrated on record and document review and statistical analysis, as well as interviews with program officials, outside groups, and experts. Why the change? The shift was largely to provide firmer documentation of the problems identified and of the approaches that might be taken to promote greater effectiveness, economy, and efficiency in departmental programs. As decision makers looked increasingly to the OIG for policy advice, especially on matters concerning possible dollar savings, it became more and more important that OIG findings and recommendations be based on a solid methodological foundation. Thus, the OIG's techniques became less those of the journalist and more those of the applied researcher drawing on a variety of analytic and reporting techniques.

Program inspections are conducted by the Office of Evaluation and Inspections and may take many shapes and forms. Some program inspections resemble SDAs: Recently the OIG issued a report describing the opinions and perspectives of 24 drug manufacturing firms in regard to FDA's review and approval of applications to market new and generic drugs. Other program inspections look a lot more like full-scale evaluations: A recent OIG report to Congress on physician ownership and self-referral involved evaluators, auditors, investigators, and lawyers within the OIG in a large-scale survey and assessment of the nature, range, and implications of financial arrangements between physicians and health care businesses to which they refer patients. Most program inspections fall somewhere in between, like recent OIG inspections on child support enforcement, which combine interviews with state program officials and caseworkers with detailed records review to assess the potential for increased collections using innovative computer matching techniques.

OIG studies vary in their approaches, sometimes finding the facts, sometimes testing a hypothesis, sometimes identifying new issues, sometimes monitoring program performance, sometimes assessing outcomes. Using these approaches, the OIG has examined such issues as the following:

- *Hospital closures.* The Secretary of HHS, concerned over media reports that hospitals were closing their doors and leaving many communities in need of acute care, requested that the OIG determine exactly how many hospitals had closed in 1987. By in-depth telephone interviews with state hospital associations, state licensing boards and state planning agencies in all 50 states, the OIG was able to provide an objective figure. In addition, through analysis of hospital data, the OIG provided information on the characteristics of closed hospitals as compared with viable hospitals.

- *The performance of state medical boards.* As a follow-up to prior work in this area, OIG examined the practices of state medical boards in disciplining physicians. A variety of techniques, including analysis of a national compilation of data on disciplinary actions, in-depth examination of disciplinary cases in eight randomly selected states, and on-site interviews with officials in the four states with the largest numbers of medical doctors, were used to assess the disciplinary practices of state boards so critical to protecting Medicare and Medicaid patients from poor quality of care.
- *Nursing home abuse.* Through a survey of 232 state complaint coordinators, state ombudsman, directors of state Medicaid Fraud Control Units, nursing home administrators, nursing home residents and advocates, and officials at professional licensure bureaus in 35 states, the OIG catalogued expert views on the types and causes of abuse in nursing homes. The OIG's survey of state laws prohibiting elder abuse found wide gaps in protection afforded elders confined to nursing homes.
- *The satisfaction of recipients with services provided by the Social Security Administration.* Staff reductions at the Social Security Administration (SSA) caused concern among some observers that SSA could no longer be responsive to its beneficiaries. The OIG surveyed a random sample of SSA clients to determine their level of satisfaction with the service provided by SSA and found that 80% felt that the service provided by SSA was good or very good.
- *Medicare coverage and reimbursement.* In a variety of studies the OIG has examined Medicare coverage and reimbursement for various medical devices and services, from Medicare coverage of seat lift chairs and power operated vehicles to reimbursement schedules and practices for outpatient laboratory services and post-operative care after cataract surgery. Analysis of Medicare payments, actual review of claims forms, modeling, and interviews are some of the techniques that have been used to study these issues.

Expanding the Traditional View of Audits and Investigations

The OIG also has expanded its view to consider the larger implications of traditional investigations and audits. For example, potential policy and program issues may be identified as a consequence of investigations. In recognition of this fact, the OIG instituted the Management Implication Report (MIR) system in 1980. Under this system, investigators expand the scope of their inquiry to assess programmatic issues when a crime has occurred; in addition to collecting evidence, investigators seek to understand the system that allowed the crime to occur and report to program managers on their findings. This system reflects the understanding that "a conviction is not simply a successful prosecution of a criminal, but is frequently a recognition of the need to change the system. . . ." (Office of Inspector General, 1984, p. 14). In addition, the OIG Office of Audit Services has turned a good deal of its attention from strict financial audits of departmental grantees and contractors to performance reviews and audits that target larger, more macro-level issues of program management and performance. In 1989, OIG audits examined such issues as how FDA reviews and approves applications to market generic drugs, how legislation to restructure SSI benefits might affect beneficiaries, how much progress has been made in systems modernization at the Social Security Administration, and what factors lead rural hospitals to financial success or failure.

Accounting for the OIG's Success

The HHS OIG has taken on an analytic and evaluative role and performed it successfully in an era when traditional analysts and evaluators in other offices have suffered budget and staff reductions. (GAO, 1988). At the same time other offices dedicated to evaluation and analysis were being stripped of employees, the OIG's evaluative staff almost tripled in size. Requests for analysis from the secretary, operating divisions, and Congress increased to account for nearly a third of all program inspections started in 1989.

What is the difference between the OIG and the program evaluation shops that have lost staff and funds in the past decade? We believe the difference lies in the OIG's institutional standing and its chosen approach to its work.

The institutional factors critical in the OIG's success include the OIG's special status as an independent authority reporting to both the secretary of HHS and Congress; the OIG's status as a cost-saver in an era of fiscal constraint; and continuity of leadership within the OIG.

First, as discussed earlier, the IG is independent and reports to both the secretary of HHS and Congress. Dual reporting was viewed by some in the early debate over how IGs would function as an impossible requirement to serve two masters. The reporting arrangement for IGs has proved to be essential to ensuring that the findings and recommendations arising from OIG work would initiate departmental action or help guide debate. On the one hand, the IG has a direct line to the secretary, a line established by law. This access allows the IG to raise and discuss important issues with the secretary personally. On the other hand, Congress is informed of findings and recommendations made by the OIG and may initiate debate or action on its own to address problems that have been identified. Dual reporting also ensures the objectivity of the OIG; since reports are not cleared through either branch of government, the IG can take the stance he or she feels is correct without bowing to the pressures of party politics. It is also worth noting that the IG is statutorily prohibited from making policy or operating programs (except for those audit, investigative, and other functions given specifically to the IG). Consequently, the IG is not a "stakeholder" in the policy decision, a position further ensuring independence.

Second, actors in both the executive branch and Congress look to the OIG as a source for cost savings, of particular importance in a decade of rising deficits and limited revenues. And the IG has responded: Between 1985 and 1989, over $26.9 billion in savings resulted from OIG activities and implementation of OIG recommendations made as a result of investigations, audits, and program inspections. Over $8 billion of program savings included in the 1989 Omnibus Budget Reconciliation Act were based on OIG recommendations. Largely because it has delivered on cost savings, a paramount issue for many engaged in the management of the federal bureaucracy, the OIG has fared well when resources were allocated to various agencies. And the OIG's reputation as a cost saver has created the necessary visibility and credibility to open doors for the OIG into other arenas, where it has provided oversight on critical questions of program effectiveness and outcomes.

Third, one person has occupied the position of inspector general since 1981. Such continuity is unusual for political leadership in Washington; during the same time period, the department has had four secretaries. This continuity has given the OIG an effective spokesman and established the office as a place where new political appointees may come for information.

Stylistically, the OIG has succeeded by formulating three guiding principles for its approach to policy analysis and evaluation: (a) work for decision makers, not other analysts; (b) expand and use all possible audiences; and (c) promote constructive change.

Work for Decision Makers, Not Other Analysts

Many complex policy matters face the federal, state, and local governments. In order to identify and develop solutions to some of these difficulties, policy analysts may need to develop in-depth knowledge of technical details and intricacies, to apply strict scientific techniques of analysis and hypothesis testing, to initiate long-term (and longitudinal) studies, to model innumerable policy decisions and possible outcomes, and to detach themselves from the political process of policy-making in order to free themselves of conventional solutions and pat answers. This type of policy analysis and program evaluation is invaluable in the contribution it makes to our common understanding of the challenges facing governmental actors today.

At the same time, decision makers have expressed frustration with the inability of policy analysts to answer their questions *now*. The average tenure of an HHS secretary is about 2 1/2 years. Within that time, the secretary must learn about the myriad of HHS programs he or she is expected to manage; respond to the complaints and questions of taxpayers, program recipients, the president, the White House staff, congressional members and their staffs, state and local officials, advocacy groups, and the media; develop new strategies and initiatives that bear his or her special imprint in order to be viewed as successful; and act effectively in times of crisis. In such an environment, the secretary (as well as lower level political appointees and program managers, who may face many of the same constraints and challenges) would trade "truth with 95% confidence" for "a reasonable course of action" in many, if not most, cases.

It is characteristic of policy analysis, performance reviews, and program evaluation undertaken by the OIG to look at problems and issues with the eyes of the decision maker. What issues are of primary importance? What level of confidence is required? How quickly does information need to be gathered? Naturally, the best policy analysis is one done in a day, assessing all issues, using the most rigorous scientific techniques available. Short of this unattainable ideal, policy analysts and evaluators traditionally have chosen to sacrifice timeliness for thoroughness, risking irrelevance in the process. While short-turnaround, broadly based studies have their own pitfalls and drawbacks, they are valued by and valuable to top decision makers, who may not be around to hear and use the results of longer term efforts. As a result, the OIG conducts its studies as rapidly as possible, generally within 4 to 6 months. On occasion, the OIG has been able to provide information to decision makers in dire need of data within a few weeks. Our inspection on Social Security client satisfaction, described earlier, took 8 weeks to complete and was delivered in time for the commissioner of Social Security to present the findings at a congressional hearing.

Expand and Use All Possible Audiences

For the OIG, given its statutory mandate, two audiences for its work are clear: the secretary of the department, and Congress. Even though this much is spelled out in law, not every OIG has capitalized on its access to these two audiences. The recent scandal at the U.S. Department of Housing and Urban Development, for example, is at least partially due to the inattention or underestimation by the HUD OIG of the need to create audiences and to publicize and create interest on significant findings and recommendations contained in their reports. We provide this example to demonstrate that audiences, even where formal relationships exist, do not necessarily sit up and pay rapt attention, IG or not. Strategies must be developed to gain and keep audience attention. To do this, we concentrate on both the substance and presentation of our work.

Attention to substance includes getting the facts right, using the right methodology to examine an issue, and pinpointing important issues. Although, as in any organization, the occasional "klunker" lands with a thud on the landscape of policy debate, audiences have come to trust the OIG's work. Credibility is a critical commodity. We are only as good as our last report; consequently, our job is much harder when we start a new study in an area in which we have just completed a piece of work that missed the mark.

Attention to presentation, although sometimes dismissed as irrelevant and superficial, can make the difference in getting and keeping a reader's attention. OIG reports are sent to people who are deluged with competing pieces of paper. To get their attention and keep it, reports are kept short (around 15 pages) and readable: A one- to two-page executive summary is provided for the busy reader, "head-lines" to make important points are used throughout the document, graphics are employed to break up the text and to demonstrate comparisons and trends effectively, and reports are formatted on personal computers so that they are attractive to look at.

Strategies must be developed also to expand audiences: The larger the audience, the larger the probability of further discussion, debate, and positive action. In order to expand its audiences, the OIG publicizes its reports to the press, speaks at conferences attended by parties affected by OIG work (practitioners and industry, state officials, recipients and beneficiaries, interest groups) and provides copies of reports free of charge to requestors.

The HHS IG has a congressional and public affairs staff that is responsible for liaison between the OIG and Congress and the media. The OIG has developed relationships with both Republican and Democratic members of Congress who value the work of the office and who, in what is becoming a more frequent occurrence, request that the OIG perform policy analysis and program evaluation on issues of interest to their committees and subcommittees. The IG has himself testified at over 100 congressional hearings since assuming the position in 1981.

Sometimes policy analysts consider audiences only when the analysis is complete and the report is written. They focus on distribution of the report as their strategy to develop and expand their audience. We have found, however, that expanding and using the audience for a report begins at the initiation of the project and continues throughout the project's life. Michael F. Mangano, deputy inspector general for evaluation and inspections, has described this approach as a "marketing approach to evaluation." One important component of the marketing approach to evaluation is preselling the product; that is, creating interest and excitement in the findings before the project is even under way. (Mangano, in press). We often meet with interest and advocacy groups active in a field when we first begin a study; often we find that our study is described in their next newsletters. The OIG also publishes a work plan that receives wide distribution and attention within various professional communities.

Promote Constructive Change

Many factors influence whether evaluation and analysis result in programmatic change and agency action. The philosophies, personalities, and temperaments of individual actors (both analysts and decision makers); timing; political climate; organizational culture; and the study methodology and findings are just a few among an inexhaustible list of other ingredients that affect the success of the policy analyst in creating action. Not all of these factors are within the power of the policy analysis office to change or even to influence. Yet certain strategies, such as negotiation with program offices, can increase substantially the potential for constructive change. For example, we often share early drafts of reports with affected offices and then meet to discuss the report and the reaction of program officials. These discussions can tell us if we need to document further some of our findings or to shore up our recommendations; they provide a forum for the further exchange of information so that points can be clarified, misstatements corrected, and objections considered. A second opportunity for affected parties to influence the report occurs when the OIG releases its draft report and solicits comments.

One of the primary advantages associated with the OIG's statutory standing is its ability, as an independent oversight agency, to force contested issues into the sunlight of open debate. Yet the IG is also a departmental actor who appreciates and appraises political considerations, administrative feasibility, and organizational factors as they affect possible solutions to identified problems. Thus, the "OIG has the institutional strength to issue recommendations which may be unpopular. . . . At the same time, because of its position within the Department and familiarity with organizational culture, the OIG is astute regarding political and other environmental dynamics that may affect the feasibility of its recommendations" (Thompson, 1989, p. 43). Both elements—strength to make needed recommendations, and rational consideration of how such recommendations might be implemented—are necessary to create an atmosphere in which effective action can take place.

Few policy analysts enjoy the position of the OIG in negotiating programmatic and managerial response to its policy recommendations. Under the departmental conflict resolution process, responsible operating and staff divisions must express formally their agreement or disagreement with policy and programmatic recommendations made by the OIG. Implementation plans must be developed for recommendations on which there is agreement; arbitration before a departmental third party must occur when there is a disagreement. Conflict resolution also helps ensure that OIG recommendations are feasible and defensible.

The OIG issues two important reports that publicize and discuss significant recommendations made by the OIG that the department has not implemented. The Cost-Saver Handbook (the "Red Book") discusses recommendations that, if implemented, would result in cost savings for the taxpayer. The Program and Management Improvement Recommendations (the "Orange Book") outlines recommendations that, while not generating specific dollar savings, would improve quality of care, program effectiveness, or service delivery. These reports are scrutinized by Congress and administration officials who can initiate or influence action on these items.

The OIG also promotes constructive change in other ways. The IG often attends meetings of the departmental policy council, along with the secretary, undersecretary, and assistant secretaries, and has been consulted regularly by past secretaries during their tenures. As discussed earlier, staff at the OIG review proposed and final regulations to be issued by the department. The IG is a member, along with other IGs, of the President's Council on Integrity and Efficiency (PCIE), which is chaired by the Deputy Director of the Office of Management and Budget. The PCIE provides a forum for IGs to review issues that cut across agency lines and to make recommendations to promote efficiency and economy and to prevent fraud and abuse government-wide.

The Risks

In our quest to produce timely reports that decision makers find useful, we obviously confront some risks. How well we minimize them is best determined by those who read and use our reports. In reflecting on our experiences, we consider two risks associated with our approach to policy analysis and evaluation as particularly significant and worthy of discussion. Each is briefly addressed below.

Rushing to Closure

In various ways, our emphasis on producing reports quickly can undermine quality. One obvious way is through the inclusion of inaccuracies—be it in citing and explaining references, presenting data, or reporting on developments. We have developed extensive internal review processes to catch such inaccuracies, but they are not foolproof, especially when decision makers are anxious to receive a product.

A second, more subtle threat to the quality of our work involves the identification and examination of issues. In the midst of an accelerated inquiry, it is possible that some important but not readily apparent questions might not be asked and that some issues might not be framed in a manner most conducive to effective policy-making. Since our staff typically are not experts on the programmatic issues they examine, it is also possible that some relevant program factors might be overlooked. (Conversely, their broader perspective might allow them to offer insights overlooked by the experts.)

Still another possible cost associated with production pressures concerns the breadth and depth of our recommendations. We tend to be best at gathering data and presenting findings. Often we find that we do not have sufficient time left to present a range of well-developed and relevant policy options and to offer sufficiently detailed recommendations for departmental action. Worse yet, in our desire to offer solutions, we may sometimes suggest courses of action without sufficiently addressing the alternatives and/or implications.

Trying Too Hard to Please

Even with the considerable independence and influence enjoyed by the OIG, we recognize that in the final analysis we are not the "doers." If we are to be successful in promoting constructive change, the "doers"—the decision makers—must respond to the findings and recommendations we present.

Herein lies a second risk intricately associated with our work. In seeking to have our work used—to have impact—we may at times try too hard, with dysfunctional consequences.

We may, for instance, lose too much control of our agenda and thus jeopardize our independence. We may at times give too much attention to what current decision makers would like us to address. In ways we may not even perceive, we may be inclined to guide the inquiry in directions that are most likely to please our "clients." Further, even though we carefully guard the objectivity of our work, we may dismiss certain types of information and certain conclusions that current decision makers are likely to find objectionable.

Similarly, and more likely, our action orientation may bias us toward studies and toward recommendations that involve short-term solutions. This "quick-fix" orientation is understandable, given the short-term tenure of most politically appointed decision makers. It almost certainly leads to some devaluing of longer term solutions, even when such solutions might be more effective.

In yet another sense, the way in which we present our reports may lead to some dysfunctional effects. In our quest to reach busy decision makers faced with overflowing in-boxes, we typically prepare very concise reports with attention-grabbing graphics. This approach has proven to be very successful in getting the attention of these decision makers. If we are not sufficiently attentive, however it may lead to some oversimplifications of very complex issues. In the process of synthesizing information and making it presentable, we can overlook or dismiss important nuances and convey some misleading impressions.

Looking Toward the Future

While we spend a good deal of time thinking about and talking about the risks associated with our work, we feel that the benefits outweigh the potential disadvantages of the OIG's chosen approach. Yet these challenges are certain to stay with us, and perhaps to increase, in an environment where the information and analysis we provide is a commodity in a full and overflowing marketplace of ideas. The advantages of institutional standing and formal authority support the OIG in that marketplace but do not guarantee its success. More important to the OIG's success is the philosophy discussed in this chapter: work for decision makers, expand and use all possible audiences, and promote constructive change.

At this time few other OIGs exploit the tools of policy analysis and program evaluation in support of their oversight activities in the way the HHS OIG does. This lack may change in the 1990s, however, as the "watchdogs" of the federal government look for powerful lenses through which to examine programs and policies and carry out their responsibilities.

Note

1. The Inspector General Act Amendments of 1988 repealed Public Law 94-505 and transferred the HHS OIG into the "umbrella" Inspector General Act of 1978, Public Law 95-452.

References

General Accounting Office. (1988, November). *Program evaluation issues.* Transition Series (No. GAO/OCG-89-8TR). Washington, DC.

Inspector General Act of 1978. (1978, August 8). Senate Report No. 95-1071.

Inspector General Act Amendments of 1988.

Mangano, M. F. (1990, April). *A marketing approach to evaluation: Four lessons for evaluators from the Honda Motor Company.* Presentation before the Society for Knowledge Utilization and Planned Change.

Mitchell, B. B., & Hendricks, M. (1984-1985, Winter). New program evaluation tools. *The Bureaucrat, 13*(4), 39.

Moore, M. H., & Gates, M. J. (1986). Inspectors general: Junkyard dogs or man's best friend? *Social Research Perspectives.* New York: Russell Sage.

Moran, W. C. (1990). Evaluation with the federal offices of inspectors general. In M. Hendricks, M. R. Mangano, & W. C. Moran (Eds.), *Inspectors general: A new force in evaluation,* pp. 9-22. San Francisco: Jossey-Bass.

Office of Inspector General. (1984, November). *Management implication reports.* Management improvement series (No. 85-01).

Omnibus Budget Reconciliation Act (1989).

Public Law 95-452.

Public Law 94-505.

Thompson, P. (1989, August). The (evaluation) role of the inspector general. *Evaluation Practice,* pp. 42-44.

5 U. S. C. App. 3.

PART 3

Legislative Units

10

The Congressional Research Service:
Policy Consultant, Think Tank, and
Information Factory

William H. Robinson

The Congressional Research Service (CRS) is the oldest and second largest of the four congressional support agencies. Part of the Library of Congress, CRS is the only department of the library whose sole purpose is to provide information and policy analysis to Congress. By statute, the agency is accorded complete research independence and maximum practicable administrative independence.

The Congressional Research Service, which traces its statutory beginnings to 1914, currently has a staff of 864 and a FY 1990 budget of nearly $46 million. The service's broad charter includes a mandate to provide a wide range of services to all members and all committees. In doing so, CRS responded to more than 500,000 requests in FY 1989. Among the services provided were information and reference, in-depth policy analyses, seminars for members and staff, training pro-

AUTHOR'S NOTE: The author owes more than the usual perfunctory thanks to colleagues who commented with such gusto and in great detail on earlier drafts of this chapter. I would like to express appreciation to Carol Davis and Royal Shipp for their continuing engagement in the process of reviewing CRS's analytical development, and Susan Finsen for developing some of the data. I owe a special debt to those who tried to correct my erroneous thinking and/or made dozens of particularly cogent suggestions—including John Moore, John Hardt, Jim Robinson, and Fred Pauls. A number of other colleagues also offered useful advice, among them Earl Canfield, Mort Schussheim, Dick Ehlke, Hugh Elsbree, Stan Bach, and Nancy Davenport. Finally, I want to thank my secretary, Annetta Tate, for her patience in producing this chapter under trying circumstances. While everyone tried to help, I remain responsible for any remaining errors in fact or interpretation.

182LEGISLATIVE UNITS

grams for staff, issue briefs, audio briefs, videotape programs, in-person briefings, and other analytical support. CRS operates in a nonpartisan fashion, providing support to both the majority and minority in the Senate and the House of Representatives. Great effort is made to ensure balance and accuracy in all products and services. The agency does not make policy or legislative recommendations. Timeliness is one of CRS' most distinguishing features, with two thirds of the 500,000 inquiries being answered within a day. A second hallmark is close involvement in the legislative process, often resulting in a confidential consultant-client relationship. As a result of that role as personal consultant, along with stringent statutory constraints on publishing its reports or studies for noncongressional use, CRS has operated with a very low profile in the policy community.

The combination of high volume and quick turnaround caused one writer to refer to CRS as a "reference factory"[1] (Goodrum, 1968). That description was only partly accurate at the time, but in some ways it continues to cover part of the reality of the CRS environment today. Since the early 1970s, however, CRS has placed greater emphasis on legislative consultation, policy analysis, the use of simulation models, and interdisciplinary analyses and anticipatory work.

Early History and Legislative Charter of CRS

The origins of the Congressional Research Service actually date back to the creation of the Library of Congress in 1800 with an appropriation of $5,000 to purchase books and to establish a room in the Capitol to house them. A later Senate report noted that the purpose of creating such an entity was "to enable statesmen to be correct in their investigations, and by a becoming display of erudition and research, give higher dignity and luster to truth"[2] (Annual Report, 1986, p. 53). It was necessary to recreate the library after the burning of the Capitol by the British in the War of 1812. The new library was launched by acquiring the private collection of 6,700 books belonging to Thomas Jefferson. With his offer to sell his wide-ranging collection, Jefferson noted, "Before a great republic there is no subject to which a Member of Congress may not have occasion to refer" (Annual Report, 1986, p. 53). With a library and staff to tend it, the thought must have occurred to busy, virtually unstaffed legislators that they could ask someone in the library to look up some fact or other information for them.

Congress decided in 1914 to recognize and set aside resources for such information support by adding language in the appropriation act for the library, creating a Legislative Reference Service "to employ competent persons to prepare such indexes, digests, and compilations of law as may be required for Congress...." (*Congressional Record,* 1914, pp. 12219-12220). This mandate was supported by Senator Robert La Follette, based on his experience in creating a similar organization in the state of Wisconsin, and received favorable testimony from Lord Bryce, author of the political classic *The American Commonwealth.* Subsequent to the 1914 enactment, Congress broadened the meaning of *legislative reference* to include gathering data "for or bearing upon legislation, and to render such data serviceable to Congress and Committees and Members thereof" (*Annual Report,* 1986, p. 59). With 1914 as the earliest explicit recognition of the need for "legislative reference services," CRS stakes its claim as the oldest congressional support agency (GAO was begun in 1921, OTA in 1972, and CBO in 1974).

The workload and fortunes of CRS followed the activities of Congress itself over the next three decades. As congressional inquiries became more specialized in nature, librarians possessing additional subject expertise were hired. In 1946, reflecting on the buildup of executive powers and staff during the course of fighting a depression and a world war, Congress sensed that it was being outweighed in the ongoing struggle to maintain the balance of power between the two branches of government. To reassert its prerogatives and streamline its committee system, Congress enacted the Legislative Reorganization Act (LRA) of 1946. Among other reforms, the LRA permanently established a Legislative Reference Service (the precursor to CRS) as a separate department in the Library of Congress, and authorized it to hire senior specialists at pay levels equal to the highest comparable positions in the executive branch. This authority, coupled with an emphasis on subject expertise rather than librarianship, provided important impetus to the service's policy analysis capability. Moreover, the LRA proposed enlarging the service and made its first listed duty:

(1) upon request, to advise and assist any committee of either house or any joint committee in the analysis, appraisal, and evaluation of legislative proposals pending before it, or of recommendations submitted to Congress, by the President or any executive agency, and otherwise assist in furnishing a basis for the proper determination of measures before the committee. (Section 203[a][1] of 2 USC 166)

The 1970 Amendments to the LRA constitute the congressional declaration of analytical independence from the executive branch. These amendments and associated reports changed the name of the Legislative Reference Service to the Congressional Research Service (underscoring its new research and analysis emphasis), foresaw a tripling of its staff and urged it to engage in "massive policy analysis" for Congress, provided for "continuous liaison" with congressional committees to tighten the tie between CRS research and the legislative activity of Congress, and provided for complete research independence and maximum practicable administrative independence from the Library of Congress.

Considering the time of its gestation, the legislation contained a remarkably prescient policy analysis charter for CRS, as well as a clear charge to keep that analysis relevant to committee needs through continuous contact:

(d) It shall be the duty of the Congressional Research Service, without partisan bias —

(1) upon request, to advise and assist any committee of the Senate or House of Representatives and any joint committee of Congress in the analysis, appraisal, and evaluation of legislative proposals within that committee's jurisdiction, or of recommendations submitted to Congress, by the President or any executive agency, so as to assist the committee in —

(A) determining the advisability of enacting such proposals;

(B) estimating the probable results of such proposals and alternatives thereto; and

(C) evaluating alternative methods for accomplishing those results; and, by providing such other research and analytical services as the committee considers appropriate for these purposes, otherwise to assist in furnishing a basis for the proper evaluation and determination of legislative proposals and recommendations generally; and in the performance of this duty the Service shall have authority, when so authorized by a committee and acting as the agent of that committee, to request of any department or agency of the United States the production of such books, records, correspondence, memoranda, papers, and documents as the Service considers necessary, and such department or agency of the United States shall comply with such request; and, further, in the performance of this and any other relevant duty, the Service shall maintain continuous liaison with all committees. . . . (Section 203[d][1] of 2 USC 166).

In the 1970s, Congress also strengthened the program evaluation capabilities of the General Accounting Office, and created the Office of Technology Assessment and the Congressional Budget Office. It increased the number of personal staff to member and committee offices. The growth in total staff on Capitol Hill is important because of the interplay between House and Senate staff and that of the support agencies. With increased numbers came greater capacity to specialize. The interaction among Hill specialists has been an important factor driving both the increased production and use of policy analysis for Congress.[3] The rise in congressional staff, however, has also increased the distance between the policy analyst in the support agency and the member of Congress or committee chair.

Institutional Development: Resources, Services, and Clients

The Joint Committee on the Library provides oversight and policy guidance to the Congressional Research Service. Committee members are drawn from the Committee on House Administration and the Senate Committee on Rules and Administration.

The Director of CRS is appointed by the Librarian of Congress, in consultation with the Joint Committee of the Library. Directors have come from within CRS in recent years, drawing primarily on former chiefs of the Government and American Law divisions. (The only exception is Gilbert Gude, a former congressman from Maryland, who served from 1977-1985.) The current director is Joseph E. Ross, an attorney and former chief of the American Law Division.

The personnel and compensation systems are separate from, but modeled on, those of the executive branch—with parallel GS levels, merit selection and tenure, and fringe benefits. The major differences flow from that separateness, including the fact that the Joint Committee on the Library authorizes the approval of any new supergrade positions (GS-16 to GS-18).

Resources and Staffing

Between fiscal years 1971 and 1977, CRS staff increased nearly 150%. Growth slowed during the economic stagflation of the late 1970s, and in 1981, CRS *lost* 19 positions. In the ensuing Gramm-Rudman-Hollings years from 1982 to 1989, 11 new staff were added. In 1989 the staff complement was 864.

Since nearly 90% of the CRS budget is invested in personnel, its appropriations have followed the growth of staff (adjusted for inflation). Appropriations for CRS rose from $4.7 million in 1970 to $27.9 million in 1980 to $45.8 million in 1990.

Organization, Staff Characteristics, and Resource Allocation

Two reference and information divisions exist—Congressional Reference and Library Services—staffed mainly by reference librarians and bibliographers. The seven policy analysis divisions are organized along both disciplinary and subject lines. Those organized by subject are Education and Public Welfare (basically human resources), Foreign Affairs and National Defense, and Environment and Natural Resources Policy. The disciplinary divisions are Government (political scientists and a few historians), American Law (all attorneys), and Science Policy (life science, physical science, engineering, etc.). The Economics Division is a hybrid. Staffed by economists, it covers subjects (transportation, housing, community development) as well as disciplinary topics (money and banking, tax policy, macroeconomic policy, etc.). Interdisciplinary teams are used to pool the resources of the divisions.

Slightly more than three fifths of the staff are allocated to policy analysis, with another 28% devoted to information and reference. The remainder is divided about equally between executive direction and the documentation and status of legislation.

The policy analysis staff are predominantly holders of graduate degrees—law, master's degrees in a variety of subjects, and many PhDs. The number of PhDs varies among the divisions, but they comprise about one quarter to one third of division research staff.

Over two thirds of the professional staff have 10 or more years of CRS experience, while an additional one fifth of the staff has 5 to 10 years of CRS experience. The average number of years of experience exceeds 12 years. The average age is 43.5. Women comprise 40% of CRS professional staff.

Workload, Products, and Clients

CRS provides information and analysis to all members and committees of Congress, not only for legislative purposes, but also for the substantial representational role that members play.

In fiscal year 1989, CRS responded to 500,000 congressional requests, or an average of over 2,000 requests per day in session (roughly 4 per day for each senator or representative). Requests in support of legislative work of members of Congress made up three fifths of the total inquiries; committees accounted for one fifth of the total volume of requests, but represented over one third of staff time. Projects that CRS launched on an anticipatory basis—before any formal request had been made by a congressional sponsor—represented 1% of the total work volume, but were accorded nearly one quarter of total staff time.

Until fairly recently, the number of inquiries roughly doubled each decade. A slowdown occurred in the 1980s, probably in part because fiscal limitations reduced the number of new program initiatives that Congress could consider and because of the greater use of omnibus legislation that reduces the access points for analysis and the time to do it.

A single division of expert reference librarians, the Congressional Reference Division, handles two thirds of all requests made to CRS, thus freeing the research divisions from a workload that surely would drive out all analysis. The division draws on CRS reports and Issue Briefs, prepackaged collections of materials called Info Packs, other off-the-shelf items, substantial clipping files, and impressive power-searching skills in computer data bases and other reference sources to locate the appropriate materials and to send them quickly to the requesting office.

The CRS product line has evolved over the years to meet changing congressional needs. The flagship of this line is the *Issue Brief,* an analytic format keyed to congressional timing needs. For each of roughly 350 to 450 issues facing Congress, CRS develops a 10- to 15-page "brief" that contains a definition of the issue and its development, an analysis of its causes and alternative solutions, descriptions of major bills in the area, a chronology of developments, references to other reading, and an initial one-page summary. Issue Briefs are updated regularly as action occurs. In 1988, about 50,000 requests specifically for Issue Briefs were received and nearly 295,000 copies were distributed, often as the best quick response to a general question on an issue.

One of the most important services offered is in-person consultation by CRS staff. Briefing a member in his or her office can be the most efficient way of tailoring CRS expertise to that member's needs, while facilitating the probing and questioning that accompanies real understanding. Moreover, the Congressional Research Service offers in-depth, continuous, and in-person support to Congressional committees. It may begin with in-person consultation with committee staff on an issue and continue through the life of a legislative proposal, such as the following:

- provision of background papers to the committee to increase understanding of the issue
- assistance in the design of congressional hearings to gather more information
- suggestions for witnesses at the hearings
- provision of possible questions for Members to ask witnesses to draw out needed information
- presence at the hearings to supplement questioning
- development of options for dealing with the problems discussed
- possible legislative specifications for implementing policy directions selected by the committee (CRS does not draft legislation)
- presence and expert consultation at committee mark-ups
- periodic appearances as witnesses to testify
- occasional availability on the floor of the House or Senate as expert resources during floor consideration
- help in preparation of conference agendas and decision documents
- attendance and assistance at conferences to resolve differences between the two houses

Institutional Culture and Values

At the core of CRS's success is its institutional culture—the values that animate it and the shared vision that inspire veteran and newcomer alike. Because culture is so binding, however, it can resist or slow desired change.

The institutional culture of CRS generally plays a positive role in providing analysis and information to Congress on a timely, usable basis. As the service undertakes to make analysis more interdisciplinary, however, its culture of decentralized operation makes that task more difficult. All policy analysis organizations face this dilemma.

Values

CRS places objectivity and nonpartisanship at the top of its value hierarchy. While total objectivity is probably impossible to achieve, the pursuit is of great value, and balance is attainable. In an environment as intensely political as Congress, nonpartisan balance is not only functional but also essential to the very survival of CRS. One of the first librarians of Congress, George Watterston, was dismissed during Andrew Jackson's presidency for being perceived as serving only "one side of the aisle" (*Annual Report*, 1986, p. 54). Beyond self-protection, this approach serves Congress well. CRS can help sort reality from fiction with a high degree of credibility because it has "no axe to grind" on the issue.

This objective, nonpartisan stance also has a philosophical base. Most important issues turn on value conflicts, not technical concerns. CRS feels strongly that only 535 people at any one time are elected to make binding value judgments for the nation. The role of the service is to inform the decision-making process, not to make the choice or to press for one set of values over another. This premise also underlies our policy of not making policy recommendations.

CRS works only for Congress. We do not undertake research for executive agencies or directly for the general public. We exist solely to help Congress maintain its role as the world's best-informed, most independent legislature. CRS maintains a sharp focus on its only client.

Confidentiality is an important mandate for CRS. The Congressional Research Service values its role as private consultant and technical advisor to Congress. In this capacity, we are enjoined to work closely with members and committees of the Congress, often on a confidential "client" basis. We do not share a memo or confidential report with another member of Congress without the explicit approval of the original requester. Moreover, a recent judicial determination ruled that CRS products are considered the works of Congress itself and, therefore, are protected by the "speech and debate" clause of the Constitution.[4] Thus, CRS is not subject to freedom of information inquiries, and it may be able to fend off injunctions seeking to obtain its analyses. Only our clients have the authority to release CRS work that is not already in the public domain.

CRS does not publish its reports. In fact, we usually do not send our products to congressional offices unless they specifically request them. (The only exceptions are "catalogues" of products available for request: the quarterly *Guide to CRS Products* and monthly *Update,* and the officially approved publications of CRS—the *CRS Review,* and *Major Legislation of the Congress.*) Congress struggles to avoid drowning in the daily deluge of incoming paper and has little desire for unsought additions to its workload. CRS also has been prohibited from publishing anything for public distribution without the prior approval of the Senate Rules or House Administration Committees. The spirit of this proscription is to ensure that CRS keeps writing solely for Congress, and not for outside groups.

A growing number of our studies are published as committee prints. Many are in-depth analyses provided to committees to support their legislative or oversight activities. These products are available to the entire Congress, the public, and are automatically distributed to all 1,400 depository libraries in the United States. A tension remains between those outside Congress who seek easy access to a broad range of CRS material, and Congress, which seeks to control the release of what it considers to be its own internal work product.

We also see our role as being research brokers—intermediaries who participate in the professional community, scan the works of academia and other sources of research, bring in what might be useful in resolving congressional policy dilemmas, fill gaps, and adapt it all for use in the congressional environment (Robinson, 1989, p. 4). In this capacity, we must understand fully the congressional environment in which we work—the political dimensions of issues, congressional organization and procedures, and the legislative process.

Timeliness is one of the essential distinguishing features of CRS. In a system of government in which any action is difficult, it is important to be able to act when the time is right (Kingdon, 1984, pp. 173-204). Congress must often move quickly when a window of opportunity is presented by the fortuitous coming together of action-forcing events, growing political consensus, and the availability of acceptable policy options. If analysis is not available when decisions must be made, analysis will be left out and decisions will be based on more intuitive techniques always available to members of Congress. CRS often negotiates with requesters, paring the ambitiousness of the analysis desired to the time available. When a deadline is agreed to, however, it is accepted as a binding commitment.

A premium is placed on anticipating issues in order to carve out sufficient advance time to do background research, to gather data, and to construct the analytical tools needed for analysis—before the issue heats up for Congress and requires speedy action.

Accuracy and authoritativeness are probably universal analytical values but take on added importance in the legislative sphere where the place of analysis is more tenuous. When the environment is open and combative and the sources of information plentiful, one mistake can spell disaster for the careless provider. Even limited access may be lost if the information provided is not seen as accurate and reliable. Thus, CRS encourages peer review and requires review of all new written products at the section and division levels and a final review in the agency Office of Policy.

Style

The environment in CRS is collegial and nonhierarchical. The same service orientation that CRS extends to Congress is present in the helpful support that CRS staff generally accord each other. Analyst-to-analyst consultation and assistance is frequent and reciprocal and often crosses division lines.

Because of this service orientation and the heavy workload of CRS, considerably less turf consciousness exists in the agency than is typical of policy analysis shops or bureaucracies generally. This comparative openness facilitates the movement toward greater interdisciplinary research. Awareness is growing about the need to attack complex problems from multiple perspectives. Moreover, Congress has a special need for such integrative analyses, given the generally fractionating nature of the congressional committee system.[5]

Personal recognition and responsibility are important CRS attributes. While all products carry the institutional backing of CRS, they also feature prominently on the cover the names of the analysts who produced them. This prominence provides personal recognition all too rare in today's bureaucratic environment and contributes both to high morale and a sense of personal responsibility for the accuracy and authoritativeness of the products produced.

CRS analysts must be entrepreneurial. With so little formal structure, and a multiplicity of aggressive information sources, each analyst must take the initiative to meet congressional staffers face to face. Even those with nationwide reputations might be forgotten quickly if they fail to "get across the street" regularly. Because of heavy reliance on the oral tradition in Congress, CRS researchers must be able also to express themselves orally, as well as in writing. Regular personal contact with staff, frequent telephone consultations, briefings, hearings support, and seminars all require analysts who can think well "on their feet" and present complex ideas clearly.

As an institution, CRS prides itself on its flexibility and capacity to innovate, all designed to stay responsive to its congressional clients.

Analytical Development

The amount and types of analysis for Congress are conditioned by a number of external factors, including: (a) the relative availability of resources to the public sector (which influences both the supply of analytical resources and the capacity to respond to public policy challenges); (b) the state of executive-legislative relations—whether the president or Congress is in ascendance (which conditions what role the Congress is both willing and able to play); and (c) congressional staff—both their numbers and training (which affects what they are prepared to ask for and able to use). For purposes of this analysis, three time periods are of interest—1946-1970 (the period between the Legislative Reorganization Act and the significant amendments in 1970), 1970-1980 (the early implementation of the amendments), and 1980 to the present.[6]

Products and Techniques

To make this section less anecdotal, top management and staff in all CRS divisions were interviewed and asked for examples of the typical and best products for three time periods (1970, 1980, and 1989). Common characteristics and trends were also discussed.

Early 1970s. The work of CRS in the period before the 1970 amendments and continuing into the early 1970s was more descriptive than analytical—and suited the environment of the times. It consisted mainly of bill descriptions and comparisons, compilations of data and information, pro-con assessments, legislative histories, reference work, speech drafts, and hundreds of one- to five-page memoranda responding directly to specific requests for information. Little quantitative work was being done, few examples of developing alternatives existed, and almost no impact analysis was done.

This output fit the typical staff available to handle the work of the period. Then, the average CRS staffer was fresh out of college, with a BA or MA, had no particular program specialty, and was likely to stay only for a few years before moving on. The biggest complaint was the immense amount of time that went into writing speeches—which were neither particularly good nor well received. Also, suspicion arose that a good bit of CRS work was being written for staff pursuing advanced degrees. At any given time, each analyst had a backlog of 15 to 30 requests on the desk.

Some outstanding qualitative analyses were done, including some probing legal analyses prepared by some of the senior staff of the American Law Division (e.g., by Killian on the constitutionality of "stop and frisk" activity, Celada on federal antibusing legislative provisions). The nature of good legal analysis has remained relatively constant across the time periods covered in this chapter.

Several divisions were regularly doing their best work anonymously in the form of committee prints. Many of these congressional publications became the equivalent of textbooks in their fields. (See for example, *Congress and the Nation's Environment*,[7] *Science, Technology and American Diplomacy*,[8] *Technical Information for the Congress*,[9] *Economic Developments in Countries of Eastern Europe*,[10] and *Congress and Foreign Policy*[11].)

Staff from several of the divisions were associated closely with the legislative process even at this early date; some served as staff directors for special committees or study groups established by Congress (e.g., Arner, Sheldon, and Kravitz). Close committee support and policy consultation were provided in such areas as agriculture and forestry (Wilcox and Wolf) and Social Security and welfare (the Education and Public Welfare Division almost since its beginning in 1957).

Mid-to-late 1970s. Responding to the staff growth of the 1970s and the mandate of the LRA, CRS began hiring more experienced, better trained, and more specialized staff. At the same time, congressional staff also began to increase in numbers. This double dose of increase resulted in a ratcheting process that led to greater specialization and expertise.

In 1973 the first in-house models were developed to handle formula grant allocations. Some simulations also were undertaken to answer "what-if" policy questions, such as a model to estimate the effects of comprehensive revision of the criminal code on the prison population.

Speech writing was eliminated. With more time available for analysis, greater emphasis could be placed on developing policy options, tracing impacts, and forging closer ties with the legislative process. With greater staff experience and additional resources, new formats also were developed, such as seminars and training institutes.

1980s. The early 1980s saw some forays into the use of microsimulation models, with an analysis that sought to assess the impact of the Reagan welfare cutbacks on the incidence of poverty by separating the effects of the policy reductions from those of a slumping economy

(House Committee on Ways and Means, 1984). An in-depth, interdisciplinary assessment of the causes for the increase in the number of children in poverty was done, in collaboration with the Congressional Budget Office (*Children*, 1985). Another notable analysis was published as a committee print entitled *Housing—A Reader (House Committee on Banking, Finance, and Urban Affairs, 1983)*.

By the end of the decade, one of the key roles played by CRS became that of policy consultant, with close attachment to the legislative process. The increased experience of the analytical staff enhanced their capacity to function effectively as policy consultants both by deepening their subject expertise and enriching their institutional memory—knowing firsthand what ideas had been tried by the committee before, the reactions of interested parties, procedural tactics tried, committee jurisdictions threatened, legislative outcomes and their impacts, and some notions about what options might be pursued usefully at the present stage of debate.

As the skill level of CRS staff rose, more work moved toward the cutting edge of the disciplines and focused on important concerns of Congress. A recent example is a three-volume study of health insurance coverage done for three committees.[12] The analysis authoritatively identified the number of people lacking health insurance coverage, their characteristics and reasons for noncoverage, an array of options for dealing with the problem, and the costs and distributional implications of the alternatives. Similar in-depth treatment was given to a study of the Federal Employees Health Benefits program and alternative measures for dealing with mounting costs. (*The Federal*, 1989). Models have been developed in the Foreign Affairs and National Defense Division to assess strategic weapon "cost to attack" scenarios.

While frequently using econometric models of the major forecasting services in their work, the Economics Division also does its own analyses of major sectors of the economy and industries. Significant new modeling work has been undertaken in the tax field, including models of capital gains taxation (Kiefer) and investment income taxation (Gravelle). Similarly, the Environment and Natural Resources Division has used national macroeconomic modeling services to simulate policy impacts on specific sectors, for example, the impacts on the farm sector of mandatory use of ethanol.

The Government Division has undertaken research using census data and university data bases, including a computer model that can forecast the reapportionment of seats in the House of Representatives, using census population estimates, the establishment of the first-ever data base of public opinion poll results from most national polling organizations, voter registration and turnout figures in presidential and congressional elections dating from 1948, regression analyses of House and Senate mailing costs, and quantitative analysis of corporate compliance with federal equal employment opportunity and affirmative action goals.

One of the most graphic examples of cutting-edge analysis by CRS had to do with the new Federal Employees Retirement System (FERS). The Education and Public Welfare Division devoted nearly a dozen analysts over a period of 3 years to the development of an analytical approach that would help the committees understand the nature of the choices available to them, and an actuarial model that could assess the costs and distributional implications of the alternatives (*Designing*, 1984). As a result, Congress's capability exceeded that of the executive branch. In fact, the executive branch lacked the ability to replicate the results of the CRS model and did not submit a contending legislative proposal.

The bulk of what CRS produces remains qualitative analysis. Two examples from the mid-1970s serve as interesting illustrations. The first was a 15-page assessment of the limited federal role in crime prevention, and a delineation of policy levers available for the federal government to influence the activity of other actors in the criminal justice system (McClure, 1976). The other example was a genuinely fresh perspective on an old issue—national health insurance. In the span of only 20 pages, this analysis outlined the problems of the health industry in the United States (cost, coverage, distribution of specialized health resources, and access) and traced the likely impact of the major national health insurance proposals at the time (Ebeler, 1976).

Forecasting Issues and Interdisciplinary Analysis

Given the time required for modeling or conducting research, issues must be foreseen far enough in advance to carve out the necessary time. Moreover, early availability broadens the role that analysis can play in the decision-making process by becoming part of the conventional understanding that shapes the way people look at the issue before party positions are solidified and legislators become committed to a particular bill or legislative approach (Robinson, 1989, p. 6).

In 1987 CRS launched a structured attempt at issue forecasting with its Major Issues Planning system. Senior managers of CRS meet twice each year to identify the top 20 or so major issues that are likely to reach the legislative stage. The preliminary list of issues is checked with congressional leadership staff to ensure its consistency with Congress's own agenda. So far, CRS has been fairly successful in selecting issues that become the focal points of congressional attention.

Once selected, the issues are addressed by interdisciplinary teams specifically created to concentrate the needed skills and disciplines on the issue—both to enhance CRS's understanding and to help congressional clients by supplying integrated analysis. This process affects not only substantive research but also seminar topics, issues presented at the annual Public Policy Issues Institute, and monthly features in the *CRS Review*, and also plays a part in staff allocation decisions. In an effort to provide a longer time horizon for Congress on developing issues, CRS includes one or more issues in the system that may take a longer gestation period than a single Congress.

CRS Style of Policy Analysis

While some variation in style exists within CRS, the service tends to place particular emphasis on structuring problems to facilitate understanding (Shipp, 1989). Impact analysis also receives comparatively more attention. On the other hand, the development of detailed options is underplayed, and policy recommendations are avoided.

CRS often offers alternatives that are generic and conceptual in approach, rather than carefully delineated options ready for translation into legislative specifications. This general approach permits members to see the essential differences among the choices available without tying up limited analytical resources in developing detailed responses that no one wants or needs. Once Congress understands the problem and the family of choices available, members are good at fine-tuning the policy options and making the political judgments. Also, since CRS assumes that it will be present at later stages of the legislative process, it can offer more detailed assistance when the broad policy directions preferred by the committee are clear.

Future Directions

The future direction of the Service will depend in part on its environment—the needs and evolution of Congress itself over the next few years—and in part on how it chooses to respond to that environment. Despite progress, plenty of tough challenges lie ahead for CRS to address in achieving still higher levels of performance. These include:

- *Pressure on resources.* For the past decade, funds available to CRS have been virtually level in real terms, while congressional requests continue to grow at 3% to 5% per year, with the real resource draw much greater still, due to more intensive analysis. The Service must find creative new ways to do more with less—or face the difficult political task of reducing services.
- *Obstacles to interdisciplinary work.* While CRS is well positioned to do interdisciplinary analysis, that position does not make it easy. The service has a strong tradition of decentralization that accords considerable autonomy to the research divisions and to individual analysts. This arrangement has many functional characteristics, including flexible responses to demonstrably different congressional markets, speed in moving products and services through the research process to the client, and high levels of responsibility and morale. These advantages turn into obstacles for interdisciplinary analysis. Thus, a need exists for new incentive systems and nonintrusive management techniques that will soften the boundaries between disciplines, divisions, and analysts and make the ongoing effort less difficult.
- *Greater need for consistency in approach and products.* Disparate services, products, and priorities grow out of CRS's decentralized culture. The trick here is to bring greater uniformity of policy and product without stultifying or driving out legitimate diversity.
- *Need for more effective market research and marketing.* Because of the mediating role of congressional staff, the service has a difficult time in determining which people in a congressional office actually use its products and services and for what purposes. CRS is trying to get at these issues, as well as to determine the reaction of users to the quality and utility of CRS products. A need also exists to provide a more focused outreach effort that assists members of Congress and committees with better understanding the services available from CRS.

The goal is to avoid strictly reactive responses, and to seek a greater measure of control over the future direction of CRS and its services to Congress.

Notes

1. Charles Goodrum, author of this phrase, is a former Assistant Director of CRS.

2. This section of the chapter owes much to the research of Daniel Mulhollan, Assistant Chief of the Government Division in CRS. Most of the material can be found in the *Annual Report* for the Congressional Research Service to the Joint Committee on the Library for Fiscal Year 1986.

3. These ideas are more full developed in Robinson, 1989. This discussion develops the notion of congressional staff and support agency specialists as "research brokers" and suggests a division of labor between them.

4. The issue arose from a controversy between the EXXON Corporation and the Federal Trade Commission. EXXON sought to subpoena material prepared by CRS for Congress. Congress resisted the move by passing S. Res. 396. In discussing that resolution, then Majority Leader Robert Byrd noted that in its role of providing information and analysis to Congress (often of a confidential nature), CRS "provides a service to the Members and committees of the Congress which is equivalent to that performed by the staffs of Members and committees." S. Res. 396 then stated that "it is the determination of the Senate that the communications of the Congressional Research Service to the Members and committees of the Congress are under the custody and control of the Congress and may be released only by the Congress, its Houses, committees and Members, in accordance with the rules and privileges of each House." The ruling by the Administrative Law Judge stated that because Congress intended "a close relationship between itself and CRS, in which CRS would play a supporting role for Congress' legislative function," CRS documents are "privileged under the doctrine of separation of powers and the speech or debate clause" of the Constitution, and the subpoena was quashed. References to the Senate Resolution can be found in the Congressional Record (Daily edition), March 27, 1980, pp. S 3162-3. The ruling in the FTC case is referenced as *In the Matter of the EXXON CORP. et al*, Docket No. 8934, decision dated June 30, 1980.

5. See, for example, *Toward a Modern Senate*, 1976, and the papers prepared for use by the Commission on the Operation of the Senate, especially Schick, 1976.

6. The author is indebted to John Hardt, Associate Director of CRS, for helping sharpen the framework for analysis.

7. An 1145-page committee print of the Senate Committee on Interior and Insular Affairs.

8. An interdisciplinary series done for the House Committee on Foreign Affairs, beginning in 1970.

9. A report prepared for the House Committee on Science and Technology and produced periodically since 1969.

10. A 634-page committee print of the Joint Economic Committee dated 1970.

11. A committee print of the House Foreign Affairs Committee produced periodically since 1974.

12. These studies were prepared for two subcommittees of the House Committee on Education and Labor (Labor-Management Relations and Labor Standards), the Health and Environment Subcommittee of the House Committee on Energy and Commerce, and the Senate Special Committee on Aging. They are entitled *Health Insurance and the Uninsured: Background Data and Analysis*, (May, 1988), 172 pages; *Insuring the Uninsured: Issues and Options* (October, 1988), 212 pages; and *Cost and Effects of Extending Health*

Insurance Coverage (October, 1988), 176 pages. All three studies were jointly printed by the House Committee on Education and Labor, and the House Committee on Energy and Commerce.

References

Amendments to the Legislative Reorganization Act of 1946. (1970). 84 Stat. 1181.

Annual Report. (1986, December). Report for the Congressional Research Service to the Joint Committee on the Library for Fiscal Year 1986.

Children in poverty. (1985, May 22). WMCP 99-8, Washington, DC: Government Printing Office.

Congress and foreign policy. 1974. (1975). Washington, DC: Government Printing Office. Congressional Research Service Reports.

Congress and the nation's environment. (1973, January 20). Washington, DC: Government Printing Office.

Congressional Record (Daily Edition). (1914, June 26).

Congressional Record (Daily Edition). (1980, March 27).

Cost and effects of extending health insurance coverage. (1988, October). Washington, DC: Government Printing Office.

Designing a retirement system for federal workers covered by Social Security. (1984, December). Committee print 98-17 of the House Committee on Post Office and Civil Service. Washington, DC: Government Printing Office.

Ebeler, J., et al. *National health insurance* (1976). Congressional Research Service Report IPP 76-5.

Economic developments in countries of Eastern Europe. (1970). Washington, DC: Government Printing Office.

The federal employee health benefits program: Possible strategies for reform. (1989, May 24). CP 101-5 of the House Committee on Post Office and Civil Service. Washington, DC: Government Printing Office.

Goodrum, C. (1968, April 15). The reference factory revisited. *Library Journal, 93,* 1577-80.

Health insurance and the uninsured: Background data and analysis. (1988, May). Washington, DC: Government Printing Office.

House Committee on Banking, Finance, and Urban Affairs. (1983). *Housing—A reader.* Committee print 98-5. Washington, DC: Government Printing Office.

House Committee on Ways and Means. (1984, July 25). *Effects of the Omnibus Budget Reconciliation Act of 1981 (OBRA) welfare changes and the recession on poverty.* WMCP 98-33. Washington, DC: Government Printing Office.

In the Matter of the EXXON CORP. et al., Docket No. 8934 (1980, June 30).

Insuring the uninsured: Issues and options. (1988, October). Washington, DC: Government Printing Office.

Kingdon, J. W. (1984). *Agendas, alternatives, and public policies.* Boston: Little, Brown.

Legislative Reorganization Act (LRA) of 1946, as amended 2 USC 166.

McClure, B. (1976). *Crime in the United States: The Federal Response.* Congressional Research Service Report #IPP76-6.

Robinson, W. (1989). Policy analysis for Congress: Lengthening the time horizon. *Journal of Policy Analysis and Management, 8*(1), 1-9.

Schick, A. (1976, June). *Complex policymaking in the U.S. Senate* (Report prepared for the Commission on the Operation of the Senate.) Washington, DC: Government Printing Office.

Science, technology and American diplomacy. (1971, October). Washington, DC: Government Printing Office.

Senate Resolution 396. (1980, March 22). Congressional Record (daily edition), pp. 53162-3.

Shipp, P. R. (1989). Anticipating future congressional action: Designing a new retirement income system. *Journal of Policy Analysis and Management, 8*(1), 13-17.

Technical information for the Congress. (1969). Washington, DC: Government Printing Office.

Toward a modern Senate. (1976). (Senate Document 94-278.) Washington, DC: Government Printing Office.

11

The Evolution of the General Accounting Office: From Voucher Audits to Program Evaluations

Harry S. Havens

The United States General Accounting Office (GAO) is a nonpartisan agency in the legislative branch of government. It was created by the Budget and Accounting Act of 1921, with the statutory responsibility (among other things) ". . . to investigate, at the seat of government or elsewhere, all matters relating to the receipt, disbursement, and application of public funds. . . ." (Budget and Accounting Act of 1921, Section 312)

Origins and Early Years

The creation of GAO was an outgrowth of the same "good government" era in the United States that gave rise to the executive budget and the U.S. Bureau of the Budget. Indeed, they were established in the same legislative act.[1] It seems clear that one of the primary motivations for including GAO in the package was the congressional view that if the president was to have the enhanced power flowing from control over budget proposals and the creation of "his" Budget Bureau, Congress needed a counterweight in the form of enhanced ability to see how the money that it appropriated was being spent.

The 1921 act included strong protections for the independence of GAO, of which the most important are those relating to the tenure of its leader, the Comptroller General of the United States. The president appoints the comptroller general, subject to Senate confirmation. Once confirmed, the comptroller general serves a fixed term of 15 years, from which he or she is removable only by impeachment or by joint resolution. Neither removal procedure has ever been attempted. On completion of his or her term, the comptroller general may not be reappointed and retires with full salary.

Initially, GAO's location in the structure of government was ambiguous. Clearly, GAO was created at the instigation of Congress, to satisfy its wishes for an independent auditor to whom it could look for information. At the same time, the presidential appointment of the comptroller general, together with GAO's inheritance from Treasury of some arguably executive functions, led some to conclude that GAO straddled the executive/legislative boundary, having a foot in both camps. Only 65 years later was the issue settled.

GAO has gone through three distinct eras since its creation. In the first period, until the end of World War II, GAO's work consisted largely of detailed auditing of individual vouchers. It was characterized by a highly formal, legalistic review of each voucher, with approval for payment and the settlement of the affected accounts being dependent on conformity with an elaborate set of rules governing the use of public funds. Some of these functions remain part of GAO's mission, such as reviewing the validity of government contracts (a responsibility now embodied in the Competition in Contracting Act) and providing advisory opinions to executive branch officials on the legality of expenditures.

Officially, GAO in the early years took no responsibility for judging the wisdom of a particular expenditure, only its legality. The conservative leanings of the first comptroller general (J. Raymond McCarl, who served out his full 15-year term from 1921 to 1936), however, brought him into frequent conflict with Roosevelt's New Deal, which McCarl saw as full of wasteful spending. In one now humorous incident, GAO questioned how the Interior Department intended to use a camera it had purchased. The penciled response to the auditors from Secretary Harold Ickes was brief and to the point, "To take pictures, you damned fool."

McCarl's retirement in 1936 created an opportunity to reassess GAO's status. The Brownlow Committee in 1937 recommended a major revamping of GAO that would have limited GAO exclusively to a postaudit role (Brownlow Committee, 1937). These proposals were rejected by Congress. When Roosevelt finally accepted this outcome, he selected a comptroller general whom he expected to be more politically sympathetic: Lindsay Warren, a Congressman from

North Carolina, who became, in effect, the second comptroller general. (Fred Brown, appointed in 1939, was officially the second but served barely a year before resigning for health reasons.)

The ideological conflict between GAO and the New Deal, which had incurred Roosevelt's wrath during the McCarl era, never surfaced with Warren. With the advent of World War II and the crushing burden of mobilization on all the institutions of government, ideological issues evaporated. Instead, Warren, who served from 1940 to 1954, eventually presided over the institutional transformation of GAO.

The Second GAO

The voucher audit process, which had begun to creak badly under the weight of a growing government during the New Deal, utterly collapsed in World War II. Even with a staff of over 14,000—most auditing clerks—GAO could not begin to keep up with the waves of paper. The GAO annual report for 1945, for example, reported a backlog of 35 million unaudited vouchers.

In 1947, after the end of the war, Comptroller General Warren joined with Treasury Secretary John Snyder and Budget Director James Webb to design a new approach to financial management and auditing. The departments and agencies would do their own voucher checking and accounting; GAO would concentrate on prescribing accounting principles and checking the adequacy of financial management procedures and controls. This concept was subsequently endorsed by the First Hoover Commission and embodied in the Accounting and Auditing Act of 1950.

This first transformation of GAO was traumatic. From a staff of almost 15,000 at the end of the war, GAO shrank to about 6,000 by the end of the Warren era. The new GAO had no use for the army of auditing clerks who had populated the organization before and during the war. Instead, GAO needed—and hired—new-style auditors (trained in accounting) who were required for the new mission.

Under the leadership of Warren and Joseph Campbell, who was appointed by Eisenhower, served from 1954 to 1965, and was the first certified public accountant (CPA) to hold the office of comptroller general, the GAO of the 1950s and 1960s was modeled on the public accounting firms of the time. It was staffed increasingly by professional accountants, many being CPAs, and a significant number were recruited directly from public accounting firms. At the same time, the overall size of the staff continued to decline and was barely 4,000 when Campbell left office.

In the early 1960s GAO had grown increasingly critical of the defense contracting community, repeatedly issuing public reports alleging overpayment and demanding that individually named contractors make voluntary refunds. This policy incurred the wrath of the defense contractors. The controversy culminated in 1965 in the Holifield Hearings, named after the chair of the Military Operations Subcommittee of the House Committee on Government Operations. Chairman Chet Holifield severely castigated GAO for its supposedly unfair treatment of the defense industry. Although these criticisms of GAO were not supported unanimously within Chairman Holifield's own subcommittee, in the committee's report (U.S. Congress, House, 1966), Chairman Holifield prevailed. Whether or not his criticism was justified, the episode had two effects: It almost certainly hastened the retirement of Campbell for reasons of health, and it probably caused GAO to become much less aggressive in its audits of defense contracts.[2]

The Modern GAO

Lyndon Johnson chose Elmer Staats as Campbell's successor. Staats was an economist and a career civil servant with almost 30 years' experience in the Bureau of the Budget, including service as deputy director under four presidents. This appointment set the stage for the second great transformation of GAO.

Staats, who served as comptroller general from 1966 to 1981, brought in analytical approaches that were gaining currency in the executive branch as part of the Planning, Programming, and Budgeting system (PPBS), a highly structured, analytically based framework for decision making. Staats believed, and convinced others, that these forms of analysis would be useful to Congress in overseeing federal programs and that providing them would be a logical extension of GAO's auditing function. The new GAO responsibilities were given a statutory foundation in the Legislative Reorganization Act of 1970 and reenacted in expanded form in the Congressional Budget and Impoundment Control Act of 1974.

Initially, the Staats initiatives required grafting onto the existing CPA and management audit functions the new roles of program evaluation and policy analysis, together with a staff having the training and the technical skills needed for this work. Over the longer run, the new functions (and the people performing them) had to be integrated into the mainstream operations of the institution, creating a truly interdisciplinary organization capable of carrying out a full range of audits, management reviews, evaluations, and other studies.

Introducing Program Evaluation

In 1967, only a year after Staats took office, GAO was asked to make its first major program evaluation. Senator Winston Prouty sponsored a provision of the Economic Opportunity Act Amendments requiring GAO to review the effectiveness of the poverty programs. This work was performed by GAO staff with the assistance of a number of consultants. The success of GAO's efforts demonstrated that we could examine complex issues affecting politically sensitive programs without great risk to the institution, so long as the work was done carefully and professionally. These were standards with which the GAO staff could be very comfortable, even though they were still learning how to apply the standards to a new type of work.

In the 1970s, program evaluations (usually called program results audits) became an increasingly common activity. GAO reviewed the effectiveness of the municipal waste water treatment construction grant program, the New Jersey negative income tax experiment, planned bed capacity of Defense Department hospitals, and the cost-effectiveness of automobile safety devices.

Other Issues

As the U.S. buildup of forces in Southeast Asia proceeded, Congress began asking questions about how the money was being spent; it became apparent that a GAO presence was needed. Accordingly, for several years GAO maintained an office in Saigon with up to 30 permanent staff, often augmented by staff from other locations on temporary duty. Its work focused on issues of supply and logistics.

The oil supply disruption of 1973 was a major factor in GAO's movement into policy analysis. As the gas lines lengthened, Congress turned to GAO for reliable information on what was happening. In a relatively traditional role, GAO began assessing the quality of available data. This assessment was formalized in the Energy Conservation and Production Act, which requires GAO to review the quality of data produced by the Energy Information Agency.

Throughout the 1970s, GAO issued numerous reports on the breeder reactor program. Finally, in 1980 and 1981, GAO advised Congress to "fish or cut bait" (GAO, 1980). GAO favored retaining the nuclear option and continued research on the breeder concept, including completion of the Clinch River Breeder Reactor project. But the current situation was a waste of hundreds of millions of dollars each year without any visible progress toward completion of the project. GAO recommended that Congress either require the Department of Energy to complete the CRBR or terminate it. Shortly thereafter, Congress terminated the CRBR.

Reemphasizing Defense in the 1980s

Charles Bowsher, the current comptroller general, was appointed by President Reagan and assumed office in 1981. Bowsher was the second CPA to hold the position. In this period GAO expanded its work on defense, in response to the defense buildup begun by President Carter and accelerated dramatically under President Reagan.

Routine assignments ranged from reviewing problems in the way the military ordered spare parts to assessing the problems in the B-1 bomber avionics systems and the resulting implications for the B-1's ability to perform its assigned strategic mission. GAO returned to detailed auditing of individual defense contracts but with a purpose very different from that in the 1950s and 1960s. The focus was on the systemic causes of contract overpricing and cost overruns. Revelation of abuses was not an end in itself, but a way of dramatizing systemic problems.

While reimmersing itself in some of the details of contract auditing, the range of GAO defense work broadened. GAO went from looking at the ability of the Aegis cruiser to perform its assigned mission to examining the vaunted 600-ship Navy, assessing potential financial and operational implications of the mismatch between the composition of the fleet and the maritime strategy it was supposed to carry out in time of war.

Financial Management and the Budget

The expanding scope of GAO's activities in the 1980s was exemplified also by its increasingly outspoken concern about the financial condition of the federal government and its fiscal policy, and by the role that Congress sought to assign GAO under the Gramm-Rudman-Hollings (GRH) deficit reduction mechanism (Balanced Budget Act, 1985). In the Congressional Budget Act of 1974, Congress assigned most of the responsibilities for supporting the congressional budget process to the Congressional Budget Office. GAO was given an oversight and assistance role with respect to budget systems and concepts and the quality of budget information. In addition, GAO retained its responsibilities for overseeing the government's accounting systems. In the 1970s GAO pursued these responsibilities in a low-key manner, but in the 1980s GAO became increasingly concerned about the government's finances.

While recognizing that the underlying problems of fiscal policy were grounded in unresolved political and ideological conflict, GAO nevertheless concluded that inadequacies in budget presentation and process were significant contributing factors. Archaic accounting and management information systems often made it impossible to obtain reliable information for managerial decisions and policy oversight, while weak internal controls created a breeding ground for the type of fraud and mismanagement that engulfed the Department of Housing and Urban Development (HUD).

These concerns culminated in the 1985 publication of the first in a series of GAO "white papers" on the federal government's financial management system (GAO, 1985a). GAO suggested a conceptual framework for a new financial management system embodying an integrated approach to the budget and accounting components. GAO also renewed its emphasis on financial auditing. It urged the departments and agencies to produce meaningful annual financial statements and to ensure the reliability of those statements through independent audit. Those views gained increasing acceptance, to the point at which GAO in 1989 audited the financial statements of the U.S. Air Force, an effort whose scope exceeded that of any previous financial audit in history.

Meanwhile, the continued inability of Congress and the president to agree on an acceptable budget policy set the stage for enactment of the GRH legislation.[3] For reasons that remain obscure, Congress chose

GAO as the agency to judge whether the deficit was going to exceed the statutory thresholds and, if so, for allocating the required spending reductions.[4] The Supreme Court, however, ruled that GAO's involvement in the GRH arrangement was unconstitutional (Bowsher v. Synar, 1986). The functions involved in implementing GRH were of an executive nature and, therefore, could not be assigned to the comptroller general. The Court finally resolved the issue that had troubled GAO from its early years of whether it was an executive or legislative agency. GAO's evolution over the past 40 years had moved the institution so much closer to Congress that its allegiance was obvious.

GAO was removed from the GRH operating mechanism after pulling the trigger once, and it stepped back to its accustomed role of monitoring the operation and reporting on results. Even so, GAO remained an active participant in aspects of the budget debate. In a series of reports prepared for the 1988-1989 presidential and congressional transition, for example, the comptroller general took a particularly strong position on the urgent need to deal with the substance of the deficit (GAO, 1988a) accompanied by a renewed call to reexamine the way the budget was presented (GAO, 1988b).

In 1989 these positions were developed further in a report on the implications of the accumulating Social Security Trust fund surpluses (GAO, 1989a, January) and in another "white paper" on the need to overhaul the budget structure and process (GAO, 1989c, October). Involvement with the budget, as with the rest of the financial management system, is assuredly part of GAO's future.

Relations With Congress

As the mission of the agency evolved, it was inevitable—indeed, it was intended—that GAO's relationship with Congress also would be transformed. GAO sought to make its work more immediately relevant to the legislative policy process. As a result, Congress and its committees became more directly interested in the scope, the nature, and the timing of that work.

From its beginnings under the 1921 act, GAO was required to perform investigations requested by Congress and its committees. For the first half century, that mandate was of relatively little consequence. As late as 1969, it is estimated that no more than 10% of GAO's reports were in response to congressional requests, and GAO officials testified only 24 times.

By 1977 congressional requests and statutorily mandated audits and reviews were absorbing 35% of GAO staff resources, and GAO officials testified before Congress 111 times. The trend was irreversible. In 1988, 80 to 100% (depending on the subject area) of GAO's resources were involved in responding to specific congressional requests, and GAO officials testified at committee hearings well over 200 times.

Staff Resources

For the most part, new ideas, new responsibilities, and new ways of doing business were introduced incrementally. Unlike the Warren-era changes, the Staats/Bowsher transformation did not require the wholesale dismissal and replacement of staff. Nevertheless, it clearly has affected the staff in several respects. The first is numbers. From a low of about 4,100 staff in the mid-1960s, GAO grew to a peak of about 5,300 in the late 1970s and then settled back to the 5,000-5,100 range, where it remained in the 1980s.

The second is the composition of the staff; it has continued to evolve. Among Staats's first initiatives were efforts to expand the base of recruiting. He included business administration graduates without substantial training in accounting and went on to such disciplines as public administration, operations research, engineering, statistics, and economics. Bowsher continued this trend and, by the mid- to late-1980s, no such thing as a "standard" GAO recruit existed. Today, the largest single group comes with a background in public administration or public policy and a strong base of quantitative skills, but virtually every academic discipline is now represented. In addition, the staff includes people with advanced academic training and line experience in virtually every substantive field touched by government, from defense to health care, energy, and tax law.

GAO still recruits accountants in significant numbers, but most of them are hired specifically to do accounting and financial auditing work. Similarly, GAO recruits economists to perform economic analysis work, computer scientists to review computer systems, and trained criminal investigators to pursue allegations of corruption.

The "promote from within" tradition established in the Campbell era has been somewhat relaxed. A large majority of GAO management is composed of people who have made their careers in the organization, and that pattern seems likely to continue. Significantly, however, almost a quarter of GAO's Senior Executive Service (SES) incumbents have had substantial professional experience with other organizations before joining GAO, and that ratio is even higher at the top. Of the 13 most senior positions in GAO,[5] more than half have prior experience in other government agencies or in the private sector. Of these positions, only one—that of comptroller general—is filled by what some would consider a political appointment. Every other position in GAO is filled through a merit-based competitive selection process, from new entry-level recruits to the top of the SES.

In the mid-1960s the professional staff was uniformly composed of white males. Top leadership became committed to change, and in time an aggressive equal opportunity and affirmative action program became successful at all levels, from entry-level recruitment to promotion into the SES. One of the important advantages of the 15-year term of the comptroller general is the ability to establish and sustain long-term agency policy directions. The GAO work force is not yet as balanced as it would like at the more senior levels, but GAO's goals are ambitious and it is moving firmly toward them.

What Makes GAO Work Special?

GAO takes a problem-solving approach to issues. When GAO identifies a problem in the design or implementation of a program, the institutional bias is to propose a solution to the problem. GAO reports routinely contain recommendations addressed to Congress or to the administering agency. The recommendations range from modest adjustments in operating procedures to major shifts in national policies. GAO's recommendations, and the analysis supporting them, become public knowledge. All GAO reports, unless classified for national security reasons, are available to the press and the public.

Other special characteristics of GAO are its field structure and its access to data. In addition to its headquarters organization in Washington, GAO has 14 regional offices in the United States and 2 overseas offices. GAO can place its staff on location, permitting direct observation of events and collection of raw data. To carry out its fieldwork,

GAO has a statutory right of access to virtually any records or other information in the possession of government agencies. In addition, GAO's reputation for objectivity and for care in handling data means that the staff often can gain voluntary access to data outside government unavailable to other researchers.

The access to information and the field staff that can examine matters at the site give GAO reports a special quality. For example, when questions arose about the condition of the nation's nuclear weapons complex or about progress in cleaning up toxic waste dumps, GAO could back up its analysis with dramatic pictures and other hard evidence, coupled with testimony based on firsthand observation.

The emphasis on "hard" evidence is characteristic of GAO. Very little of GAO's work involves speculation, and GAO rarely relies on expert opinion as the principal support for conclusions and recommendations. The usual GAO report relies heavily on data that GAO has either gathered itself or tested for reliability. This approach reflects GAO's grounding in the auditing profession. In auditing, the reliability of data must be assured before it is used for decision making. Thus, GAO is comfortable using existing data in its work so long as the quality of that data can be established with reasonable confidence. In its program audits and evaluations, GAO is a frequent user of the large-scale data bases maintained by the departments and agencies and, when needed, by organizations outside government. GAO will invest substantial time and effort in testing the data before using them or in collecting original data when existing data are inadequate.

In one recent case, GAO was asked to assess the effect on air fares of increasing concentration in the airline industry. In particular, GAO was asked to examine the consequences of one or two airlines' achieving dominance in serving a city. GAO compared the fare per passenger-mile for those enplaning in 15 airports dominated by one or two airlines with 38 airports that were not so dominated, using fare data collected routinely by the Department of Transportation. In checking that data, however, GAO discovered not only the usual random errors that are found in almost any large data base but also some outdated edit controls that systematically were screening out valid fares. Once these problems were corrected, GAO was able to proceed with the analysis.[6] GAO found that fares were strongly and positively related to concentration; they typically rose significantly after an airline established a dominant position.

In many cases, existing data are inadequate to answer the questions posed by Congress. In 1981, for example, Congress enacted significant restrictions on eligibility and benefits in the program of Aid to Families with Dependent Children (AFDC). It then asked GAO to assess the impact of these amendments in terms of (a) AFDC caseload and cost, (b) work effort of affected families, and (c) economic well-being of affected families. GAO examined the available data, including data bases maintained by academic and other nongovernment researchers. After careful consideration, GAO concluded that while the data provided useful insights, they were inadequate to establish cause-and-effect relationships. Accordingly, GAO supplemented available data with the results of detailed evaluations at each of five sites, chosen to reflect diversity in program characteristics, economic context, and so on. At these sites, GAO collected data from thousands of case records and hundreds of interviews with people who had lost AFDC benefits because of the 1981 amendments. The analysis showed a significant, nontransient decline in AFDC caseload and cost, no indication that people quit work to regain lost AFDC benefits, a significant loss of income for the families affected, and a special hardship for some families from loss of Medicaid coverage (GAO, 1984 and 1985b).

Assuring Institutional Credibility

GAO's reliance on hard data and its insistence on establishing the reliability of data before using them are visible indicators of the institution's concern for credibility. That credibility is built on GAO's values of independence, objectivity, and accuracy.

Independence and objectivity can be threatened by a committee that is convinced of the rightness of a particular policy position and wants a GAO report not to illuminate the issue but to support that position. Accuracy can be threatened by the temptation to take short-cuts in order to satisfy a committee's demand that GAO meet an unrealistic deadline. Recognizing these risks, GAO goes to great lengths to protect against them.

Safeguards start with the GAO strategic planning process, in which GAO defines the issues it judges to be of central importance, identifies the questions it believes should be pursued, and allocates available staff resources. Judgments about priorities are formed from extensive discussions both with committee staff concerning the anticipated legislative calendar and with subject matter experts and agency officials about emerging trends, problems, and policy initiatives. The dialogue, particularly with the committee staffs, is mutually beneficial. GAO learns what concerns are uppermost in the minds of committee members and staff. At the same time, GAO observations about emerging problems often lead a committee to adjust its agenda to take account of an issue of which the committee was not previously aware.[7]

Not all committee requests, of course, fit neatly into GAO's internal sense of relative priorities. And priorities change as events and problems emerge. In any year, GAO initiates well over 1,000 new assignments. The first step, in the case of a congressional request, is for staff to meet with the committee's or member's staff to define the request. Experienced congressional staff usually call an informal meeting before sending the official request. In these discussions, GAO's staff negotiate agreement on a study that can be performed in a balanced fashion (no hatchet jobs, please), is technically feasible (please do not ask GAO to count the number of illegal drug abusers), and involves a reasonable claim on GAO's limited staff resources (GAO would rather not duplicate the efforts of the inspectors general or Defense Contract Audit Agency). Usually, discussions at the staff level are successful. In the event of problems, however, GAO is never reluctant to elevate the issue to a discussion between senior officials of GAO and the Congressperson or the Senator initiating the request.

Once the request has been negotiated, the assignment goes through GAO's internal review processes. Each assignment is reviewed by the leadership of the division in which the work will be performed and (separately) by the comptroller general and the senior management team. The reviews center on certain key considerations. Is the assignment appropriate for GAO? Is someone else already working on the issue? Questions about estimated budgetary costs, for example, would be more properly directed to the Congressional Budget Office. GAO staff are responsible for ensuring the absence of unnecessary duplication. Is the issue worth the resources needed to explore it? Is the right question being asked? Does GAO have an efficient and a reliable way of developing the data needed? Is the proposed analytical approach likely to yield a valid result? Are the right people working on the assignment? Will the results be available in time? These questions are inherently subjective, but the process of asking them and debating the answers is an essential safeguard against waste of scarce resources and, more importantly, against the risk of starting a study that is biased or technically flawed from the outset.

As the fieldwork and analysis are performed, routine supervisory reviews take place on the progress of the job. Usually, these reviews center on assessing progress against the assignment plan and solving the inevitable problems that arise. In addition, on congressional request assignments, contact with the requesters is frequent to ensure that they are informed of progress and problems and that the requested work is still relevant to congressional needs.

As an assignment nears completion, the safeguards become intensified, focusing on the written product (formal report, statement for hearings, etc.). Multiple independent reviews are made before the product can be published. These reviews take several forms, but the intended cumulative effect is (a) to provide the functional equivalent of the professional peer review to which academic research is commonly subjected, and (b) to apply sufficient tests to the content of the report to ensure that it meets GAO quality standards. The more important or complex the issue, the more reviews the report receives.

Each report is also "referenced." A fully qualified staffer must check every number and every statement of fact in the report, identifying the source in the fieldwork or the analysis (the "workpapers" in GAO parlance) and confirming that the report accurately reflects the information in the workpapers.

Unless explicitly prohibited by the requester, written comments on GAO's findings, conclusions, and recommendations are requested routinely by GAO from the agency on whose activities it is reporting. When these official comments are received, they are published as part of the report. If an agency's comments indicate disagreement with the contents of the draft, the GAO staff must analyze those comments and respond to them before the report can be published. This response also is published as part of the report. If, as sometimes happens, the agency provides information that was previously not available to GAO or points out flaws in analysis or logic, GAO reexamines its conclusions. If GAO decides that the agency arguments are valid, it makes an appropriate change before publishing the report.

Another type of independent review is given to reports that involve complex forms of analysis or deal with sensitive policy issues. For example, any report dealing with questions of economics or relying on economic analysis must be reviewed by GAO's chief economist, who is independent of the operating divisions and reports directly to the comptroller general. When issues are tricky or politically sensitive, the comptroller general and members of the immediate staff routinely review the reports.

To ensure that safeguards on quality remain strong, GAO has instituted a mechanism for systematically reviewing its procedures for conducting studies. The Post Assignment Quality Review system (PAQRS) involves an independent staff that selects a sample of reports and examines in detail how the assignments were planned and carried out. For each step of the assignment, actions by the GAO staff are compared with the required procedures. Any deviations are analyzed to determine why they occurred and what effect they may have had. The results of the PAQRS reviews are reported to GAO senior management both to reinforce the importance of the quality control procedures and to identify procedures that may need modification.

The laborious, tedious, and often time-consuming lengths to which GAO goes to ensure the quality of its products are a frequent source of frustration both to the GAO staff and to congressional clients. They are one of the reasons, along with the complexity of the work itself, that the average GAO assignment takes 9 to 12 months to complete.

When GAO issues a report or when GAO officials present testimony before a congressional committee, the comptroller general and GAO as an institution stand behind that product. Conclusions and recommendations are supported by GAO's institutional stature, not just the professional reputation of the individuals who produced them. Indeed, it is a relatively recent innovation for GAO even to identify in a report the people who worked on it. This acknowledgment is being done now as a means of providing individual recognition, but no diminution of institutional responsibility has occurred.

Conclusion

Today's GAO is an organization of about 5,000 people who take pride in carrying out a modern version of the original mandate from the 1921 act: ". . . to investigate, at the seat of government or elsewhere, all matters relating to the receipt, disbursement, and application of public funds. . . ."

As the world has changed around us, the work needed to satisfy that mandate also has changed, as has the institution of GAO. The work and the staff performing it have become more sophisticated technically, more policy oriented, and more closely attuned to the needs of Congress. But the purpose of the mandate, GAO's central mission, has not changed. To GAO, it means always finding a way to learn the facts, no matter the issue about which Congress has inquired, and putting those facts together into a story that is accurate and balanced and with recommendations that are appropriate for solving any identified problems, no matter whose ox may be gored.

Fulfilling that mandate is a challenge that can take GAO people anywhere in the world, from examining files and records in an agency's Washington headquarters to observing the tests of a new weapon system and analyzing the results to following the cash of a foreign assistance grant in the third world to assessing the role of computer failures in the 1987 stock market crash to evaluating the effects of new, federally mandated procedures in a local welfare office. Wherever GAO must go to learn the facts, there you will find the GAO staff.

Notes

1. For a more detailed examination of the history of GAO, see Mosher, 1979 and 1984. Frederick C. Mosher's work is the primary basis for the historical discussion in this chapter. Another valuable source is Wilbur, 1988.

2. Other factors undoubtedly contributed to GAO's lessened interest in contract auditing, including the creation of the Defense Contract Audit Agency (DCAA), an organization devoted exclusively to that task.

3. The Balanced Budget and Emergency Deficit Control Act of 1985, Public Law 99-177, approved December 12, 1985. For a more detailed discussion of this episode, see Havens, 1986.

4. The decision was made in a late-night session of the conference committee, and no formal record of the discussion was made. Most observers believe the principal consideration was a legacy of distrust of the executive branch and especially of what was seen as a politicized Office of Management and Budget.

5. The comptroller general, the special assistant to the comptroller general, the general counsel, and 10 assistant comptrollers general.

6. Statement by Kenneth M. Mead, GAO, before the Subcommittee on Aviation, Senate Committee on Commerce, Science, and Transportation. See GAO, 1989b.

7. Needless to say, these efforts do not always have the expected effect. For a number of years, GAO and the inspector general of the Department of Housing and Urban Development had been warning about weak management and lax controls in HUD. For various reasons, the committees chose not to follow up on these matters until the HUD scandal broke in the spring of 1989.

References

Accounting and Auditing Act of 1950. (1950, September 12). Public Law 81-784 at 64 Stat. 834.

Balanced Budget and Emergency Deficit Control Act of 1985. (1985, December 12). Public Law 99-177.

Bowsher v. Synar, 106 S. Ct. 3181 (1986).

Brownlow Committee. (1937). *Report of the President's Committee on Administrative Management*. Washington, DC: U.S. Government Printing Office.

Budget and Accounting Act of 1921. (1921, June 10). Public Law 67-13.

Competition in Contracting Act (1984, July 18). Public Law 98-369 at 98 Stat. 1175.

Congressional Budget and Impoundment Control Act of 1974. (1974, July 12). Public Law 93-334.

Economic Opportunity Act Amendments (1967, December 23). Public Law 90-222.

Energy Conservation and Production Act (1976, August 14). Public Law 94-385.

General Accounting Office. (1980, September 22). *U.S. Fast Breeder Reactor Program needs direction* (No. GAO/EMD-80-81). Washington, DC.

General Accounting Office. (1984, April). An evaluation of the 1981 AFDC changes: Initial analysis (No. GAO/PEMD-84-6). Washington, DC.

General Accounting Office. (1985a, February). *Managing the cost of government: Building an effective financial management structure* (No. GAO/AFMD-85-35 and 35A, 2 vols.). Washington, DC.

General Accounting Office. (1985b, July). *An evaluation of the 1981 AFDC changes: Final report* (No. GAO/PEMD-85-4). Washington, DC.

General Accounting Office. (1988a, November). *The budget deficit* (No. GAO/OCG-89-1TR). Washington, DC.

General Accounting Office. (1988b, November). *Financial management issues* (No. GAO/OCG-89-7TR). Washington, DC.

General Accounting Office. (1989a, January). *Social Security: The trust fund reserve accumulation, the economy, and the federal budget* (No. GAO/HRD-89-44). Washington, DC.

General Accounting Office. (1989b, June). *Air fares and service and concentrated airports* (No. GAO/T-RCED-89-37). Washington, DC.

General Accounting Office. (1989c, October). *Managing the cost of government: Proposals for reforming federal budgeting practices* (No. GAO/AFMD-90-1). Washington, DC.

Havens, H. S. (1986). Gramm-Rudman-Hollings: Origins and implementation. *Public Budgeting and Finance, 6*(3), 4-24.

Legislative Reorganization Act of 1970. (1970, October 26). Public Law 91-510.

Mosher, F. C. (1979). *The GAO: The quest for accountability in American government*. Boulder, CO: Westview.

Mosher, F. C. (1984). *A tale of two agencies*. Baton Rouge: Louisiana State University Press.

U.S. Congress. House. (1966, March 23). *Defense contract audits*. 90th Cong., 2nd sess. House Rept. 1132.

Wilbur, M. H. (1988, March). *An early history of the General Accounting Office, 1921-1943*. (No. GAO/OP-1-HO). Washington, DC: General Accounting Office.

12

The Congressional Budget Office: On the One Hand, On the Other

James L. Blum

Institutional Background

The Congressional Budget Office (CBO) is the youngest of the four analytic support agencies of the U.S. Congress. It was created by the Congressional Budget Act of 1974 and started operations on February 24, 1975, with the appointment of its first director, Alice M. Rivlin. In comparison with the charters of the other support agencies, CBO's mission is relatively narrow: to provide economic and budgetary information in support of the congressional budget and legislative processes. The subject matter of the agency's work is quite broad, however, since the budget of the U.S. government covers a wide range of activities and plays a major role in the national economy.

The Congressional Budget Act was intended to strengthen the ability of Congress to deal with the federal budget and to restore the balance of budgetary power, which many people felt had tipped too much toward the executive branch. The act established a new process for setting congressional budget targets, with the aim of providing more discipline to the passage of appropriations, other spending measures, and tax legislation. It also created three new congressional institutions to carry out the process: a Committee on the Budget in both the House of Representatives and the Senate, each with its own staff, and the Congressional Budget Office.[1]

AUTHOR'S NOTE: Helpful data and comments were provided by Earl Armbrust, Elizabeth Clark, Mark Desautels, Robert Hale, Roy Meyers, Frederick Ribe, and Paul Van de Water.

Legislative Responsibilities

Although the Budget Act spelled out the functions of CBO, many of the descriptions were quite general and remained to be worked out. Basically, CBO's functions can be divided into three categories: budgetary assistance, economic analysis, and policy analysis. The act is more specific on the first function than on the other two. Budgetary activities include cost estimates on pending legislation, scorekeeping reports, and 5-year budget projections. For the economic and policy analysis functions, the act directs CBO to produce an annual report "with respect to fiscal policy. . .taking into account projected economic factors," that would also discuss "national budget priorities" and alternative allocations of budgetary resources. CBO is also directed to produce such additional reports as "may be necessary and appropriate (Congressional Budget Act, 1974, section 202(f))."

Even more generally, the act states that the duty and function of CBO is to provide the budget committees, the appropriations and taxing committees, and all other committees with whatever information may be requested on budgetary or other matters within their respective jurisdictions. Priority is to be given to assisting the budget, appropriations, and taxing committees; and work for the other committees—aside from cost estimates and other budgetary information—is to be provided "to the extent practicable."

CBO Products

A major CBO product is its annual report to the budget committees. This report has evolved over time to consist of two separate documents: one providing economic and budget projections for the next 5 years, and the other presenting a collection of spending and revenue options for reducing the budget deficit.[2] The economic and budget volume often includes a discussion of a current fiscal policy issue, such as the implications of federal deficits for economic growth. The Budget Act requires that the annual report be submitted by February 15. The economic and budget projections are updated customarily in mid-August.

Economic Forecasts

The Congressional Budget Office is the only entity of the legislative branch that makes economic forecasts and projections. CBO's forecasts are usually fairly close to the consensus of private forecasters, but they are generally less optimistic than those made by the administration, particularly as they relate to budget estimates.

For many years, the budget committees used the CBO forecast and projections as the basis for their annual budget resolutions, but lately those of the administration have been used. Two probable reasons for this change in practice are (a) the Office of Management and Budget (OMB) now makes the final determination of whether spending reductions are needed to reach the annual deficit targets specified by the Balanced Budget Act, and (b) using CBO's less optimistic assumptions would make reaching a fixed deficit target more difficult.

Deficit Reduction Options

Since 1982, CBO has included in its annual report a separate volume on options for reducing the federal deficit. This document discusses alternative strategies for reducing the deficit and provides specific spending and revenue options for Congress to consider. The first of these reports was prepared in 1980 at the request of the House Budget Committee and proved to be so popular that it was made part of the CBO annual report two years later. It is still the most widely distributed of all CBO publications. The report has been used by many members of Congress, as well as outside groups, to develop deficit reduction proposals and to educate the public about the difficult choices involved in reducing the deficit.

Analysis of the President's Budget

Another popular CBO report is the annual analysis of the president's budget. The proposed budget is recast, using CBO's economic assumptions and estimating techniques. In recent years the analysis has shown that the president's budget proposals implied much larger deficits than estimated by OMB, if CBO's less optimistic (many would say "more realistic") assumptions were used.

Program Analysis

At the request of various congressional committees, CBO analyzes specific program and policy issues that affect the federal budget. These analyses, usually resulting in published reports and studies, examine current policies, develop alternative approaches, and project how the alternatives would affect current programs, as well as the federal budget and the economy. Program analyses do not offer policy recommendations. "On the one hand" and "on the other hand" are phrases used frequently in CBO reports and studies, and they characterize much of CBO's analytic work. Many CBO publications have had an influence extending beyond Capitol Hill, helping shape the public discussion of issues addressed in them.

CBO's published reports and studies typically take 9 to 12 months to complete, or even longer. Analyses conducted in a shorter time frame may result in unpublished staff papers or memoranda. The output of published reports and studies reached a peak of 38 in 1982, and unpublished papers numbered 49 in that year. The numbers have declined somewhat in recent years, as the focus of legislative activity has shifted because of budgetary pressures, and more analytical work has been produced in the form of papers, staff memoranda, or letters to committees.

Bill Cost Estimates

CBO prepares cost estimates for virtually every public bill reported by congressional committees to show how these legislative proposals would affect spending or revenues over the next 5 years. Other cost estimates are prepared for use in earlier stages of bill drafting, for floor amendments, and for conference committees. Since 1980 the number of federal cost estimates has ranged from 553 to 861, with an average of about 700 per year. A large part of CBO's bill-costing activity from 1981 through 1987 was for House and Senate committees receiving reconciliation instructions in the annual budget resolutions.

The CBO bill cost estimates have become an integral part of the legislative process. Committees refer to them increasingly at every stage of bill drafting. They often have an impact on the final outcome of legislation because they are used to determine whether the committees are in compliance with the annual budget resolutions and reconciliation instructions.

Scorekeeping

One of CBO's most important functions is to keep track of all spending and revenue legislation that is considered, so that Congress can know whether it is acting within the limits set by the annual budget resolutions. CBO's staff provide the budget and appropriations committees with frequent computer tabulations of congressional action on appropriation and other spending bills (and also on tax bills). The scorekeeping system keeps track of all bills affecting the budget from the time they are reported from committee to the time they are enacted into law. The scorekeeping data base is quite large (more than 1,000 separate spending accounts), and keeping it current takes a major effort.

Scorekeeping sounds like a relatively easy task, but it is in fact quite complicated and often controversial. Virtually no written rules exist, and scorekeeping conventions are challenged frequently by committees that feel pinched by the limits set in the annual budget resolutions. The two budget committees are the ultimate scorekeepers for Congress, for it is they, not CBO, that advise the parliamentarians on whether a point of order (used to prevent departure from a budget resolution) should apply to a particular revenue or spending bill. Scoring disputes are settled often by political compromises between the committees. Nevertheless, the budget committees look to CBO to provide the necessary technical judgments and numerical estimates that go into the scorekeeping decisions.

Congressional Testimony

In addition to providing published reports and studies, unpublished papers, staff memoranda, letters, and computer tabulations, CBO is asked frequently to testify before a variety of congressional committees. Numbers of hearings at which CBO testifies range from about 20 to 50 a year. This testimony is often in connection with an ongoing or completed report, though sometimes new analyses are prepared for such appearances.

Major CBO Clients

The Congressional Budget Office naturally is associated closely with the House and Senate Budget Committees. The Budget Act stipulated that the two committees get first priority for CBO services, that the two committees are responsible for providing congressional oversight of CBO activities, and that the two committees make recommendations on who should be appointed CBO director. But the budget committees are by no means the only clients. Budgetary assistance is provided to all the other committees in the form of bill cost estimates and scorekeeping tabulations. The majority of requests for CBO policy analyses that result in published studies come from the appropriations, taxing, and authorizing committees. Demands for CBO services, particularly for budgetary assistance, are about equally divided between the House of Representatives and the Senate.

Organization and Staffing

After considering recommendations received from the two budget committees, the Speaker of the House of Representatives and the President pro tempore of the Senate jointly appoint the CBO director. The appointment is required to be made without regard to political affiliation and solely on the basis of a candidate's fitness to perform the director's duties. The term of office is 4 years, with no limit to the number of terms a director may serve. The deputy director is appointed by the director, as are all CBO staff members. All appointments are made without regard to political affiliation and solely on the basis of professional competence.

So far, the CBO has had three directors, each a well-known economist with expertise in the federal budget process. Alice Rivlin served two terms, from 1975 to 1983; Rudolph G. Penner served one term, from 1983 to 1987; and Robert D. Reischauer became the third director in March 1989. During the 2-year hiatus between the Penner and Reischauer terms, two persons served as acting director: Edward M. Gramlich, who had been Penner's deputy, and James L. Blum, the Assistant Director for Budget Analysis.

Organizational structure has been very stable throughout CBO's short history. A choice was made at the outset to separate the "budget" and the "program analysis" staffs in order to ensure that CBO could fulfill its budgetary assistance responsibilities and also provide indepth policy analysis. The primary responsibility for preparing bill cost estimates, 5-year projections, and scorekeeping tabulations was assigned to the Budget Analysis Division. The Fiscal Analysis Division is responsible for preparing CBO's economic forecasts and longer run economic projections and for responding to requests for analyses of fiscal policy and other macroeconomic issues. The Tax Analysis Division is responsible for revenue estimates and for preparing requested studies on tax policy issues. Finally, three program divisions, representing broad areas of legislative concern and organized along functional lines, are responsible for preparing requested policy and program analyses: Natural Resources and Commerce, Human Resources and Community Development, and National Security. The director's office, a general counsel's office, and a central support staff (which includes a small general government program analysis unit) complete the staffing.

The number of CBO employees is limited by the agency's annual appropriations.[3] The limitation has risen from 193 positions in fiscal year 1976 to 226 positions in 1989. The initial plan was that about 45% of CBO's staff would be assigned to the program divisions and only 20% to budget analysis. As the work load for budgetary assistance proved greater than expected, resources were shifted. Today, 36% of the staff positions have been allocated to the Budget Analysis Division, which provides the bulk of CBO's budgetary assistance services. The program divisions include 31% of the staff; the Fiscal and Tax Analysis divisions, 17%; and the central support units, 16 percent.

CBO's Budget

CBO's 1989 appropriation was $18.4 million, slightly more than the $17.9 million appropriation for the Office of Technology Assessment (OTA), about 40% of the $44.7 million appropriation for the Congressional Research Service (CRS), and only 5% of the General Accounting Office's (GAO) $347.3 million appropriation. By comparison, the Office of Management and Budget's (OMB) appropriation for 1989 was $42.0 million. Measured in constant dollars, CBO's 1989 appropriation was about equal to the 1977 appropriation.

The largest part of CBO's expenditures is for personnel. During the past 5 years, personnel costs have risen from 56% of total obligations to 75%. The second largest component is computer costs, which have fallen sharply because of the large-scale use of microcomputers (every CBO analyst is provided a personal computer), the use of more efficient data base management software, and lower charges for computer time-sharing services as the result of reduced hardware costs.

Institutional Culture

The institutional culture has been conditioned by CBO's legislative mandate, its directors, and the congressional environment in which it operates. The legislative mandate was fairly general, allowing the first CBO director, Alice Rivlin, wide latitude. It was clear, however, that CBO was to operate in a nonpartisan manner. This nonpartisan stance was reinforced by emphatic instructions in the first CBO appropriation that the office was not to take a position on any policy issue. The results of CBO's work were to be made available to all members of Congress and to the public, unless the committee requesting a particular product explicitly directed otherwise. A further impetus toward nonpartisanship stems from the fact that CBO works for both houses of Congress, each with its own traditions and mores, and serves both the majority and minority in each house.

No Policy Recommendations

The nonpartisan stance has been instrumental in preserving CBO's reputation for professionalism and has enhanced the credibility of its budget estimates and analyses. Taking a policy position on a particular budget issue could bring charges of bias and would jeopardize the agency's usefulness to Congress.

The constraint against making policy recommendations is not universal among legislative agencies. It seems to apply to CRS but not to GAO. Perhaps the size of the GAO and the long tenure of its comptroller general protect it from the pressures felt by CBO and CRS. At other levels of government, however, legislative budget staffs similar to CBO often make policy recommendations (for example, the legislative analyst for the California state legislature routinely takes policy positions). This behavior would be unacceptable for CBO because of the intensely political nature of the congressional budget process.

CBO occasionally offers technical recommendations. It is directed sometimes to do so in making certain studies, but these relate only to technical areas in which the agency's recommendations are presumed to be based on professional expertise and not reflect political views. CBO is also generally recognized as having a quasipolitical role to play as a defender of budgetary integrity and rational planning. Accordingly, the agency has endorsed a multiyear approach to budgeting and has favored a comprehensive budget as against one fragmented into different parts for Social Security and other programs. On a more technical level, CBO has recommended that the budgetary treatment of credit programs should focus on subsidy costs and not cash flows and has suggested a number of technical provisions, such as the definition of a budget baseline that came to be included in the

Balanced Budget Act. Although those matters are sometimes controversial, CBO's recommendations usually are regarded as politically neutral.

Full Disclosure

CBO routinely discloses the assumptions and methods used for its cost estimates, budget projections, and program analyses. Some bill cost estimates are quite detailed because the basis for the estimates is complex. Occasionally, when there is no time to write up a formal cost estimate (this often happens with reconciliation bills), staff papers will be prepared later to explain important estimates.

This willingness to publish the methods underlying its cost estimates and other analyses adds to the general acceptance of CBO's work as objective and impartial. It also contributes to an openness among U.S. government analytic agencies that is the envy of many foreign government analysts. Occasionally, charges are made that CBO's work is biased, but the general view in Congress and the media is quite the opposite—that the work is unbiased and expertly done. Errors occur from time to time, sometimes spectacular ones, but these are disclosed when they become apparent.

Responsiveness

Three rules for success cover staff work on Capitol Hill. The first is to respond to the needs of members and committees. Analytical work must be completed and delivered in time for use in a committee markup or report. It was mainly for this reason that budgetary assistance and program analysis functions were assigned to separate staff units in CBO. (At OMB, to a large extent, budgetary work has crowded out program analysis.) Being responsive often means that work must be anticipated and started in advance of a committee request for a specific product. CBO usually gets high marks for responsiveness in both its program analyses and its cost estimates. It frequently communicates the results of analytic studies to committee staff through informal briefings in advance of published reports and often supplies informal cost estimates by telephone.

The second rule is to be clear and concise in presenting reports. This rule sometimes is referred to as "meeting the subway test"; that is, a member of Congress should be able to grasp the gist of an analysis in the time it takes to ride the subway between the House or Senate office buildings and the Capitol. CBO places great importance on readability and employs four full-time editors to enhance the quality of its written output. Good writing has become part of CBO's culture, in part because the first director insisted on clear exposition.

The third rule is not to surprise key members or committees with the unexpected findings. Committee chairs, ranking minority members, and staff directors like to know about critical budget estimates or analyses before they appear in the press, so that they will be able to respond to questions—particularly if the results are unfavorable to policies they champion. CBO, therefore, gives great attention to distributing its products to all interested parties and, if possible, simultaneously.

Independent Role

Although CBO is identified closely with the two budget committees, it has established an independent role in the legislative process. This independent role derives in part from serving a large constituency. Alice Rivlin established the principle that CBO worked for all of Congress and not just for the budget committees. CBO is not just a budget office that estimates the cost of legislative actions, but also is a policy analysis office that helps shape the content of legislation.

Another important part of establishing an independent role was the first director's success in publicizing CBO's products. The Budget Act makes clear that the public is to have access to CBO estimates and other information, but Rivlin went further by distributing copies of completed reports to the media, holding briefings, giving interviews, and making speeches. CBO quickly developed its own identity and became a source of stories on major public policy issues. Today, CBO remains a popular source of information, and press reports are an important vehicle for communicating the results of CBO studies to Congress.

Congress was concerned at the outset that CBO's policy analyses would duplicate the work of CRS, OTA, and GAO. To allay such concerns, the four agencies have established an interagency coordinating group and notification process designed to prevent unwarranted duplication of effort. Occasionally, they produce joint studies, but CBO has focused on establishing its own niche in the policy analysis field by emphasizing its comparative advantage in quantitative economic and budget analysis.

In the final analysis, CBO's independent role and credibility rest on the quality of its budget estimates and projections. CBO is regarded as having the best budget numbers in town, largely because the agency is seen as impartial and more realistic than its executive branch counterpart, OMB. Comparison of the economic and technical errors made by CBO and OMB in their budget estimates in recent years shows that CBO's estimating errors have been smaller than those of OMB in 6 out of the last 7 years.

Management Style

Since CBO is small, as government agencies go, it does not need—and does not have—a lot of bureaucratic procedures. Managers are relatively few, and assistant directors are given wide latitude in supervising their divisions and hiring and firing personnel. A collegial atmosphere exists in the agency at all levels. Executive staff meetings are relatively infrequent, and much internal coordination of agency work is achieved in hallway conversations.

Probably the most systematic procedure involves the publication of reports. Drafts go through a rigorous internal review, and usually other comments are solicited from outside experts. Meetings are held to discuss the comments of reviewers and to reach a consensus on revisions. After agreement is reached on content, the report generally goes through an extensive editing process and a final review by the director. Despite the rigors of the review process, it is faster and more streamlined than at many other agencies.

Staff Profiles

CBO is an agency dominated by economists. All CBO directors have been economists, and about 60% of the professional staff have either majored in economics at the undergraduate level or have acquired graduate degrees in economics. Nearly all the professional staff have completed 4 years or more of college, and nearly 70% have graduate degrees. People with PhDs are numerous in all CBO analytic divisions, although in the largest division, Budget Analysis, a majority have master's degrees. About 12% of the professional staff have master's degrees in public administration or public policy, and two thirds of these work in the Budget Analysis Division.

CBO employees are relatively youthful, and a large proportion are women. The average age of the professional staff in July 1989 was 37, and 35% of the professional staff were female. The average age and the proportion of women have both increased somewhat since 1980. About 15% of total staff, but only 6% of the professional staff, are from minority population groups. Half of the professional staff have been at CBO for more than 5 years, and the average length of employment is about 6 years.

Analytic Style

CBO's analytic style is determined by what it does. Budgetary assistance requires quantitative analysis and statistical models. CBO uses data generated by federal agencies and other sources in its cost estimation and program analysis work, including agency program data, periodic censuses and population surveys, and research studies by private groups. Computer simulations of large microdata sets, and spreadsheet analysis on personal computers, are used frequently. Mainstream economic theory provides the basic framework for most of CBO's analytic work. Much of the bill costing, scorekeeping, and program analysis focuses on baseline projections.

Quantitative Analysis and Modeling

CBO discovered that it had to develop its own capability for making detailed budget estimates. Not only did its economic forecasts usually differ from those of the administration, but the administration's budget estimates were not always accurate enough for the purpose of the new congressional budget process. Also, it was essential to have independent projections of entitlement programs in order to develop cost estimates for proposed changes in eligibility and benefits. Consequently, CBO devoted a lot of effort to developing quantitative methods and models for estimating and projecting budget revenues and outlays.

In-House Models

Three examples of the fairly elaborate modeling work that CBO has done in making budget estimates are the models for interest costs on federal debt, farm commodity price supports, and individual income tax receipts. The CBO interest model is designed to produce budget estimates quickly under a variety of economic and fiscal policy assumptions. It contains data on all outstanding Treasury debt issues (including amounts, interest rates, and maturity dates for all outstanding issues) and makes projections of interest outlays on a monthly basis, based on assumptions about such factors as future interest rates, budget deficits, and the length of maturity of new Treasury debt issues. The interest model can be used to project the date on which federal debt limits will be reached and to analyze the dynamics and economic effects of federal debt and interest costs.[4]

Similar detailed work has been done in order to project spending by the Commodity Credit Corporation (CCC) on farm price support programs. The outlay projections start with the provisions in current law governing the basic parameters of the farm programs (such as target prices and nonrecourse loan rates) and are based on detailed assumptions about future market conditions for each supported commodity, including levels of farmer participation in government programs, farm production, domestic use, exports, government and market stocks, and market prices. It is necessary to have projections for each supported farm commodity in order to estimate the cost impact of proposed changes in farm law or administrative policy.[5]

The Tax Analysis Division has developed a model for estimating individual income tax receipts, combining macroeconomic assumptions about national income levels and other variables with microdata drawn from the Treasury Department's public use sample of federal individual income tax returns. CBO's new income tax calculator can be modified to reflect actual or proposed changes in tax law. It has been used for a number of tax policy studies, as well as for projecting tax returns.[6]

CBO also constructs quantitative budget models for program analyses. A good example is the Defense Resources Model (DRM), which is a projection model for estimating the impact on operating costs of changes in the composition of the military forces. The model has been used to estimate the costs of developing a 600-ship Navy, returning Army divisions from Europe and elsewhere, increasing the Air Force to 40 tactical wings, and many other options. The model computes both direct and indirect costs for separate program elements, such as B-52 bombers or submarines, infantry or armored divisions located stateside or overseas, and nuclear or conventionally powered aircraft carriers (Congressional Budget Office, 1988b, Appendix A).

Other Models

CBO also uses models built and maintained elsewhere. For example, it uses the Transfer Income Model (TRIM) maintained by the Urban Institute for analyzing proposed changes in income support programs, such as aid to families with dependent children (AFDC). It employed this model in analyzing the potential costs of various welfare reform proposals in the late 1970s (CBO, 1977a, 1978). CBO used the National Coal Model, maintained by the Energy Information Administration in the Department of Energy, to analyze the budget and economic effects of various options for curbing acid rain (CBO, 1986).

Computer Simulations

CBO increasingly uses computer analyses and simulations of large microdata sets. One recent analysis projected the costs of the catastrophic drug insurance program (CBO, 1989c). The potential costs of this new program were quite uncertain when it was enacted in 1988. CBO used the data from the 1987 National Medical Expenditure Survey, a nationally representative survey of the noninstitutionalized population, to determine the distribution of spending on prescription drugs for elderly and disabled Medicare enrollees living in their communities. Simulations of drug spending by Medicare enrollees who live in such institutions as nursing homes were done with data from the 1985 National Nursing Home Survey. The analysis showed that prescription spending by the Medicare population had increased by more than had been projected in CBO's 1988 cost estimate, and consequently costs for the new catastrophic drug insurance program would be much higher than estimated. This is an example of one of CBO's more spectacular cost estimating errors, and it became a factor in the debate to repeal the catastrophic program.

The Current Population Survey (CPS) produced by the Bureau of the Census provides data on the economic and social status of families. CBO has used CPS, for example, in a study of trends in family income since 1970. The study revealed that families as a whole were markedly better off in 1986 than they had been 16 years earlier but that some classes of families, particularly low-income single mothers with children, and families with heads under age 25, became worse off during the period. The inequality of incomes among families increased during the period (CBO, 1988a).

CBO also used CPS data in conjunction with Internal Revenue Service (IRS) tax files to examine how changes in tax laws and changes in income have affected the distribution of federal tax liabilities. This study revealed that the distribution of total federal taxes has become less progressive since 1977 (CBO, 1987b).

While quantitative models and computer simulations are used in many CBO budget estimates and program analyses, much analytic work still consists of reading agency reports and other relevant studies, developing good agency contacts and reliable sources of information, and keeping abreast of economic and programmatic data as they are reported each month. Budget analysts, for example, generally spend more time on the telephone gathering information than they do at their personal computers in developing bill cost estimates. CBO's estimates and analyses usually depend more on access to the best available information than on elaborate statistical modeling.

Mainstream Economics

Many of CBO's program analyses and budget estimates require making assumptions about the performance of the U.S. economy. These assumptions are based on CBO's economic forecasts and medium-term projections. CBO does not maintain its own econometric model of the economy. Its economic forecasts are derived judgmentally. They can be characterized as middle-of-the road and are usually quite close to the consensus of private forecasts reported monthly in the *Blue Chip Economic Indicators.* This outcome is not surprising since CBO's forecasting starts with a review of other forecasts. Staff judgments and advice from CBO's Panel of Economic Advisers usually result in only minor changes from the consensus outlook.[7]

CBO's analyses of other macroeconomic issues also are based on a consensus of economists' views, when this exists. The consensus was quite Keynesian in character in the 1960s and 1970s, but in recent years it has been modified, following the rise of other schools of thought. CBO's economic analyses have reflected this trend in macroeconomic thinking.[8]

In analyzing issues affecting particular sectors of the economy, CBO's approach is based on standard microeconomic methodology. Recent CBO studies have included the GATT negotiations and U.S. trade policy (1987), how federal policies affect the steel industry (1987), the use of federal R&D to promote commercial innovation

(1988), the prospects of the U.S. space program in the 1990s and beyond (1988), the risks and benefits of building the superconducting super collider (1988), and trends in educational achievement (1986).

The Importance of Having a Baseline

Much of CBO's analytical work is incremental in nature; that is, it tries to determine the net effect of a change in law or policy on the economy or the budget or both. To do this type of analysis, it is usually important to have a baseline—a benchmark measure of what would happen if no change occurred in law or policy. CBO's economic forecast often serves as such a baseline for CBO's economic analyses, and CBO's baseline budget projections serve a similar purpose for many budget estimates. A major example of the latter is the annual volume devoted to deficit reduction options, which is part of CBO's annual report to the budget committees. This volume lists over 100 different policy options for reducing spending or raising revenues and shows for each the impact it would have on the budget, measured in terms of incremental changes in CBO's baseline budget projections.

The baseline approach is used also in analyzing the economic effects of possible legislation in various areas. For example, in CBO's acid rain study, the effects of different strategies to lower sulfur dioxide emissions from the nation's power plants were measured as changes from a projected baseline of what would happen under current policy (CBO, 1986). The baseline concept is a key part of the congressional budget process. Budget resolutions are constructed in terms of changes from a baseline. Budget committee instructions to other committees to raise taxes or to reduce spending are stated in terms of incremental changes from the budget resolution baseline. In the Balanced Budget Act (Gramm-Rudman-Hollings) process for reducing deficits, the required budget calculations start with baseline budget estimates and use incremental changes to determine whether across-the-board spending reductions will be required to meet the annual deficit targets.

Conclusion

In creating CBO, Congress has established its own source of information on the budget and the economy, information that may be used for policy decisions or to challenge information supplied by the executive branch. Analysts of the federal government, such as Hedrick Smith, observe that "the CBO represents the most important shift of power on domestic issues between the executive branch and Congress in several decades" (Smith, 1988, p. 290).

CBO has received much attention in the media during the past decade for its budget projections, economic forecasts, and policy analyses. Most of the attention has been favorable; generally, CBO is viewed as providing useful and objective information. In part, CBO's reputation has been gained at the expense of OMB, which has lost some of its credibility for accurate budget estimates and realistic economic assumptions. OMB had no competition 15 years ago, and its budget projections were used widely by the press, Wall Street, academia, international organizations, and state and local governments. Now, preeminence is given to the CBO projections.

Many international officials have visited CBO over the years, and several have expressed interest in establishing a similar staff capacity in their own governments. CBO is, however, very much the product of a federal regime in which the executive and legislative branches are independent and have separate powers. An agency like CBO would not fit into most parliamentary forms of government in which the legislature does not play much of a role in the budget process. Nevertheless, the idea of an independent source of information on the budget and the economy, produced by a government agency with no policy agenda, intrigues many policymakers abroad.

In the end, of course, CBO is only a staff arm of Congress, with no independent source of political power. It cannot force Congress to use its economic forecasts, budget estimates, or policy analyses. Its influence derives only from the credibility of its work. To remain influential, CBO must continue to produce forecasts, estimates, and studies that are perceived to be unbiased and authoritative.

Notes

1. For an excellent overview of the Congressional Budget Act, the new budget process, the budget committees, and CBO, see Schick, 1980.

2. Before 1985 the economic and budget projections were published also in separate volumes.

3. The initial staffing request for 259 positions in fiscal year 1976 was scaled back to 193. The appropriations committees were concerned that CBO analytic work would duplicate the activities of other congressional support agencies and believed that too many positions had been requested for policy analysis work. See Schick, 1980, and Kates, 1989.

4. See Congressional Budget Office, 1984, for a detailed discussion of the CBO interest model. Additional work has been done to streamline the model.

5. Recent projections of CCC outlays are discussed in Congressional Budget Office, 1989a.

6. For a more detailed discussion of CBO's income tax calculator, as well as the models used by the Treasury Department and the Joint Committee on Taxation, see Strauss, 1989.

7. For a discussion of the accuracy of CBO's economic forecasts, see Congressional Budget Office, 1987a, Chapter III.

8. The change can be seen by comparing CBO's earlier studies, such as 1977b, with more recent ones such as August 1989.

References

Congressional Budget and Impoundment Control Act of 1974. (1974, July 12). P. L. 93-344, 88 Stat. 297.

Congressional Budget Office. (1977a, July). *Welfare reform: Issues, objectives, and approaches.* Washington, DC.

Congressional Budget Office. (1977b, August). *The CBO Multipliers project: A methodology for analyzing the effects of alternative economic policies.* Washington, DC.

Congressional Budget Office. (1978, April). *The administration's welfare reform proposal: An analysis of the program for better jobs and income.* Washington, DC.

Congressional Budget Office. (1984, September) *Federal debt and interest costs.* Washington, DC.

Congressional Budget Office. (1986, June). *Curbing acid rain: Cost, budget, and coal-market effects.* Washington, DC.

Congressional Budget Office. (1987a, August). *The economic and budget outlook: An update.* Washington, DC.

Congressional Budget Office. (1987b, October). *The changing distribution of federal taxes: 1975-1990.* Washington, DC.

Congressional Budget Office. (1988a, February). *Trends in family income: 1970-1986.* Washington, DC.

Congressional Budget Office. (1988b, July). *Operation and support costs for the Department of Defense.* Washington, DC.

Congressional Budget Office. (1989a, May). *The outlook for Farm Commodity Program spending, fiscal years 1983-1984.* Washington, DC.

Congressional Budget Office. (1989b, August). *Policies for reducing the current-account deficit.* Washington, DC.

Congressional Budget Office. (1989c, October). *Updated estimates of Medicare's catastrophic drug insurance program.* Washington, DC.

Kates, N. D. (1989). Starting from scratch: Alice Rivlin and the Congressional Budget Office. Cambridge, MA: John F. Kennedy School of Government, Harvard University.

Schick, A. (1980). *Congress and money: Budgeting, spending and taxing.* Washington, DC: The Urban Institute.

Smith, H. (1988). *The power game.* New York: Random House.

Strauss, R. P. (1989). *Micro-simulation models and taxpayer behavior: Understanding current law and its alternatives.* Pittsburgh, PA: Carnegie-Mellon University.

13

Process, Prescience, and Pragmatism: The Office of Technology Assessment

Nancy Carson

OTA embodies the marriage of a visionary approach to policy analysis—technology assessment—to the most pragmatic of American political institutions, the U.S. Congress. This marriage has produced a continuing tension between the hope for a better tomorrow and the need for a better today that is reflected in OTA's history, agenda, and functions. Disavowing a methodology, this young agency has developed instead a process that allows for incorporating diverse opinion, utilizing expert information and analysis, and generating a timely product.

History and Description

Charter and Mandate

The Office of Technology Assessment was created by Congress in 1972, through Public Law 92-484. OTA's job is to provide congressional committees with objective analyses of the emerging, difficult, and often highly technical issues of today. Specifically, Congress wished to: ". . . equip itself with new and effective means for securing competent, unbiased information concerning the physical, biological, economic, social, and political effects of such applications. . . ." In addition to organizational language, PL 92-484 specifies the duties of the agency in these words:

(c) The basic function of the Office shall be to provide early indications of the probable beneficial and adverse impacts of the applications of technology and to develop other coordinate information which may assist the Congress in carrying out such function, the Office shall: (1) identify existing or probable impacts of technology or technological programs; (2) where possible, ascertain cause and effect relationships; (3) identify alternative technological methods of implementing specific programs; (4) identify alternative programs for achieving requisite goals; (5) make estimates and comparisons of the impacts of alternative methods and programs; (6) present findings of completed analyses to the appropriate legislative authorities; (7) identify areas where additional research or data collection is required to provide adequate support for the assessments and estimates described in paragraph (1) through (5) of this subsection; and (8) undertake such additional associated activities as the appropriate authorities specified under subsection (d) may direct.

History

OTA was conceived in the reform era of the mid-1960s, the same era that produced the Congressional Budget Office and drastically altered CRS. Technology assessment as propounded by the academic community was understood as a mechanism for seeing into the future and thus avoiding the "bad" effects of technology. The idea was that rational thinking and futurist techniques could be combined to anticipate the impacts of technology and to steer a course toward better use of resources. In addition to academic interest, the public was concerned deeply in this period about resources and the environment, and a commitment to citizen participation grew. The struggle in Congress over authorization of the supersonic transport was intense. Earth Day and the strength of the environmental movement heightened the belief, which recurs in American history, that technology had the bit in its teeth and was galloping ahead of wisdom. The result was a desire for ways to pull back on the reins and to ensure that technology was not out of control and driving national decisions.

In addition to environmental and citizen enthusiasm, Congress itself was experiencing a need for expert support. The rapidity with which the executive branch, particularly Secretary of Defense McNamara, had adopted quantitative analysis made possible by increasing computer capability placed many congressional members in a difficult situation. The discussion and personal negotiations of an earlier period were no longer sufficient; executive branch witnesses would now arrive with printouts, calculations, and convincing projections. Further, the tradition of high intelligence and informal decision making that characterized congressional staff no longer seemed sufficient to deal with complex technology problems. The staff were certainly smart enough, but as subcommittees increased and problems multiplied, no one had time or resources to spend analyzing the future.

Hearings on the need for new institutional capacity continued from 1966 through 1972. Harvey Brooks, Jerome Weisner, and others provided intellectual support for a new agency that would assist the government by doing long-range, objective analysis. The location of the agency—within the executive or the legislative branch—was debated hotly. Interestingly, until the authorizing bill reached the House floor, it contained a governing board that included both members of Congress and private citizens. This move toward citizen participation disappeared at the last moment, and the actual agency was to be governed by a Board of Senators and Representatives (Technology Assessment Board [TAB]) but advised by a committee composed of private citizens (Technology Assessment Advisory Council [TAAC]). The desire for broad and direct participation, however, was to remain with the agency and to influence its development.

In July of 1974 the first product of the new agency, *Drug Bioequivalence*, was published. An assessment of automobile collision data needs appeared in February 1975, and a full report, *Analysis of the Feasibility of Separating Exploration From Production of Oil and Gas in the Outer Continental Shelf,* was printed in May 1975. OTA was up and running.

The Daddario Period—Birth Pangs (January 1974–Spring 1977)

OTA has had three directors (named by TAB) and three distinct periods. The first director, former Congressman Emilio Daddario, was chosen after his unsuccessful run for the Senate. Already the congressional champion of the new agency (he had chaired the authorizing hearings in the House), Mim Daddario brought congressional savvy and the support of his former colleagues to the work of structuring a new institution. All members of the new Technology Assessment Board (six from the House and six from the Senate, equally divided by party) were entitled to one employee in the new agency, and many of these people were the original key staff of the agency. The involvement of members of TAB was high; members of Congress were interested but tended to request studies on rather limited topics.

Having sustained OTA through its early years, Daddario left in May of 1977.

The Peterson Period—Adolescent Separation and Independence (January 1978–April 1979)

Daddario was replaced by Russell Peterson, former governor of Delaware and director of the Council on Environmental Quality. A chemist by training, Peterson was well known as a committed environmentalist and a strong leader at CEQ. He was interested in futurist techniques and deeply committed to raising "quality of life" issues. Peterson wanted to define an issue agenda for OTA that he believed should also constitute a congressional agenda, and he wanted all studies to reflect holistic thinking.

Russell Peterson was also committed to ensuring that the work of OTA would be objective, nonpartisan, and completely without bias or the appearance of bias. He believed strongly that the existence within the agency of people who had been selected by members of TAB and whose loyalty must therefore be to those members meant that the agency could never achieve the critical level of objectivity. He also believed that the director must have an entirely free hand in running the agency.

Thus, he made clear to TAB that change was needed. After a struggle, the board consented to place all hiring and firing decisions solely in the hands of the director and agreed that all staff worked solely for the director. Peterson thus contributed importantly to the reputation of the agency as independent but set in motion a serious test of wills between the director and the board. If the agency was to serve Congress, and the board was to approve studies, board cooperation was vital. But if the director was to be independent and saw the board as reflecting parochial interests, problems were inevitable.

As the stage began to darken in this institutional drama, fate intervened. For many years, Russell Peterson had longed to become president of the Audubon Society. A long-time birder and interested in citizen involvement, Peterson had explored the possibility of leading this largest environmental group before coming to OTA. Suddenly, in early 1978 the job became vacant and he was called by Audubon. Although he had been at OTA for just over a year, he felt that this was the opportunity of his lifetime and accepted the offer. Having altered the agency to protect it against political manipulation, he departed the scene.

John H. Gibbons—Growth and Maturity (June 1979—present)

The third director of OTA is John H. Gibbons, a physicist and environmentalist from Tennessee. Gibbons had served in the first Federal Energy Office (just prior to the oil disruption of 1973) and knew something about Washington. He was committed to energy conservation and resource management. He was the quintessential gentleman scientist—someone who could speak with grace and ease to almost anyone on a complicated question. He had served as chairman of OTA Advisory Panels, including a study on energy conservation in buildings, and knew well the energy program, then the largest group at OTA. He was thoughtful about politics but not strongly identified with any party or politician. His work at Oak Ridge National Laboratory and with the National Academy of Sciences on its major energy study had established his standing in the scientific community. His selection as director for the agency was greeted widely with enthusiasm. (It would not be an overstatement to say the staff were stunned with their good fortune.) Under Gibbons, the productivity of the agency increased, disparities between programs lessened, quality improved, and the authority and credibility of the agency grew.

The Technology Assessment Board

Six Senators and six Representatives, representing both political parties and the political spectrum within both parties, constitute OTA's board of directors—TAB. Prognostications in the early days were that TAB would not work; it would either be a disinterested body, unwilling to defend the new agency, or it would become divided along political lines, as are most committees. A major achievement is that this has not happened. TAB has become a strong supporter of OTA's work, and disagreements within the board over proposals seldom reflect party or ideological lines. TAB members, appointed by the leadership in each House, are powerful people, who have many demands on their time. The fact that the turnout is strong at TAB meetings, which occur about every 6 weeks, reflects their view of the importance of OTA.

Technology Assessment Advisory Council

TAAC members are distinguished private citizens from many walks of life. TAAC meets twice a year, and its charge is to advise TAB on the strength and direction of OTA. The group occasionally has become involved (as individuals) in OTA studies. Because they do not have a direct function in the running of the agency, it has been difficult to develop a clear and compelling role for TAAC. They constitute a reservoir of guidance for OTA, and during Gibbons's term they have become similar to a visiting committee for a university, advising TAB and the director as needed.

Resources

In 1989, OTA obligations totaled just under $17.9 million, with a full-time employment ceiling of 143. The staff is extended substantially by temporary employees, in-house contractors, and a few people detailed from executive branch agencies. This method offers flexibility to define staff based on project needs. As the agency entered fiscal year 1989, 140 people were employed doing analytical work on studies at OTA.

The staff balance has shifted over time from an original concentration in the "hard" sciences to a wider mix; a look at the initial degrees held by staff shows a continuing preference for a technical background but a broadening of fields since the early days. From 1984 to 1988 the proportion of staff with final degrees in engineering, physics, biology, and other sciences declined slightly, from about 40% to 31%. The difference was made up by a corresponding rise in those with final degrees in political science, law, economics, and other social and policy sciences. If one counts the type of initial degree, the proportion of the staff with technical degrees increases by about 15%. In 1989, for example, of 128 permanent and temporary full-time research staff, 40 had final degrees in so-called hard disciplines. The number who had either a final degree or an earlier degree in these fields totaled 64. As studies are interdisciplinary, study teams are composed purposely of complementary skills, and the skilled, experienced generalist—who tends to flourish in Washington in any event—appears in many OTA programs.

OTA has always had close to 50% female analysts. They are concentrated, however, in midlevel positions. The number of men in the top four OTA salary levels is 39, the number of women is 22 (1989 figures). Turnover has been high at OTA if all employees, both temporary and permanent, are counted. Turnover rates declined in the mid-1980s to 5% for all permanent staff and 2% for permanent analytical staff. This trend seemed to be shifting upward in 1989. Of the permanent analytical staff, 4% to 6% have been at OTA for 7 years or more.

By the early 1990s, a substantial number of OTA's senior management staff will have reached the 20-year point in their federal careers. This period also coincides with the conclusion of the second term held by Gibbons. It is, therefore, entirely possible that major staff change could occur. As OTA is within the legislative branch, no job security or protection is guaranteed.

Workload

The definition of the OTA product has changed over time. In its effort to be comprehensive and objective, many studies, and particularly early documents, tended to be extremely long, detailed, and technical. As the agency learned the importance of communication as well as analysis, the product became shorter, more sophisticated, and more attractive. Summary documents are provided for general readers; very few users actually require the extensive documentation that goes into the preparation of a report.

The number of documents published annually has increased over time, reaching the low 20s in 1978 and 1979, somewhere in the 30s from 1981 to 1985, and hitting 50 published studies in 1988. The type of document produced also has shifted. In recent years, staff papers and special reports have become more common, to complement the full-fledged assessment report. Assessments remain the principal agency product. Shorter documents, such as special reports and staff papers, are intended to be responsive to Congress on more and more topics. Publications tend to cycle with Congress, with more studies completed in the second year of a session. OTA has produced video versions of reports and has worked on training staff for effective writing and presentation in hearings, speeches, and work with the press and citizen groups. Given the technical training of most staff and a bias toward comprehensiveness that often works against effective communication with Congress, retraining the staff to translate their work effectively will be a continuing OTA effort.

OTA study requests have been dominated by the House Committee on Energy and Commerce; the House Committee on Science, Space, and Technology; and the Senate Committee on Commerce, Science, and Transportation. These three committees have asked for over 200 studies. OTA has made a sustained effort to broaden its utility, and requests for 10 or more studies have been received from these committees:

House Committees	Senate Committees
Appropriations	Appropriations
Agriculture	Banking, Housing and Urban Affairs
Education and Labor	Energy and Natural Resources
Foreign Affairs	Environment and Public Works
Government Operations	Finance
Judiciary	Foreign Relations
Merchant Marine and Fisheries	Governmental Affairs
Post Office and Civil Service	Labor and Human Resources
	Ways and Means
	Special Committee on Aging
	The Joint Economic Committee

OTA testifies extensively on its reports, both in release and initial use of the report and in follow-up. In fiscal year 1988, OTA staff testified 55 times; for fiscal year 1989, 35.

Culture

Values

OTA's credibility rests on its objectivity, its comprehensiveness, and its rigor. As the agency responds to study requests only from full committees and members of TAB and requires approval by the board for most work, it is somewhat protected from overly circumscribed projects. An essential aspect of the OTA process is the ability of the agency to formulate the question. A committee may request a study that is self-serving or overly narrow; the OTA staff receiving the request will outline a broader approach and discuss with the committee why this approach will lead to a more useful study. In most cases the new approach can be worked out with the requesters. In a few instances it has not been possible, and the study has not gone forward. As the agency has become more well known (and the press coverage of reports has increased), the demand for studies has grown, and it has become somewhat more difficult to filter requests and to ensure that studies are as comprehensive as they need to be.

Increasingly, the director has been asked to select members for such legislatively mandated groups as the Prospective Payments Assessment Commission, the Physician Payment Review Commission, and the Prescription Drug Payment Review Commission. It is challenging to undertake such a selection process, which includes the need to consider and balance expertise, diversity, geographic, and other considerations, and to understand the political needs of decision-making bodies. Although making assignments is difficult and the agency has not sought this task, the choice of OTA to make hard decisions of this kind indicates respect for OTA's objectivity and stature.

An additional concern for OTA planners and researchers is that there be a balance between the direct utility of a study to Congress and the more "visionary function" expected of the agency. In practice, studies will combine greater or lesser aspects of these approaches but generally will try hard at least to look into the future of the issue. Building some foresight into each study has been more successful, in general, than trying to isolate some studies and using those to look deeper into the crystal ball.

Style

OTA is interdisciplinary, open, and works by extensive internal and external review. Agency studies are truly joint products; this collaboration works against the development of individuals as experts in one field. Staff become somewhat specialized but must be able to move to new issues, and sometimes new fields, as the congressional agenda changes. This readiness reinforces the openness of the agency to ideas. The fluidity in assignment probably contributes to the rejection of standardized methodology by most OTA staff; each study is approached as a new challenge.

In the early 1970s an OTA division prepared a notebook showing background, hobbies, and interests of staff; the wide variety of education, interests, and experience was striking. Almost no one on the staff had followed a traditional "career ladder." A more typical background might include an undergraduate degree in science, some time spent in the Peace Corps or in trying to run a cooperative business, independent travel, a year or two in the private sector, a graduate degree in a discipline different from the original degree, followed by a job with an environmental lobby group while writing book reviews on the side. In essence, OTA staff are smart people with broad curiosity who have done many interesting things. They have strong intellectual drive and sufficient chutzpah to take on a major study in a new field with confidence. Coming fresh to a study also reinforces the institutional value of listening.

The agency structure is flat, congenial, and receptive to ideas, making for a collegial environment, but it is difficult for mid-level people to rise in the organization. OTA does not attract many people who are interested in organizational power. Little emphasis is placed on management, and few OTA managers have had any formal training in this art. Given the lack of structure and methodology, and the general openness to alternative views, the agency is better understood as a collection of programs than as a single, unified organization. Over time, the nine OTA programs and their program managers have developed distinctive ways of dealing with problems, preferences for different types of employees, varying degrees of hierarchy, and idiosyncratic approaches to employee development. Essentially, the management philosophy is, "Let 1,000 flowers bloom."

How Does OTA Think of Itself?

OTA considers itself the congressional agency with the mandate for doing the most comprehensive analytical work. The ability to control and affect the work load, and the legislative charge to consider positive and negative impacts of technical, economic, social, and political decisions makes for an environment in which all important aspects of an issue can be analyzed fully and fairly. To support this approach, OTA needs clients (standing committees) who can take a long view and are sufficiently brave to accept a conclusion that can neither be known in advance nor suppressed. It also requires that staff believe in the value of information as a constructive force in legislation.

Studies develop slowly and carefully, and short documents generally can be produced only when a knowledge base has been built. The length of time in preparation (a major assessment requires about 2 years) and depth of analysis, combined with an objectivity among outcomes, means that OTA does not tend to be "high profile" in its work. Independence and quality are more highly valued than timeliness or celebrity.

OTA's work was adopted with enthusiasm early on by foreign governments. The science attachés of embassies in Washington have long been first in line for new reports, and studies are often well known abroad. Over the past 10 years many European governments have explored the possibility of creating an OTA and have spent time visiting the agency and trying to arrange for a variety of cooperative efforts. Particular enthusiasm has been shown by the West Germans, the French, and the British. Spain has launched a small effort, and the European Parliament has an OTA-like body, as do the Netherlands and Austria. Interestingly, replicating an OTA within the parliamentary construct has proved difficult, if not impossible. The tension that exists in the United States between the executive and legislative branches and between the various factions in both parties creates a situation in which the agency is most effective and protected when objectivity is pursued. In a parliamentary structure, the legislative branch cannot undertake a study that might come up with results displeasing to the executive branch unless the study is initiated by the opposition. OTA staff have observed also, in working with foreign visitors and visiting their countries, that the American attitude of easily combining people with different standing, training, and background is still uncomfortable in many other countries. Explaining how to assemble an advisory panel, as done by OTA, produces incredulous stares.

Analytical Development

Development of the OTA Process

The framers of OTA believed that answers to many complex problems were already available in either academia or the private sector; much of OTA's work was anticipated as simply bringing in this information, thought to be sidetracked by the traditional bureaucracies. The early approaches to preparing reports relied on large contracts with private firms and groups. This approach failed totally, and OTA was forced to invent a way to respond on little money to complex questions with assurance and objectivity.

By 1980 the OTA process was well established and continues to be the heart of the agency's work. It is based on an unusually eclectic and open approach, purposeful attention to diverse views, interdisciplinary work teams, and the cost-effective use of private and public resources. In addition, the process generates interest in issues and knowledge of the agency among groups and individuals who participate. This interest leads to an amplifying effect that carries study results to Congress through many channels.

The Advisory Panel and Workshops

For each assessment, OTA assembles an expert advisory panel of people representing various attitudes and interests in the topic. Much attention is given to the selection of the panels. The job of the panel is to guide the study, to oversee the general approach, to ensure that attention is given to all concerns and all factions, to provide expert technical review, and generally to contribute to the development of the project. Most panels meet three times over the course of a study, and all members have full access to project materials and draft reports. Comments by panel members are examined with great seriousness by OTA staff. Responsibility for the report, however, always remains with OTA itself. Advisory panel members are free to associate themselves with results or not, as they prefer.

While advisory panels based on this model are now more common, the early use of such panels by OTA was a substantial change from most early advisory committees used by research organizations. Those groups generally had been made up of technical experts, and often the groups had been designed to elicit consensus. OTA panels combine very different expertise and opinion, and consensus is not sought. The object is rather for OTA to hear and understand truly the positions stated around the table.

Workshops are a more focused version of an advisory panel. They provide a great deal of material for OTA studies, often by commenting on draft material circulated prior to the workshop. Sometimes workshops identify new study needs; sometimes they validate or redirect initial conclusions by the agency. They are always valuable. Through the panel, workshop, and review process, OTA engages about 2,000 people a year in its work. All of these people become more informed about the issue, come to know OTA, and often come closer to understanding the views of others. The value of their time and effort is enormous.

Contracts

OTA is free to contract with any group or individual for the provision of information. In practice, most contracts are with individuals or small firms. The overhead rates of large research organizations cannot often be absorbed within the OTA budget, and the need to be certain that carefully selected people are actually doing the work also factors against large contracts.

Executive Branch

The resources and data of the executive branch are available to OTA (as prescribed by the authorizing legislation), and much information is gathered in this way. Often, OTA can effectively reanalyze data from executive branch agencies. Members of the executive branch do not serve on advisory panels but are sometimes ex officio members and frequently participate in workshops. OTA is not charged with investigating or reviewing the effectiveness of the executive branch (a study on this topic would be referred to GAO), but aspects of these issues arise. In many instances an OTA report has assisted groups within executive agencies to make changes they have long sought. For example, OTA's work on safety in aviation is credited frequently with improving the allocation of funds and the emphasis given to human factors research within the Federal Aviation Administration.

Review

OTA studies are not proprietary; once initiated, a study "belongs" to OTA, and its contents cannot be controlled by any member of Congress or committee. Draft documents are circulated to a wide variety of reviewers and interested parties as they develop. Comments are sifted carefully by OTA staff, and many changes result. In some instances the difference between an early draft and a final report has been interpreted as reflection of political pressure. In fact, changes are common and tend to reflect increased knowledge by the staff and their sensitivity to comments. Contractor reports submitted to OTA are reviewed by people in the related field. (A small portion of OTA work is classified and, therefore, dealt with somewhat differently.) Reports are iterated and reviewed internally as well, by the originating unit in OTA and by those whose work is related closely. Final submission of a report to TAB prior to release includes a statement by the director, restating the review process—who said what, and how OTA responded to those comments. TAB, thus assured that OTA has been faithful to its own process, approves the release of major assessments.

Congressional Relationship

Most OTA studies are conducted in close cooperation with staff of the requesting committees. OTA seeks to interest in each study all those committees with a role to play in the policy outcome. For example, the OTA transportation studies are of interest to many committees and subcommittees. Often a study is endorsed by several committees, and OTA makes an effort to provide information to all requesters as the study develops. In some instances this dissemination may mean that some of the findings of the study have already been used by Congress and have become conventional wisdom by the time of publication; this incorporation is seen as a success within the agency. Committee staff are invited to panel and workshop meetings and are briefed as they wish on study progress. Sometimes an interim document is prepared if it will be helpful to the requesting committee and can be accommodated within the project structure.

Policy Analysis: The If-Then Construction

OTA is not prohibited from making recommendations to Congress, but seldom does so, primarily because few complex issues have a clear resolution. In most studies some assumptions or recommendations may be included, but policy options tend to take on an "if-then" construction. For example, *if* the principal objective of legislation on basic research is to accelerate leading-edge science, *then* an option might be to confine research funding to the leading institutions in that discipline. *If* an object of basic research is to broaden the nation's capacity for research, *then* an option would be to institute a geographic distribution element in funding.

The "if-then" construction allows members to determine their own prevailing objective and to see how to reach it. For instance, many choices will have to be made in rethinking the national approach to building and maintaining infrastructure. If one's ultimate objective is to shift costs to users or to improve environmental quality quickly or to integrate needs coherently on a regional basis, different strategies will be needed. This approach yields a meaty report for Congress. OTA's history contains instances in which the same document was used by opposing sides in a floor argument. The choice of complex policy analysis and resulting lower profile is a central aspect of the agency's philosophy. It does not make for simple headlines. In general, the agency would rather be criticized for having too many hands than for oversimplifying a difficult task or favoring one set of values or objectives over another.

Dissemination and Use

Studies generally are released by the requesting committee at a hearing, but they quickly move into the public arena and are used widely. Groups who have been part of the OTA advisory or review process use the documents. These people may participate in hearings or lobbying activities. A great many OTA documents have been reprinted privately for direct sale; many are used as classroom texts. OTA cooperates in these efforts, making copy available to publishers. Videotapes have been reproduced and distributed widely, and made available through public television. As major OTA studies are comprehensive and detailed, they have a long "shelf life" as reference documents. The thorough review and nonpartisan tenor of the agency make the documents acceptable to most audiences. Short, attractive summary documents are provided free for most studies. OTA staff are working to become more proficient at speaking concisely and effectively about study results. Staff are made available to interest groups, conferences, universities, and local meetings to share the information widely.

Criticism and Evaluation

What Happened to the Crystal Ball?

Critics of OTA often state that the agency is not looking far enough ahead, doing what "technology assessment" was supposed to do. Some within the agency agree with this statement but believe it results from two realities: (a) Looking ahead is hard, and just planning to do it does not get you there; and (b) Congress is concerned with today, and moving their horizon slightly ahead may be the best contribution possible while serving their immediate analytical needs. Recently, senior OTA staff engaged in a lengthy review of this question. Finally, when a survey was made to see if anyone could identify a "futures" issue that could not be undertaken within an existing study, nothing was identified. This finding may also reflect a pragmatic staff.

Future

A growing demand for OTA products is both the good news and the bad news. It is always wonderful to have people wanting an OTA product; it is difficult to sort among requests, to tell committees to wait, and sometimes to convince a requester that the question is not exactly right for OTA. It seems unlikely that any substantial change in the OTA way of doing business will occur in the near future. Dealing with comprehensive problems requires the type of widely cast net that has been developed by the agency. One possible response to increasing demand for studies is to take on some number of even more ambitious studies, such as the continuing work under way on global warming, to build upon the agency's experience base. The deep philosophy behind OTA—that information counts and that we as a nation can and do shape our future—will continue to push the agency toward ambitious work for decision makers. Participation by many people will continue to result in studies that reflect those beliefs, attitudes, and perspectives. And OTA will continue to reflect the healthy tension between the hope for a better tomorrow and the need for a better today.

References

Technology Assessment Act of 1972. (1972). Public Law 92-484.

Office of Technology Assessment. (1974, July). *Drug bioequivalence.* Washington, DC.

Office of Technology Assessment. (1975, May). *Analysis of the feasibility of separating exploration from production of oil and gas in the outer continental shelf.* Washington, DC.

14

The Congressional Support Agencies: Comments

James M. Verdier

Introduction

Each of the four congressional support agencies faces a common set of questions:

- Who is our audience?
- What is our product?
- What constitutes success?

Audience

The obvious answer to the audience question is "Congress," but Congress is made up of 535 individuals, each of whom plays multiple roles and has multiple interests and concerns. To communicate effectively, an analyst sitting down at a word processor must be able to envision the audience as specific human beings with specific knowledge, capacities, and concerns.

The congressional support agencies vary in their ability to give their staffs this realistic sense of their audience.

- CBO is probably closest to its congressional audience, if only because it is most closely plugged in to congressional decision making and deadlines.
- CRS is next closest because of its tradition of quick turnaround responses and temporary staff loans to committees.

- GAO is more remote because of its depersonalized "institutional" authorship style and its time-consuming review processes.
- OTA is perhaps most remote because of its more academic approach to issues and its concentration on issues that do not have close decision-making deadlines.

When the nominal audience is shadowy and distant, analysts have a tendency to write instead for the audience that seems most tangible and real to them: other experts, reviewers, advisory panels, academics, interest groups, issue networks, or whatever.

This tendency is especially the case when the author gets no direct feedback from the congressional audience, or feedback that is so attenuated, diffuse, and hard to interpret that the author does not know what to make of it. Determining cause-and-effect links between congressional action and support agency reports or testimony is the stuff of political science doctoral dissertations; few support agency staff people can do it on their own.

For most people, operating in a feedback-free world is frustrating and unsatisfying. It also makes it difficult to produce a product that the audience finds useful. The congressional support agencies have developed, therefore, a variety of approaches to product definition that provide guidance and support to their analysts. The need for these special efforts depends mainly on the agency's closeness to its congressional audience.

Product

Each agency's product is a reflection of its institutional history, the demands of its audience, and the capabilities of its staff.

- CBO does budgeting, forecasting, and policy analysis. It is grounded firmly in the discipline of economics; it does what economists do.
- CRS is more eclectic in terms of disciplines. It provides information and responses to congressional questions, with products that have evolved from factoids to broader frameworks.
- GAO also is evolving, from accounting to program evaluation, but its signature products still bear the stamp of its accounting tradition ("accuracy, independence, and objectivity").
- OTA does the future, with a disciplinary grounding in science and technology. Its products expand horizons rather than seeking to solve immediate problems.

CBO has little problem with product definition. Its closeness to its audience, its budgetary focus, and its grounding in economics make it reasonably clear to both insiders and outsiders what is expected. CRS has little problem with the large mass of products in the middle of its product line—issue briefs, reports, info packs, bibliographies, and other "reference factory" items. The congressional demand is great, and it is clear what is needed to satisfy it. What the "think tank" product should look like is less clear, however. With both an eclectic disciplinary base and an eclectic congressional audience, carving out a niche and an identity for this product will not be easy.

GAO has an even greater product identity problem in moving beyond its traditional auditing, accounting, and financial management products. The traditions and routines of accounting sometimes conflict with the requirements of program and policy evaluation. It is possible to be accurate and precise about the past and about things that can be measured easily in dollars. Congressional policy decisions, however, are about a future filled with uncertainty and about costs and benefits that cannot be measured with precision. GAO's elaborate, cumbersome, and time-consuming review process may be a way of seeking an accountant's precision and objectivity in the uncertain and subjective world of program and policy evaluation. If so, the goal is unachievable, and the price in delay and unresponsiveness may be more than the congressional audience is willing to pay.

Lacking a long history, a disciplinary base, or a clearly defined congressional demand, OTA has sought to define its product with the help of an elaborate advisory and review process. Although final decisions are made by OTA's congressional board, the products themselves seem shaped much more by the technical and professional reviewers from universities, industries, and interest groups. The process itself seems to distance the product from its nominal congressional audience.

Success

How an institution defines success helps shape its products, its reputation, and the job satisfaction of those who work in it.

For CBO, success in the early years was visibility, impact on decisions, and high-quality professional work. Now that Gramm-Rudman-Hollings has removed CBO's budgeting and economic forecasting staff from the front lines (at least temporarily), some question exists about how success should be defined for those staffs. For CRS, success in its "reference factory" capacity is well grounded and assured. Success in its "think tank" capacity still remains problematical, however, with major open questions about staff recruitment and product development.

For GAO, success in program and policy evaluation is likely to remain elusive as long as the accountants' standards of "accuracy and objectivity" remain as dominant as they now are. The accountants' culture in GAO needs to be confronted more systematically by economists, with their techniques for dealing with uncertainty and probability, and by people with direct congressional experience, with their understanding of congressional needs and deadlines. The emphasis on "problem solving" also might bear some rethinking. In a complex political environment, only narrowly defined technical problems can be "solved" on the basis of substantive analysis alone. Options are better than solutions in a political world.

For OTA, success seems now to be defined mainly as influencing a larger policy community, with the hope that the perceptions of that community ultimately will shape those of Congress. Directly shaping congressional perceptions and decision making remains inherently difficult for OTA, given the agency's focus on a more distant future than Congress is inclined to deal with.

Recruitment and Motivation

The history, institutional characteristics, disciplinary bases, comparative advantages, and aspirations for the future of each of the congressional support agencies determine the kinds of people they seek to recruit and the sources of satisfaction of their current staffs.

The "development, analytical style, and institutional culture" of each institution should, therefore, be captured in the recruiting pitch that each agency uses and in the motivational tools that each uses for internal management.

15

The California Legislative Analyst's Office

Elizabeth Hill

Introduction

One of the most distinctive types of policy advice institutions is the nonpartisan legislative fiscal organization. At the state level, approximately 30 such offices serve state legislatures. The oldest of these state institutions is the California Legislative Analyst's Office (LAO), established a half century ago.

This chapter examines the LAO and its impact on policy-making. It first provides some background on the office: history, organization and culture, and products. It then reviews the ways in which the office's analytical work has an impact and some of the constraints under which we operate. I conclude with comments on where the office is moving to maximize its impact in the future.

Background

History of the Office

The LAO was established in 1941 through a change in the joint rules of the legislature (the governor had vetoed a bill that would have accomplished this through statute). Prior to that time, the legislature basically had no fiscal staff to review independently the executive branch's proposals or to evaluate its administration of legislative enactments.

In 1951 the governor signed legislation codifying the joint rule, thereby providing a statutory basis for the LAO and the Joint Legislative Budget Committee (JLBC), which oversees the office. The office's mandate is to:

> . . . ascertain facts and make recommendations to the Legislature . . . concerning the state budget; the revenues and expenditures of the state; and the organization and functions of the state, its departments, subdivisions and agencies, with a view of reducing the cost of the state government and securing greater efficiency and economy (*California Government Code*, 1951, p. 3803).

While broad in scope, the language focuses on a fiscal role. Consequently, the office has always concentrated on fiscal-related issues, primarily through its analysis of the state budget and proposed legislation. As noted above, the office is charged in statute with making recommendations, a function not commonly performed by nonpartisan analytical institutions (such as the Congressional Budget Office and the Congressional Research Service). These recommendations often serve as a lightning rod for legislative debate on issues.

By 1955 the office staff had grown to 41 (30 analytical and 11 support). At that time, California had a population of 13 million and a General Fund budget of under $1 billion. The legislature was in session for only a limited time—six months during the first year of the session and only two months during the second year. As a consequence, analysts had plenty of time to develop budget issues, to learn about the operations of state programs, and to perform special evaluations for policy committees.

Also at this time, the legislature had very few employees—either on personal or committee staff. As a result, analysts at the LAO often served as the key policy advice staff to members. The office's credibility was also greatly enhanced by having a strong leader—A. Alan Post—as the legislative analyst during its early years. Post, who headed the office between 1949 and 1977, developed great rapport with legislative leaders and, consequently, had the ability to influence significant policy issues. For all the above reasons—strong leadership, no competition from other staff, access to members, and time to develop extensive program expertise—the office was highly influential during its first two decades.

Since 1960 several significant developments have altered the policy advice world in which we operate.

- During the Pat Brown administrations of the 1960s, the executive branch became more activist.
- At the same time, Assembly Speaker Jesse Unruh began adding significant numbers of legislative employees. The growth in this staff enabled the legislature to develop its own programs and solutions to state problems rather than only to react to the administration's proposals.
- The one-person, one-vote U.S. Supreme Court ruling in 1964 dramatically changed the California senate, diminishing the very strong budgetary role played by a few key senators. As the office's influence was in part tied to providing staff support to these fiscal players, its role changed when the assembly exercised more influence in fiscal matters.
- The legislature became a full-time body, meeting generally from January to the first of September of each year. This schedule has limited the time available for analysts to undertake in-depth fieldwork projects.
- The state budget became much more complex following the passage of Proposition 13 in 1978. It is now much more intermeshed with the financing of local governmental services and also is subject to numerous constitutional and statutory constraints and funding formulas.
- Finally, the level of partisanship in the legislature has risen, especially over the last 10 to 15 years. This rise has tended to lessen the impact of nonpartisan analysis in policy-making.

Currently, the office has a staff of about 100 employees (75 analytical and 25 support staff) that reviews a state General Fund budget of over $40 billion. When the state budget is compared with the *Fortune* 500 list of largest corporations, California ranks fifth in size between IBM and General Electric. The budget has grown not only in size during the last two decades, but also in complexity.

Organization and Culture

The JLBC

As noted above, the LAO is the staff to the JLBC. The 14-member committee is made up of seven senators and seven assembly members. Throughout its history, the JLBC has been strictly bipartisan, with representation accorded key minority party members. The rules also provide that all actions of the committee require approval of four senate and four assembly members, thus ensuring that its actions reflect the views of both houses.

By tradition, most of the work of the committee is handled by correspondence. Decisions that come before the committee—such as

LAO administrative matters and budget control analyses (see below)—are made by the chairperson after appropriate consultation with other members. Consequently, the JLBC seldom holds formal hearings. (As such, it is similar to the Congressional Joint Committee on Taxation.)

Fiscal Committees

The main work of the office—budgets and bills—is done for the legislature's fiscal committees: Assembly Ways and Means, and the Senate Budget and Fiscal Review Committee (Budget Bill) and Senate Appropriations (other fiscal bills). While these committees all have their own staffs (majority and minority), the LAO is a key source of fiscal and program information, as well as analysis for each of them.

Organization

Most of the analytical staff is assigned to one of nine operating sections, with each section responsible for fiscal and policy analysis in a single program area (such as health). Analysts within a section are assigned a particular department or program within the section (for example, the state Medicaid program). The individual analyst becomes, in effect, the office expert in that program, responsible for all products pertaining to that subject.

The sections are headed by directors, the "line" managers responsible for supervising analysts, and serving as the office's institutional memory in the respective policy area. The top management of the office consists of the legislative analyst and three deputies, each with a particular functional responsibility (administration, bills, budgets).

Recruitment

Currently, the office hires most of its analytical employees out of graduate schools, primarily public policy programs. These schools tend to provide people who have solid quantitative (economics, public finance, and statistics) and communication (writing and speaking) skills and who understand government. This hiring strategy generally has been a successful one. What the new employees lack in experience, they make up for in energy to handle a demanding work environment. Given the organizational "flatness" of the office and the intensity of the work experience, many analysts leave after 3 to 5 years. This turnover has several negative effects: increased workload pressure on the directors, less program knowledge resident in the office, and high training costs. On the positive side, this turnover has resulted in an extensive "alumni network" of trained professionals who continue to work in or with state government. These alumni often serve as an informal conduit for distributing the office's nonpartisan advice and analysis.

Culture

Most people who work—or who have worked—at the LAO would give the office high marks on work environment. It is a highly professional organization, known for the quality of its products and staff. Analysts (even new ones) are given much responsibility and considerable autonomy in the way they meet that responsibility. Furthermore, it is a merit-based office, with salary and promotion decisions based on performance.

Recently, the office went through some internal soul-searching, reexamining its mission and direction and the values that are important to us. Several specific products resulted from our rather lengthy review process, including a statement of our "vision/mission/values" (see Table 15.1), and a more formalized process for setting office-wide workload priorities.

Products and Their Audiences

The LAO produces many different products, each "consumed" by a slightly different audience. Clearly, our products are geared first and foremost for our "bosses", the 120 members of the California legislature. In fact, many of our documents are used actively by a much smaller subset of the entire legislature—members of the leadership and fiscal committees. Almost as important an audience are the legislative staff advisors to this subset of members. Given their influence with key legislators, it is critical for us to assist them on both a formal and informal basis.

The key products of the office, and their main audiences, are described below.

Table 15.1 Legislative Analyst's Office
Statement of Vision, Mission, and Values

Vision	Serving the public through independent analysis to meet the challenges of tomorrow.
Mission	We provide analysis and nonpartisan advice to the legislature on fiscal and policy issues.
Values	As an organization, the Legislative Analyst's Office values:

Service
Contributions that make a difference
Integrity
Intellectual honesty and ethical behavior
Initiative
Seeking opportunities to contribute
Excellence
Expertise and quality in all we do
Creativity
Innovative approaches to problem solving
Camaraderie
An environment in which people enjoy working together

Teamwork
Working together to achieve our goals
A Supportive Environment
An environment that recognizes individual needs and fosters personal and professional growth
Respect for the Individual
Appreciation for each person's contribution and individuality
Open Communication
Direct discussions that promote understanding and trust

Budget Analysis

Each February the office publishes a detailed analysis of the Governor's Budget. This book, which typically runs 1,400 pages, critiques the governor's proposed spending plan for each item of state expenditure for the coming year and makes recommendations regarding spending cuts, legislative oversight, and program changes. For most analysts in the office, the annual *Analysis of the Budget Bill* is the major task and product and governs how they spend much of their time during the legislative session. For instance, the fall is spent planning issues for the coming *Analysis* and doing appropriate field work. Much of November and December is spent reviewing specific proposals the administration is considering or has approved for the coming budget year; January and February are spent preparing our specific issues for inclusion in the book; and the spring is spent testifying on those recommendations before legislative committees.

The *Analysis* is geared specifically for use by the fiscal committees that hear the budget (that is, subcommittees of the Ways and Means, and Budget and Fiscal Review Committees). The issues raised in the book help set the agenda for legislative hearings at which each department's budget request is reviewed.

While the fiscal committee members and staff are the crucial audience for the *Analysis,* other consumers of the product are state departments, local government, lobbyists and the Capitol media.

Bill Analyses

The office prepares fiscal analyses for every piece of legislation that has a state or local fiscal impact, almost half of the bills introduced. In recent years, the office has produced almost 3,500 such analyses a year, all of which are public documents. Most of these products are short (two to three pages) and briefly describe the bill and summarize the key fiscal impacts on the state and local governments.

The key audiences for our bill analyses are the authors of the legislation and the fiscal committees (members and staff) that hear the bills. A member of our staff provides oral testimony on each bill during the fiscal committee hearings. Just as important as the published analyses, however, are the informal discussions between LAO staff and fiscal committee and author staff prior to a hearing. Analysts discuss the basis for our fiscal estimate, point out problems with a bill, and suggest possible amendments.

Other key consumers of LAO bill analyses are lobbyists, local government, and state agencies.

Assignments

The office responds on a confidential basis to specific requests for information from legislative members. These requests range from the simple (determining how much money a particular department spent on a certain activity) to the complex (explaining a structural problem with the state budget). Given the confidentiality considerations, these responses basically have an audience of one. Many members, however, release the contents of our responses, expanding the list of consumers to the legislature as a whole, as well as the public.

Perspectives and Issues

Published simultaneously with the annual budget analysis each year is a smaller document entitled *Perspectives and Issues (P&I)*. The *P&I* provides an overview of the state's fiscal picture (spending and revenues) and identifies some of the major policy issues confronting the legislature. These self-generated issue pieces, which run between 10 and 25 pages, serve many purposes: frame a problem (e.g., concerns about health care delivery in rural areas), address crosscutting issues involving several policy areas (e.g., drug-related problems), offer alternative ways of approaching problems (e.g., market incentives to improving air quality), and offer policy options (e.g., treatment of juvenile and adult offenders).

Reports

For lengthier products (over 30 pages), the office issues reports. Examples of recent reports are: *A Perspective on the California Economy* (LAO, 1988), *AIDS Education in Correctional Facilities* (LAO, 1990), and *A Perspective on Housing in California* (LAO, 1990). As with *P&I* issues, reports are more policy-oriented (as compared with the strong fiscal slant of budget and bill products) and tend to address issues more comprehensively.

Policy Briefs

Recently, the office has used a new product, entitled *Policy Beliefs*, to disseminate information on policy issues (such as, a review of the governor's housing initiative and an overview of the state budget situation). What differentiates these self-generated briefs is that they are short (four pages or less) in order to improve their accessibility with legislative members and are generally geared to a specific event (for example, a key hearing) in order to maximize their usefulness.

Budget Control Analyses

The office produces various budget control analyses during the course of the year. After the annual budget is adopted by the legislature, the administration can make certain changes in the budget (e.g., spending unanticipated federal funds, moving dollar amounts within a budget item, and entering into long-term leases) only after a 30-day notification of the JLBC. In effect, the committee provides oversight of the budget for the entire legislature, which is especially important when the legislature is out of session. The LAO performs the staff work on these notifications and provides a suggested response to the administration for the chairperson of the JLBC. Typically, the chair acts on behalf of the full committee and generally accepts our recommendations on issues to raise with the executive branch.

Initiative and Ballot Write-Ups

In the case of all the above products, our primary clients are clearly the members of the legislature. We do have two products, however, for which the primary audience is the public at large. State law requires the Department of Finance (the executive branch budget office) and the LAO to prepare jointly the fiscal estimates of all initiatives before they are circulated among the voters for signature. Our estimates are designed to assist voters in evaluating whether to sign a proposed initiative petition. In addition, for initiatives that qualify for the ballot, the office has the sole responsibility to prepare an analysis and fiscal estimate of the state and local impact of each measure for inclusion in the statewide ballot pamphlet that is distributed to all voters. (This responsibility was given to us through the approval of an initiative.) With the increased use of initiatives in California, this work load has grown significantly in quantity, as well as complexity, in recent years.

Impact on Policy-Making

One of the most important values that the office has adopted is that of service, which we have defined as "contributions that make a difference." In other words, we want not only to produce high quality, objective products, but also we want them to be used to frame and influence policy discussions and to help legislators make better decisions.

Ways in Which the LAO Has an Impact

Critiquing

Perhaps the most important way the office contributes to policy-making is through its critical reviews of proposals. Much of what we do, especially in the annual *Analysis*, is reacting to a proposal and pointing out the problems with the request. With the budget, this process means our reviewing departmental requests to increase programs at the margin and often results in our making recommendations to reduce or delete the funding or to amend the proposal in some way.

This is a "negative" type of influence in that it focuses on what does not work and forces the administration to do a better job in making its case. It is a role at which the office excels, due in large part to our ability to hire and train "professional skeptics," analysts who know how to ask the right questions, challenge underlying assumptions, and seek alternatives. Given that the critiquing function involves saying "no" a lot, it is also a role that many other legislative staffers do not want or desire.

The LAO's impact in this regard varies dramatically with the type of proposal involved. For instance, members are more likely to follow our recommendation to cut or amend if (a) it is a new or expanded program, (b) a tight fiscal situation exists, or (c) no strong partisan interests are involved. Conversely, we have relatively less influence in cases in which we "take on the base" (that is, recommend reductions in previously authorized expenditure levels).

Setting Budget Agendas

As noted above, the LAO's annual *Analysis* plays an important role in setting the legislative budget agenda for each agency. For example, recently the office raised serious concerns regarding the way both a resource and a health agency were managing their programs and carrying out their statutory mandates. In subsequent budget hearings, these themes dominated the proceedings. Thus, the annual *Analysis* is a powerful tool for getting issues on the legislative platter and assisting the legislature with its oversight functions.

Reliance for Program/Technical Detail

Another key way the office affects policy-making is through the huge reservoir of technical and program information that analysts accumulate. Because LAO staff tend to know departments and their programs well as a result of extensive fieldwork, they often are tapped for their knowledge in formal and informal ways. For example, the office receives many requests asking us to review some aspect of an agency's operations, and analysts receive numerous calls from other legislative staff for background information on a department or for "reality checks" on how a proposal might affect a department. In these ways LAO staff serve as the "eyes and ears" of the legislature, accumulating firsthand information about government operations that can be used for oversight, evaluation, and review.

Neutral Third Party

As a nonpartisan institution, the office is in a unique position to assist the legislature in resolving certain issues. For instance, the LAO is asked often to perform a desired study of a program or agency in cases in which the legislature does not trust the administration to perform the job adequately. Similarly, the office typically plays a strong role during the conference committee on the Budget Bill. Members are often looking for a "neutral" voice that can frame the issue before them, provide factual information about program operation, and offer ways to resolve differences between the two houses and/or the two parties. The ultimate "third party" role played by the office is in our analyses of initiatives and ballot measures for the statewide voter pamphlet. The LAO was given this responsibility because of its nonpartisan fiscal advice function.

Crosscutting Issues

Given the committee structure of the legislature, it is often difficult for members to deal with problems that do not fit neatly into that structure. For instance, the president's national drug strategy provided additional funds to the state through three programs: health, criminal justice, and schools. Since these programs come under the jurisdictions of three different budget and policy committees in each house, it is institutionally difficult for the legislature to take a comprehensive approach to targeting and spending these funds. Although the LAO is divided also by program area, we have been able to assemble staff teams using officewide resources in order to provide the legislature with some perspective on crosscutting issues. In the case of the drug funding, we prepared three *P&I* pieces that tried to help the legislature see the "bigger picture" in each program area. We have attempted to provide this larger perspective in other ways as well. For example, we recently have inventoried programs that cross traditional subject lines (such as programs that aid the elderly and provide child care assistance) and identified areas of overlap. In addition, we are now in the process of examining the fiscal and programmatic relationship between the state and its 58 counties, a large undertaking aimed at giving the legislature a wider perspective on the existing problems with the state/local partnership. It is our belief that the office has a comparative advantage in tackling these types of "big picture" issues because of our program and fiscal expertise, as well as our nonpartisan role.

Idea Dissemination

The office also influences policy-making by proposing specific courses of action. Recently, the office has spent considerable effort in conveying the need for the state to develop a comprehensive capital outlay plan. While the issue of infrastructure has received much legislative attention, it has focused often on a particular concern (e.g., is the state issuing too many bonds?) instead of a more comprehensive approach that considers asset needs, maintenance requirements, financing alternatives, and priority setting.

The office also disseminates ideas to the legislature by offering alternative ways of approaching problems. For instance, in recent *P&I*s we have suggested how market incentives (as opposed to strict regulatory actions) could be an effective way to improve air quality and the electrical generation industry.

Institutional "Watchdog"

Another role the office plays is that of institutional watchdog. Tension will always exist between the legislative and executive branches regarding the operation of government. We try, however, to guard jealously certain legislative functions and responsibilities. For example, the legislature uses various budgetary control mechanisms so that funds appropriated in the Budget Bill are spent in particular ways. An important part of our budgetary review is ensuring that the administration has complied—in both letter and spirit—with legislative intent. As a long-standing legislative organization, we have the institutional memory and history to identify issues that challenge the powers of the legislative branch.

Policy Alternatives

Finally, the LAO is able to affect decisions by offering various policy and program options. For instance, given the state's tight fiscal condition for 1990-1991—a gap of approximately $3 billion between projected revenues and expenditures—we prepared two detailed volumes for the legislature, presenting both revenue-raising and expenditure-reduction options. This is a task for which we are well suited, as we have the program knowledge to identify reasonable alternatives and to describe their impacts (such as tax burden effects or service reductions), as well as the technical ability to make the fiscal estimates for budget-balancing purposes. In addition, the annual *Analysis* is a rich source of policy options for decision makers. In past documents we have provided options on the expenditure of desegregation funds, the allocation of state funds to local districts for school construction, and the ways to cut the state's health care costs.

The options approach is a realistic way to assist the legislature when no analytical basis exists for choosing among alternatives. For instance, how does a policy advice institution tell a committee the appropriate way to raise $1 billion in new revenues until there is a policy decision about how the tax burden should be shared? An options approach allows nonpartisan staff to assist their bosses—by providing the range of possibilities and identifying the impacts of their implementation—and still maintain objectivity and neutrality.

Constraints of the Nonpartisan Advice World

As the above indicates, the office does affect policy-making—in small and large, direct and indirect ways. Constraints exist in the nonpartisan advice world that affect our impact, as described below.

Crowded Advice World

The increasing complexity of government and partisanship of the legislature have resulted in a crowded advice world. Legislators now have personal aides, policy committee consultants, fiscal committee consultants, offices of research, and party caucus staff. In addition, many nonlegislative policy advice institutions exist with a strong presence in Sacramento: business-supported entities (e.g., "Cal Tax"), tax policy groups (e.g., California Tax Reform Association), and consumer interests (e.g., Common Cause). Given the plethora of sources of advice, not to mention the policy analysis available from academia and national institutions, it is difficult for any one entity to establish itself as a dominant analysis source.

Nonpartisan Approach in a Partisan World

Many California legislators come to Sacramento with a fairly strong perspective reflective of their district's constituency. As such, they tend to associate closely with definable interests and groups and rely on them for guidance in dealing with policy proposals. It is understandable that members, whose schedules are incredibly overburdened, come to rely on partisan "shortcuts" to help them make a myriad of decisions. Anything that challenges these shortcuts, as nonpartisan analysis will do often, can be viewed by members as being unhelpful or even counterproductive.

Problem-Solving Orientation

Another constraint faced by the LAO may be the many differences between policy analysts and policymakers. Analysts by training (and perhaps also by disposition) tend to be quantitatively oriented, to rely on written products, and to devise comprehensive solutions. Members, on the other hand, tend to be qualitatively oriented, to rely on personal communication, and to focus on solutions that can fix the immediate problem. In other words, some fundamental differences exist in the way the two groups address issues.

Limits of Analysis

In many cases the constraints of the advice world in which we operate simply reflect the limitations of analysis. For example, the office can do nothing to resolve an issue that is dependent on unquan- tifiable information. Often, the LAO must prepare fiscal estimates of legislation that imposes short-term costs in order to achieve some type of savings or benefits down the road. Unfortunately, those longer term savings/benefits may be impossible to quantify (usually because one cannot predict certain intended behavioral effects) and thus can only be acknowledged as *potential* outcomes. In these cases, a member trying to change a state law is confronted by a bill analysis with an *identifiable* cost estimate potentially offset by an *unquantifiable* savings. The net effect of the measure remains unknown.

Similarly, many issues transcend policy analysis. For instance, no basis exists for the office to say what is the "appropriate" level of progressiveness in the state's income tax or to draw conclusions about comparable redistribution issues. As nonpartisan advisors, we cannot take a position of substituting our policy preferences for those of the decision makers.

Reputation as "Nay-Sayers"

While our ability to critique proposals is one of our strengths, a flip side exists to having a propensity for saying no. The office has some- what of a reputation for being a nay-sayer. The allegation contains some truth, as the office, by typically being in a reactive mode, is not always in a position or does not have the time to offer constructive alternatives.

By comparison, policymakers tend to shun the naysaying role, preferring instead to negotiate solutions. Clearly, both critical evalu- ation and creative new solutions are needed in policy-making. If, however, the LAO is perceived as capable of doing only the former, it will not have the audience for the latter.

Steps to Improve Our Role in the Policy-Making Process

During the past 4 years, the office has taken several steps to enhance the efficacy of the LAO as a policy advice institution.

Clarify the Office Mission

The first and most important step the office took was to reevaluate its role and purpose. This was a time-consuming task that involved

the entire staff; but in retrospect, it was a critical starting point. Through this internal review process, we were able to achieve a fairly good consensus about our mission. As a result, the office plans to do more analysis on major policy and fiscal issues and to make contributions to the process in a more timely and relevant way.

Maintain Comparative Advantages

While we want to make changes in the way the office operates in order to improve our contributions, we also recognize that we must continue to perform well the tasks we do better than others. As described above, the LAO's comparative advantage is in budget-related work and fiscal analyses of bills. While these tasks are not always glamorous, they are our bread and butter and the key to our influence on policy discussions.

Find Other Niches

We can make unique contributions to other areas of policy advice. We noted above that the legislature currently has a need for analysis of crosscutting issues. Given the size and breadth of experience in the office, this is an area in which we can excel.

Take Some Risks

We also recognize that to be influential in the policy-making process entails taking some risks. In carefully protecting the nonpartisanship and independence of the office, at times we have been too cautious in the roles we have taken. We need to be more forceful in tackling sensitive issues, in taking more stands on important fiscal and public finance issues, and in providing our judgment for legislative members in cases for which pure analysis falls somewhat short.

Manage Resources

Given the short-term, crisis nature of almost any legislative environment, it is easy for staff to become captive to the day-to-day workload demands that exist in that environment. We have tried, however, to respond to these workload requirements, while still keeping resources dedicated to longer term projects, through better management. This attempt has involved responding more flexibly to

changing workload needs (e.g., moving staff around to meet temporary peaks), reducing our efforts on low-priority projects, and working with legislative members to limit the scope of our response to
some requests.

We have tried also to better anticipate the issues that will be before
the legislature in the near future by holding more strategic planning
meetings and by early designation of staff teams to address the key
issues identified.

Respond to Opportunities

We have tried to capitalize on analytical opportunities in several
ways. For example, we created a specific document (the aforemen-
tioned *Policy Brief*) to respond quickly to issues. The briefs are short
and can be published quickly, which make them well suited for
getting out our perspective on issues prior to key hearings.

Write for the Members

In preparing our documents, we have made a conscious effort to
write for legislative members. This focus has meant framing the issue
up front, limiting the analytical arguments to the most important
ones, leaving out the technical detail and terminology, highlighting
the recommendations, and ensuring that they are action oriented.
These efforts have served also to shorten our products, a crucial goal
in making them accessible to the members.

Improve the Look of Products

An important step the office has taken in improving its usefulness
was to acquire (and develop) desktop publishing capabilities. It
improved the look of our documents immeasurably by allowing
enhanced use of graphics, better layouts, and more professional
designs. It has helped us think more "visually" in the way we respond
to members and generally has made us more aware of the importance
of the way we present information.

Think About the "M" Word

Finally, we have spent more time on improving the coverage and attention that our published products receive (what most would call marketing). As analysts, we tend to react negatively to the notion of marketing, what with its connotations of manipulation and advocacy. We have, however, learned to accept the notion that the world is not going to beat a path to our analytical door. Consequently, we are trying to be more methodical about what we must do after the presses stop rolling: (a) make a list of the people who should receive the document, (b) consider briefings and/or personal letters to members and staff who would be interested, (c) increase distribution to the media, (d) try to arrange presentations at hearings where appropriate, and (e) follow up more carefully on reactions to the documents.

These are some of the things the LAO has done and is doing to improve the use of policy analysis in legislative decision making and the way the office serves the California legislature. We realize that constraints exist in the nonpartisan advice world that will always work to limit the policy influence we can have with members. At the same time, however, nonpartisan offices can play unique roles—the institutional watchdog, the neutral third party, the storehouse of program and technical expertise and information—that can ensure their usefulness to legislative bodies.

References

Governor's budget. (yearly).

California Legislative Analyst's Office. (yearly). *Analysis of the Budget Bill.* Sacramento, CA: Author.

California Legislative Analyst's Office. (yearly). *Perspectives and issues [P&I].* Sacramento, CA: Author.

California Legislative Analyst's Office. (1988). *A perspective on the California economy.* Sacramento, CA: Author.

California Legislative Analyst's Office. (1990). *AIDS education in correctional facilities.* Sacramento, CA: Author.

California Legislative Analyst's Office. (1990). *A perspective on housing in California.* Sacramento, CA: Author.

Proposition 13 (1978). Initiative measure passed by California voters at the June 6, 1978, election that added Article XIIIA to the California Constitution.

Index

274

About the Authors

James L. Blum has been the Assistant Director for Budget Analysis at the Congressional Budget Office since 1975, when CBO was established. He also served as the acting director of CBO for 14 months in 1988-1989. Previously, he worked for the Office of Management and Budget, the Department of Labor, the Council on Wage and Price Stability, and the Organization for Economic Co-operation and Development. He studied economics at the University of Michigan, satisfying all requirements except completion of a dissertation for a doctoral degree.

Nancy Carson is Program Manager for Science, Education, and Transportation at the Office of Technology Assessment (OTA) of the U.S. Congress. OTA provides analysis of the positive and negative impacts of technology choices for Congress. She has extensive experience in both the legislative and executive branches of the Federal Government, including policy and implementation responsibility for water quality, open space and neighborhood development, historic preservation, and recreation planning. She holds a bachelor's degree in general studies from the University of Washington in Seattle, and a master's degree in public administration from the John F. Kennedy School of Government at Harvard, where she was a Littauer Fellow. She is a member of the Committee on Science, Engineering, and Public Policy of the American Association for the Advancement of Science, and was a member of the National Academy of Sciences delegation to Bulgaria in 1988.

Patrick Ford is a managing director for public affairs and senior vice president of Burson-Marsteller, a worldwide public relations consulting firm. Based in New York, he directs client service teams working with major global companies in insurance, telecommunications, defense, biotechnology, consumer products, and other industries. Before joining B-M/Washington in 1989, he served as vice president for public affairs at the American Enterprise Institute for Public Policy Research. He was associated with the institute as consultant or employee for nearly 10 years, managing much of its external outreach efforts. He also served as secretary of AEI's Board of Trustees. His earlier professional experience included managing the Media Operations Center at the 1984 Republican National Convention; serving on the Board of Directors of CapitalCare, a wholly owned subsidiary of Blue Cross/Blue Shield; and reporting for several news organizations in New Jersey. He holds a bachelor's degree in political science from Rutgers University.

Susan H. Fuhrman is a professor at Eagleton Institute of Politics at Rutgers, The State University of New Jersey, and director of the Consortium for Policy Research in Education (CPRE). CPRE, a consortium of Rutgers University, the University of Southern California, Harvard University, Michigan State University, Stanford University, and the University of Wisconsin-Madison, conducts research on the implementation and effects of state and local education policies to improve schooling. CPRE is funded by the Office of Educational Research and Improvement of the U.S. Department of Education. She is the author of numerous articles, research reports, and monographs on education policy and finance. She was a consultant to the Ford Foundation's program on educational management and finance for 10 years and currently serves as a school board member in Westfield, New Jersey.

Robert Greenstein is founder and Executive Director of the Center on Budget and Policy Priorities, a nonprofit organization established in 1981 to analyze budget and policy issues affecting low- and moderate-income Americans. Over the years, he has been responsible primarily or jointly for many of the Center's research reports and analyses. Most recently, he was principal author of *Drifting Apart: New Findings on Growing Income Disparities Between the Rich, the Poor, and the Middle Class*, published in 1990. He has contributed chapters to a number of books, including a recently published Brookings Institution book on the underclass. He also has written articles for such publications as *The New York Times, The Washington Post,* the *Los Angeles Times,* and *The New Republic.* He has been a guest on "The MacNeil/Lehrer Newshour," ABC's "Good Morning, America," the CBS "Evening News," C-SPAN, and other network, cable, and local television and radio programs. He received his undergraduate degree from Harvard University and has done graduate work at the University of California at Berkeley.

Harry S. Havens was appointed Assistant Comptroller General in the U.S. General Accounting Office on April 18, 1980. He now handles a variety of special assignments for the Comptroller General. Most recently he directed the study leading to GAO's report *The Budget Deficit: Outlook, Implications and Choices,* published in September 1990. Before that, he led GAO's work under the Gramm-Rudman-Hollings legislation and GAO's study of the 1987 stock market crash. He also serves on a number of internal management boards and committees. Prior to his present assignment, he served in the U.S. Navy from 1957 to 1964, with the Bureau of the Budget (now Office of Management and Budget) from 1964 to 1974, and as Director of GAO's Program Analysis Division from 1974-1980. He graduated from Duke University in 1957 with a bachelor's degree in economics. He attended University College, Oxford, England, from 1957 to 1959 as a Rhodes Scholar, receiving a bachelor's degree in politics and economics in 1959 and a master's degree in 1963.

Elizabeth Hill earned a bachelor's degree with honors in human biology from Stanford University and a master's of public policy degree from the University of California, Berkeley. Following her academic training, she was a Fulbright Scholar in Stockholm, Sweden, conducting research into innovative Swedish transportation policies. She commenced a career in state government in 1976, joining California's Legislative Analyst's Office as a Program Analyst focusing on criminal justice. Following specializations in other policy areas, she was appointed state Legislative Analyst by the Joint Legislative Budget Committee in 1986. As Legislative Analyst, she oversees the preparation of annual fiscal and policy analyses of the State of California's budget and proposed legislation considered by the state legislature. She also is charged with the responsibility of preparing analyses for all initiatives and constitutional measures qualifying for the state's ballot. She has been an active member of the Association for Public Policy Analysis and Management, serving on its Policy Council, and the National Association of Legislative Fiscal Officers, serving as President of the Western regional organization. She currently serves on the advisory boards of the Center for California Studies and *California Policy Choices.*

Robert H. Nelson is a member of the economics staff of the Office of Program Analysis (formerly Office of Policy Analysis) of the U.S. Department of the Interior. While serving in the Office since 1975, he has worked closely with the livestock grazing, timber management, and coal leasing programs of the Bureau of Land Management and the economic development and education programs of the Bureau of Indian Affairs. On temporary assignments from Interior, he has been the Senior Economist of the congressionally chartered Commission on Fair Market Value Policy for Federal Coal Leasing (Linowes Commission) and the Senior Research Manager of the President's Commission on Privatization. Several leaves from Interior have included terms as a Visiting Scholar at The Brookings Institution, a Visiting Senior Fellow at the Woods Hole Oceanographic Institution, and a Visiting Scholar at the Political Economy Research Center. His articles have appeared in *The Washington Post, Wall Street Journal, Forbes, Technology Review, Regulation,* and other publications, and he has written three books: *Zoning and Property Rights* (1977), *The Making of Federal Coal Policy* (1983), and *Reaching for Heaven on Earth: The Theological Meaning of Economics* (1991).

Malcolm A. Palmatier is an Editorial Consultant to The RAND Corporation, with a long-standing interest in RAND's contributions to the field of policy analysis. He is coeditor of *Perspectives in Economics* (1971) and holds degrees in mathematics (B.S., Western Michigan University), English literature (M.A., University of California, Los Angeles), and economics (M.A., University of Southern California).

Kathryn H. Porter is Research Director for the Center on Budget and Policy Priorities, an independent nonprofit research and analysis organization located in Washington, DC. She supervises the center's research into welfare reform, employment and training, poverty, hunger, and other policy issues affecting low- and moderate-income Americans. Among her recent publications are *Real Life Poverty in America: Where the American Public Would Set the Poverty Line, Making JOBS Work: What the Research Says About Effective Employment Programs for AFDC Recipients,* and *Poverty in Rural America: A National Overview.* Prior to her current position at the center, she was a senior research analyst for the Office of Research, Planning, and Evaluation of the Department of Public Welfare, Commonwealth of Massachusetts. She also held research positions with the Food and Nutrition Service of

the U.S. Department of Agriculture and the U.S. Senate Select Committee on Nutrition and Human Needs. She holds a Master of Public Administration degree from the John F. Kennedy School of Government, Harvard University.

Beryl A. Radin is a Professor of Public Administration at the Washington Public Affairs Center of the University of Southern California. Her major research and teaching interests focus on the implementation of national policies in a complex, federal system. Her publications deal with education policy, human services policy and administration, and advice giving. They include several books (including *The Politics of Federal Reorganization: Creating the U.S. Department of Education* with Willis D. Hawley, 1988); chapters in recent books on women's policy, public administration, and intergovernmental relations; and articles in *Public Administration Review, Public Administration Quarterly,* and the *New England Journal of Human Services.* She has been a consultant to a number of federal agencies, including NASA, the Social Security Administration, the Office of the Assistant Secretary for Planning and Evaluation in the Department of Health and Human Services, and the Office of Management and Budget. During the past several years she has taught at public policy programs at the University of California at Berkeley and the Australian National University. She served as a Fulbright Scholar at the Indian Institute of Public Administration in New Delhi in 1990.

Alice M. Rivlin, an economist, is a Senior Fellow in the Economic Studies Program of the Brookings Institution. She was Director of the Economic Studies Program at the Brookings Institution from September 1983 through June 1987. Before returning to the Brookings Institution, she served for eight years as the first Director of the Congressional Budget Office (CBO). She also has been Assistant Secretary for Planning and Evaluation in the U.S. Department of Health, Education, and Welfare. During the spring semester of 1988, she was a Visiting Professor at the John F. Kennedy School of Government at Harvard University. She has written extensively on the U.S. economy, the budget, and public decision making. She is the editor of *Economic Choices 1984* and a coauthor of *Economic Choices 1987.* She is the author of *Systematic Thinking for Social Action* (1971), coauthor of three volumes on the federal budget entitled *Setting National Priorities* (1971-1973), a coeditor of *The Swedish Economy* (1987), and coauthor of *Caring* *for the Disabled Elderly: Who Will Pay?* (1988). She is currently a Director of the Unisys Corporation, the Union Carbide Corporation, TJ International, and Chair of the Board of The Wilderness Society.

William H. Robinson has been the Deputy Director of the Congressional Research Service for the past 4 years. As Deputy Director, he has overseen a complete review of the CRS product line, developed the major issue tracking system for focusing CRS analytical resources on pressing congressional issues, and promoted a Strategic Planning Process for CRS. He is currently Vice President of the Association for Public Policy Analysis and Management. Before coming to the Library, he with the U.S. Office of Management and Budget (OMB), where he served as a Fiscal Economist from 1963 to 1970 and subsequently as Assistant Division Chief for Income Maintenance and Veterans. As research manager, he has remained active in the research process—with several publications and numerous presentations before professional groups and congressional audiences. He earned a bachelor's degree in political science from Brigham Young University in 1959 and was awarded a master's degree in government and political economy by Harvard University in 1963. He has completed all requirements for a doctoral degree except a dissertation.

Isaac Shapiro is a senior research analyst at the Center on Budget and Policy Priorities, a nonprofit organization located in Washington, DC. The center analyzes federal and state budget and policy issues, with an emphasis on those affecting low- and moderate-income Americans. His areas of research include low-wage employment policies as well as broad analyses of trends in poverty and welfare programs. He is the author of the center's 52-volume study, *Holes in the Safety Nets: Poverty Programs and Policies in the States,* and two recent center reports on the rural working poor, *Laboring for Less: Working but Poor in Rural America* and *Fulfilling Work's Promise: Policies to Increase Incomes of the Rural Working Poor.* Prior to his current position, he was a research associate at the Center for Social Policy Studies. He also has worked as a legislative assistant to a member of Congress, for the Congressional Budget Office, and as a neighborhood organizer. He received his undergraduate degree from Washington University in St. Louis and his master's degree in public policy from Harvard University's John F. Kennedy School of Government.

Penny R. Thompson is a Senior Program Analyst in the Office of Evaluation and Inspections, Office of Inspector General, U.S. Department of Health and Human Services, where she has received the Excellence in Program Evaluation and other achievement awards. During her tenure with the OIG, she has conducted numerous program inspections on various topics of interest to HHS and the OIG: patient "dumping" (1987 and 1988), financial arrangements between physicians and other health care businesses (1988-1989), clearance of home testing devices by the Food and Drug Administration (FDA) (1989), FDA product review for new and generic drugs (1989-1990), and expansion of user fees at FDA (1990). She is the author or coauthor of numerous federal reports emanating from these studies. She also provides technical assistance and guidance to OIG regional offices conducting inspections. She previously has authored articles and made presentations at evaluation conferences on the OIG's work in evaluation and policy analysis. She received her MPA from the George Washington University in Washington, DC. She holds a bachelor's degree from the University of Virginia.

James M. Verdier is currently Deputy Commissioner for Medicaid and Administration in the Indiana State Department of Public Welfare. He is responsible for Medicaid policy, planning, and administration, and for the department's overall budgeting and financial management. He was previously Deputy Director for Strategic Planning and Finance in the Michigan Department of Management and Budget from 1989 to 1990, and taught public policy and management at the John F. Kennedy School of Goverment at Harvard from 1983 to 1989. He served in the Congressional Budget Office (CBO) from 1975 to 1983, heading the Tax Analysis Division from 1979 to 1983. Before coming to CBO he served as a legislative assistant for 6 years in the U.S. House and Senate. He is a graduate of Dartmouth College and Harvard Law School and attended the Queen's College at Oxford University. He is the author of a number of articles on policy analysis, tax policy, congressional behavior, and budgeting.

Carol H. Weiss is a Professor at Harvard University in the Graduate School of Education. In the 1960s and 1970s she conducted evaluations of social programs and consulted for federal agencies on program evaluation and policy research. On the basis of that work, she wrote two books on program evaluation and has continued to publish on the subject. She early became concerned that the results of evaluation and policy research were being ignored when decisions were made, and she did a series of studies on the uses of research in policy making and factors other than information that influence the substance of policy. She has published three books and scores of articles on the uses of social science research, including *Social Science Research and Decision-Making* (1980), and edited a book on "making bureaucracies work." Her recent work has looked at the channels that bring social science research into the policy arena, which has led to a book on the media, *Reporting of Social Science in the National Media* (with Eleanor Singer, 1987), articles on Congressional staffs, and now this volume on policy analysis organizations. Her most recent book, co-edited with P. Wagner, B. Wittrock, and H. Wollman, is a cross-national inquiry entitled *Social Sciences and Modern States: National Experiences and Theoretical Crossroads* (1991). She holds a doctorate in sociology from Columbia University.

Barbara R. Williams is a Vice President of The RAND Corporation and Co-Director of its Drug Policy Research Center. She holds doctoral and master's degrees in sociology from the University of Illinois and a bachelor's degree from Austin College. She joined RAND in 1971. From 1973 to 1979, she was Director of the Urban Policy Analysis Program. In 1974 she was appointed Deputy Vice President of RAND's Washington Office and Director of its Domestic Programs; she served in this capacity until 1982. In February 1982, she returned to Santa Monica to become Head of RAND's Behavioral Sciences Department. In addition to those duties, she directed RAND's Criminal Justice Program from 1981 to 1988. She was appointed Vice President in 1989. Prior to joining RAND, she served 2 years in Washington, DC, in the Research and Plans Division of the Office of Economic Opportunity, authoring numerous reports on crime, poverty, and juvenile issues. Her publications at RAND cover a variety of urban policy problems and general concerns of policy analysis.

Walter Williams is a Professor in the Graduate School of Public Affairs at the University of Washington. He headed the Research and Plans Division in the Office of Economic Opportunity during the Johnson administration and has been a visiting scholar at the London School of Economics and the University of Bergen. He has written several books on policy analysis and federal policy implementation, including *Social Policy Research and Analysis* (1971), *Government by Agency* (1980), *The Implementation Perspective* (1980), and *Disaster Policy Implementation: Managing Programs under Shared Governance* (with Peter May, 1986). His most recent books, *Washington, Westminster and Whitehall* (1988) and *Mismanaging America: The Rise of the Anti-Analytic Presidency* (1990), are part of a decade-long study of policy-making capacity at the top of the United States and United Kingdom governments. The two books focus on the structure and staffing of policy units serving presidents and prime ministers.

Mark R. Yessian is Regional Inspector General for Evaluation and Inspections in the Department of Health and Human Services (HHS) in Region I (New England). He also serves as the Regional Coordinator for the Office of Inspector General in Region I. He joined the federal government in 1971 in Washington, DC, serving as a Special Assistant in the Office of the Secretary for the Department of Health, Education, and Welfare. Subsequently, he worked in the Office of the Regional Director and the Office of Inspector General in Region I. In his current position, he is responsible for the development, conduct, and preparation of short-term national evaluations and policy analyses addressing health and human services issues. As Regional Coordinator, he is responsible for representing interests of the Office of Inspector General (OIG) as a whole in Region I. In addition to the Office of Evaluation and Inspections, the OIG includes the Office of Audit Services and Office of Investigations. He was the cofounder and copublisher of the *New England Journal of Human Services (NEJHS)* a national publication that was a benefit of membership of the human services section of the American Society for Public Administration. From 1980 to 1988, he wrote a regular column of commentary for *NEJHS*. He also has had articles published in other journals, including *Public Administration Review, American Behavioral Scientist, Social Service Review,* and the *Journal of the American Medical Association.* He received a doctoral degree in political science from the Maxwell School of Citizenship at Syracuse University.